Business Schools, Leadership and the Sustainable Development Goals

Business Schools, Leadership and the Sustainable Development Goals: The Future of Responsible Management Education is the second book in the series Citizenship and Sustainability in Organizations: Exploring and Spanning the Boundaries. It contains chapters from various scholars and practitioners in the field of responsible management education (RME). Through introspection, through celebrating successes and learning from failures (retrospection) and through looking forward (prospection), it aims to inspire a future of management education and leadership development that demonstrates its relevance to sustainable development. In doing so, it touches upon the grand societal challenges of our time, as illustrated by the United Nations Sustainable Development Goals, and discusses how business schools, and other providers of management education, could and should contribute to overcoming these challenges. It argues that management education needs to educate future leaders in a way that no longer hampers but truly accelerates the process of sustainable development. This book offers a collection of thought-provoking ideas, vivid stories (including personal accounts and experiences), and appealing and engaged forecasts, visions and ideas about management education and leadership development for sustainability. Hence, it is a must-read for anyone interested in or involved in RME.

Lars Moratis is Professor of Sustainable Business at Antwerp Management School and the Chair in Management Education for Sustainability, a joint initiative of Antwerp Management School (Belgium) and Breda University of Applied Sciences (the Netherlands).

Frans Melissen is Professor of Sustainable Experience Design at Breda University of Applied Sciences and the Chair in Management Education for Sustainability, a joint initiative of Antwerp Management School (Belgium) and Breda University of Applied Sciences (the Netherlands).

Citizenship and Sustainability in Organizations
Series Editors: David F Murphy and Alison Marshall

Exploring how organisations and citizens respond to and influence current and future global transformations, this book series publishes excellent, innovative, and critical scholarship in the fields of citizenship, social responsibility, sustainability, innovation, and place leadership in diverse organisational contexts. These contexts include commercial businesses, social enterprises, public service organisations, international organisations, faith-based organisations (FBOs), non-governmental organisations (NGOs), community groups, hybrids, and cross-sector partnerships. The role of the individual as citizen may also be explored in relation to one or more of these contexts, as could formal or informal networks, clusters, and organisational ecosystems.

Business Schools, Leadership and the Sustainable Development Goals

The Future of Responsible Management Education

Edited by Lars Moratis and Frans Melissen

Routledge
Taylor & Francis Group

NEW YORK AND LONDON

First published 2023
by Routledge
605 Third Avenue, New York, NY 10158

and by Routledge
4 Park Square, Milton Park, Abingdon, Oxon, OX14 4RN

Routledge is an imprint of the Taylor & Francis Group, an informa business

ISBN: 978-1-032-15602-6 (hbk)
ISBN: 978-1-032-15604-0 (pbk)
ISBN: 978-1-003-24490-5 (ebk)

DOI: 10.4324/9781003244905

Typeset in Bembo
by MPS Limited, Dehradun

Contents

Tables

Figures

Contributors

Guénola Abord-Hugon Nonet is Assistant Professor at Jönköping International Business School (JIBS), where she teaches, researches, and leads projects and teams to help accelerate the sustainability transition. Guénola is the former United Global Compact PRME Chair for Scandinavia. She is JIBS Champion for Responsibility in Action and has also chaired Jönköping University Sustainability Network from 2019 to 2022. Her pioneering doctoral research from 2013 studied responsible management education and the needed changes in management education to co-create sustainable societies. Guénola is Board member of Jönköping County Sustainability Board.

Ruth Areli García-León is a lecturer and researcher at Ostfalia University of Applied Sciences and the University of Hamburg in Germany. Her research interest focuses on sustainable consumption and Responsible Management Education. After working in the marketing and communication fields in the public and private sectors, Dr. García-León moved to academia where she has occupied different management positions. She has accumulated more than 20 years of experience lecturing communication, marketing, and management courses for graduate and undergraduate students in Spanish, English, and German at different universities in Latin America and Europe. She is part of the steering committee of the PRME DACH Chapter (Germany-Austria-Switzerland) and the steering committee of the PRME Working Group on Climate Change and Environment. She holds a Ph.D. in Education Sciences, a Master in Marketing, an M.Sc. in Communication, a Licentiate in Communication Sciences, and is a certified coach and trainer of cross-cultural competencies.

Muhammad Atif is an Associate Professor at EDC Paris Business School, France, and leads the school initiatives in corporate social responsibility and sustainability areas. He received his Ph.D. in Management Sciences from the University of Paris Dauphine (France) and an MBA degree from IBA, University of Punjab (Pakistan). His research work is focused on corporate social responsibility and sustainability, with a special interest in textile industry and developing economies. In addition to his teaching and research experience, Dr. Atif has worked for over eight years in the textile industry at managerial positions.

Elaine Berkery is a Lecturer in Management and a researcher at the Kemmy Business School in the University of Limerick, Ireland. She teaches on a wide range of programmes at both undergraduate and post-graduate level in the area of management, international management and strategic management across health, public, and tourism sectors. Elaine's main research interests are in the area of diversity and flexibility in the workplace. These include gender in management; investigating the use and benefits of flexible working arrangements; and the talent management of international nurses and midwives. Elaine regularly presents her research to international audiences and publishes her research in International Journals such as European Management Review, the European Management Journal, the Journal of Nursing Management, and Gender in Management: An International Journal. She is a Senior Associate Fellow of the Academy of World Business, Marketing and Management Development, a member of the Irish Academy of Management and British Academy of Management.

Joanna C. Carey is an Associate Professor of Earth & Environmental Science at Babson College. Her research focuses on answering fundamental questions regarding ecosystem processes in the context of global change and she teaches courses related to ocean systems and climate change, among other topics. Joanna received her Ph.D. in Earth Science from Boston University (2013), her M.S. in Environmental Science from Yale University (2007), and her B.S. in Environmental Policy & Planning from Virginia Tech (2005). Before joining Babson in 2017, Joanna completed several post-doctoral fellowships, including an NSF Earth Science Fellowship and a USGS Powell Center Fellowship, both hosted at the Marine Biological Laboratory in Woods Hole, MA.

Karen Cripps is Lecturer in Business Management in the Department of Responsible Management at the University of Winchester Business School. She has a role as PRME Champion and lectures and researches in responsible management and education.

Afrodita Dobreva received her M.Sc. degree (cum laude) in International Management/CEMS from Rotterdam School of Management, Erasmus University in Rotterdam, The Netherlands. Alongside her studies, she was involved in research on non-profit management and responsible management education. Currently, she works as an associate at a management consultancy firm that focuses on helping executives develop themselves, their teams, and their businesses.

Enrico Fontana is a Lecturer at Sasin School of Management (Thailand) and an Affiliated Researcher at the Mistra Centre for Sustainable Markets at Stockholm School of Economics (Sweden). He received his Ph.D. in Business Administration from Stockholm School of Economics and MBA degree from McGill University (Canada). His Ph.D. and current work are focused on corporate social responsibility and corporate sustainability, with a focus on South and Southeast Asia. Enrico has published his work in multiple academic outlets, such as *Journal of Business Ethics, Journal of Business Research, and Business Strategy and the Environment.* Before embarking on his Ph.D. studies, Enrico has worked for six years as market manager in the apparel industry in Asia and Europe.

Alex Hope is Deputy Pro-Vice Chancellor and Associate Professor of Business Ethics at Newcastle Business School, Northumbria University. He is responsible for the strategic leadership of education across the faculty and undertakes teaching, research, and consultancy across topics such as education for sustainable development, responsible business, business ethics, and the Sustainable Development Goals. Alongside his work at Newcastle Business School Dr Hope is Co-Chair of the United Nations Principles of Responsible Management Education (UN PRME) Climate Change and Environment working group and past Vice-Chair of the UN PRME UK and Ireland Chapter. He is a member of the Chartered Association of Business Schools Learning and Teaching Committee and sits on the Northeast board of Business in the Community, the Prince of Wales Responsible Business Network. He holds a Ph.D. in Sustainable development, an MA in Academic Practice and B.Sc. (Hons) in Environmental Management.

James Hunt is an Associate Professor of Management at Babson College where he teaches organisational behaviour and sustainability. James is the co-author of two books, *The Coaching Manager: Developing Top Talent in Business* (third edition), and *The Coaching Organization: A Strategy for Developing Leaders.* James is a former Chair of the Management Division at Babson. He is also a fine art and environmental photographer, focusing on the interaction of humans and the environment.

Lucas Meijs is full professor of Strategic Philanthropy and volunteering at Rotterdam School of Management, Erasmus University in the Netherlands. His research focuses on issues related to volunteer/non-profit management. He has served for six years as the first non–North-America editor of the journal *Nonprofit and Voluntary Sector Quarterly,* the premier journal in the field and is a board member of several Dutch non-profit organisations, including a corporate foundation fighting digital exclusion.

Mirjam Minderman supports higher education for sustainable development through strategy development and implementation, process facilitation, training, education, and research. In her role as Policy Adviser & Lecturer

Business and Society at TIAS School for Business and Society, Mirjam is responsible for the integration of 'Business and Society' in the school's education. She designs and implements the TIAS strategy and policies in this regard, based on the Business & Society Competency Framework that she developed. This includes facilitating faculty to integrate the related competencies and contents in their programs and courses, and designing and delivering related courses. Several Appreciative Inquiry-related trainings enable Mirjam to be more effective in her work. With a Master's degree in International Relations, Mirjam initially worked in the field of microfinance, fair trade, and responsible investing. She gradually shifted towards sustainable development and CSR – and specifically towards training and education on these issues. She specialised in Higher Education for Sustainable Development and worked with several Dutch higher education institutions. Mirjam is active in various Dutch and international networks related to CSR and RME.

David F. Murphy is Associate Professor of Sustainability and Collaborative Leadership and the academic lead for the Initiative for Leadership & Sustainability at the University of Cumbria. David has extensive global-local experience working on multi-stakeholder engagement and collaboration with senior leaders and change agents in business, government, NGOs, and the UN system, including related consultancy and academic work in teaching and applied research on responsible business practice and partnerships for sustainable development.

Nuala Ryan is a lecturer and researcher in the Department of Management and Marketing at the Kemmy Business School in the University of Limerick. Her areas of focus include Strategic Management, Leadership and Organisational Behaviour. She has been a lecturer at the University College Cork, UCD Michael Smurfit Graduate Business School, University College Dublin, The National College of Ireland, NUI Galway and currently in University of Limerick. Prior to becoming a full time lecturer Dr. Ryan has worked in industry where her main responsibilities included HR Business Management, Organisational Development, Team Development and Learning Organisation Management. This experience has led to a wide range of teaching, research and publication interests in the broad area of gender, leadership development, strategic management, and general organisational behaviour. She is currently carrying out research in the healthcare sector in the area of leadership and strategic management.

Hugues Séraphin is Senior Lecturer in Event/Tourism Management Studies and Marketing. He holds a PhD from the Université de *Perpignan Via Domitia* (France) and joined The University of Winchester Business School in 2012.

Simon M. Smith is Principal Lecturer in Business, Management, and Enterprise at Oxford Brookes University. He has expertise and interests in leadership and management, responsible management, human resource management, organisational behaviour, organisational analysis, and international business. His current research interests encompass Organisational Ambidexterity, Sustainable Development Goals (SDGs), overtourism, global talent management, resilience, emerging-market economies, and training and development. He has published in *Human Resource Management, International Journal of Human Resource Management, Human Resource Management Review* and *Thunderbird International Business Review.*

Ranjit Voola is an Associate Professor in Marketing, at the University of Sydney. He is passionate about engaging in Responsible Management Education which is transformational in re-imagining the purpose of business and marketing, where alleviating societal issues and making profits are not mutually exclusive. He believes that the SDGs provide a viable framework for re-imagining the purpose of business. He has developed novel curricula relating to Marketing and the SDGs and Poverty Alleviation and Profitability. His scholarly work challenges marketing scholars to tackle critiques relating to its lack of relevance and impact of scholarly marketing research by holistically, strategically, and explicitly engaging with the SDGs.

Lauren Verheijen is a lecturer and researcher of Management Education for Sustainable Development at Breda University of Applied Sciences. Lauren holds a Masters in Global Business and Sustainability from Erasmus University Rotterdam and a Research Masters in Arts and Culture from Leiden University. Her interests lie in exploring the intersection between sustainability transitions and culture, interpreting individual and societal transformation to go hand-in-hand. Current research focuses on the implementation of transformative learning in higher education.

Sarah Williams is Senior Lecturer in Leadership and Sustainability at the University of Cumbria. She leads the MBA module 'Local–Global Challenges in Ethics, Responsibility and Sustainability' and redesigned the module from an on-campus residential to online during the Covid-19 pandemic. Sarah has over 30 years' experience of working with business and public/voluntary sector partners, largely to develop and support sustainability programs. She has a particular interest in personal values and sensemaking.

Preface

This is exactly the book I would have liked to read when I started teaching business school students about the role of business in society. The book is a true gem of thought-provoking chapters that call educators to reflect, examine taken-for-granted assumptions, and search for novel ways of engaging our students to become those critically thinking responsible leaders that the world needs. In other words, this book is about how to create contexts for 'student agency.'

The two book editors, Lars Moratis and Frans Melissen, are both Professors of Responsible Management Education (RME). They are world-leading scholars in the RME context and they are known among peers to invite critical debates and enjoy a provocative discussion. Personally, I have had the pleasure of working with both of them over the past two years, as they have developed the PRME Responsible Management Education Webinar Series and currently serve as Editors in Chief of the PRME BLOG. The critical twist and the invitation to turn around arguments and old routines is very much the spirit of this book.

Today business schools have a responsibility to educate business leaders who are able to identify novel solutions to some of the world's grandest challenges, some of these are described in the United Nation's Sustainable Development Goals (SDG). It is no longer sufficient to train business school students in the techniques to develop growth, consumption and shareholder value and become what Harvard professor Khurana has called 'mere craftsmen' who know their mathematics and can calculate the return on investment (Khurana, 2010). Today, there is a global need for a private sector that is able to think beyond 'do no harm' and instead can rethink the concept of economic growth and generate new business models. With the development of the SDGs in 2015, the Secretary General of the United Nations, Antonio Guterres, made it clear that businesses are part of the solution to repair the world and create an inclusive and sustainable future for all. Scientists have again and again supported this vision: the corporate sector may be part of the problem but it is also a central part of the solution to develop a sustainable world (Rockström, Steffen, Noon and Persson, 2009). To take on this responsibility, businesses need leaders who know how to rethink economic models and how to generate novel business models that will mutually benefit the business and the world.

The book is set in a world of global 'wicked problems' of climate change and rising inequalities where there are no predefined solutions to how business leaders shall operate. The editors emphasise the modern business school's responsibility to educate business leaders, who not only have the knowledge to address these problems but also importantly the skills to 'learn to learn,' i.e., the capacity to ongoingly set goals in new complex situations, critically reflect and responsibly act to help put the world on a better future track.

There is a growing awareness and support by business school deans to transform the curriculum and many business schools have already significantly done so. Several of the business schools that have signed up to PRME Principles have reviewed their entire curricula and insisted to integrate sustainable development into all program across all management disciplines. This is a key part of the journey.

However, much less focus has been given to the pedagogies with which the curriculum is brought into the business school classrooms. The way to engage students in innovation and critical thinking is not by 'telling them' what to do. It is rather to make them curious and to let them explore themselves how to identify problems and novel solutions. Such curiosity is not encouraged when the professor is simply 'profess'ing,' i.e., positioning him/herself centrally in front of the students in the classroom, going through the texts, that the students have already read, supported by a PowerPoint presentation. Yet 'profess'ing' is still the pedagogical habitus that is preferred among many professors when teaching the curriculum. Because that is the way we were taught ourselves.

The recent OECD report 'Student Agency for 2030' defines student agency as 'the capacity to set a goal, reflect and act responsibly to effect change. It is about acting rather than being acted upon; shaping rather than being shaped; and making responsible decisions and choices rather than accepting those determined by others' (OECD, 2019: 2). The report refers to studies that show how students, when they are agents in their learning and they play an active part in what they learn and how they learn, they show not only greater motivation and wish to pursue the objectives for their learning, they become better at 'learning how to learn.'

This book critically insists on turning old pedagogical habits upside-down. Not by telling professors the best way to teach the future generation of business leaders. But by bringing in a group of highly experienced and skilled professors who have all reflected on their own pedagogies over many years and who perseveres on the journey to engage students as active learners. The book chapters are admirably inspiring in their different ways of conceptualising successes and failures in engaging (or not) students and

The tone of the book is set on the very first page in the very first chapter that asks: 'Are we *irresponsible* in delivering responsible management education?' This fundamental question engages a debate about our role as educators to prepare students to navigate in a profit-focused capitalistic society while at the same time engaging them to aspire to transform business to achieve the SDGs. The authors are asking us as educators to self-critically rethink how we try to balance such complexity in the classroom.

In that same spirit the other book chapters alert us as educators to rethink how we engage our students to navigate with complexity, paradoxes, and ambiguities. All the invited authors share the same ambition: to help 'equip' our business school students to become those change makers that will develop make sustainable development the norm for new economic thinking in the private sector and beyond.

As I read the book chapters, I began to imagine what business schools would like if the examples and ideas from this book were actually brought into the classroom as a pedagogical habitus. If business schools students were actually invited to re-imagine themselves what the role of business in society could be. And most importantly, how enjoyable it would be to be a business school student invited to engage to reimagine positive social, economic, and environmental impact.

It is a book like this that will contribute to the urgent need to train and reward business school faculty for their pedagogical achievements. I am very honoured to be invited to write the preface of this admirable book, and I am convinced that this book will inspire not only professors to become better teachers but also business school deans to rethink how to give more emphasis and prestige to their professors' pedagogical efforts and achievements.

Mette Morsing
Head of PRME
United Nations Global Compact, New York
August 2022

Introduction

Frans Melissen and Lars Moratis

The future of management education is inextricably intertwined with the grand challenges of our time. On the one hand, management education has been instrumental 'in the destruction that modern-day business and economic thinking have brought upon the planet and the human and non-human life inhabiting it' (Moratis and Melissen, 2022a, p. 30) through teaching and research activities that propagate the principles on which our current socioeconomic system is founded. Consequently, management education is anything but an innocent bystander when it comes to the various crises that are threatening humanity. Obviously, this role in the origin of today's most acute and urgent threats comes with great responsibility – a moral responsibility to clean up the mess it helped make.

Simultaneously, business schools and other providers of management education have long since claimed that they educate the leaders of the future and help build tomorrow's business world. Living up to this promise against the background of the grand challenges of our time only reinforces and amplifies this moral responsibility. However, as many have stated before us, this will require nothing short of a paradigm shift in the way sustainability is addressed in management education (see e.g., Kelly et al., 2022; Teerikangas et al., 2022) and a re-purposing of education in general (see e.g., Stewart et al., 2022). It not only requires a complete rethinking of teaching and research activities from a content perspective, but also from a pedagogical–didactical perspective.

The relevance of the latter becomes painfully clear from recent research that shows how young people suffer from anxiety, grief, fear, and anger, and up to 45% of them reporting that negative emotions linked to climate change (and other socioecological crises) impact their daily functioning (Hickman et al., 2021; Dooley et al., 2021). Some of them are the very same young people that management education providers aspire to teach how to become the leaders of our common future. Just imagine the emotional affect that comes with being educated to shape tomorrow's business world and wider society while worrying and hurting about whether you will have any future at all. Educating these young people will have to be a lot more and something very different than simply addressing

DOI: 10.4324/9781003244905-1

some sustainability aspects within the context of the very same curricula and pedagogical-didactical approaches that contributed to creating the crises that threaten their future in the first place.

Exploring what these curricula will have to look like and what pedagogical-didactical approaches will do justice to management education's moral responsibility to not only shape a sustainable business world but to truly facilitate today's young people in taking leadership in shaping our common future is the topic of this volume in the series 'Citizenship and Sustainability in Organizations' and the chapters included in this edited collection of perspectives on this key challenge of our time.

The role of the Sustainable Development Goals

The United Nations' Sustainable Development Goals (SDGs) have now become the 'de facto sustainability standard' (Moratis and Melissen, 2022b, p. 213) for addressing the grand challenges mentioned earlier and, consequently, they also constitute an important guideline for rethinking and redesigning management education. In essence, the SDGs represent a blueprint for creating a sustainable and just socioeconomic system by operationalising how to address poverty, inequality, climate change, environmental degradation, peace and justice (United Nations, n.d.), to name just a few of the wicked problems that are included in this framework. Today, despite critiques (see e.g., Biermann et al., 2022), the SDGs remain a central lever in the way companies and other organisations, together with their stakeholders and broader society, search for effective responses to and solutions for these problems.

The SDGs and the challenges they represent, including the urgency to address them, have certainly been helpful in pushing the envelope when it comes to interpreting the concept of 'sustainable business.' Nowadays, companies are increasingly expected to not only make their internal processes more *green* and limit their environmental impacts, but to also develop products with a societal purpose, consider if they want to become a B-corporation, and even experiment with entirely new business models that rely on sustainable ways of value creation (Moratis et al., 2018). Companies leading the sustainability revolution, such as Patagonia, are now even taking an activist stance towards sustainability, aiming to further redefine conceptions of corporate sustainability and showing and inspiring others what roles and responsibilities business can take in making system change happen. These (fast) evolving conceptions of (corporate) sustainability also highlight the need for a different approach to leadership and point towards new types of leadership.

As such, the SDGs might prove helpful in doing the same for management education – to assist in moving (far) away from reproducing harmful assumptions about the creation and distribution of economic value and the relationships between firms, their stakeholders, and wider society that are not only incompatible with sustainability (Springett, 2005; Høgdal et al., 2019) but have actually created the problems addressed in the SDGs in the first place. Similarly, educating future leaders cannot be based on the values on which our current socioeconomic system is founded; management education will have to facilitate tomorrow's leaders in adopting sustainability as a leading value and acting on it (cf. Weybrecht, 2017). Taking the SDGs as its dominant sustainability perspective and main context, this edited collection therefore brings together examinations of academics and practitioners on how (1) to develop visions of the roles and responsibilities of business schools and other providers of management education, (2) to reflect critically on responsible management education (RME) and the assumptions that guide it, and (3) to share ideas for and experiences with creative applications of management education and leadership development for sustainability, and their implementation in practice.

The chapters providing these examinations present a variety of perspectives on these visions, assumptions, and ideas. Together, they represent a rich palette of interpretations of what management education's curricula and pedagogical-didactical approaches should look like, given the trade-offs, tensions and paradoxes represented by the SDGs, the emotional affect that comes with addressing them, and the systemic activism that is required to realise them (Moratis and Melissen, 2022b). Similarly, through these interpretations, these chapters also put forward important reference points for critically reflecting on and further developing sectoral guidelines, such as the Principles for Responsible Management Education (PRME), and the way accreditation bodies deal with providers of management education and actually assessing them based on delivering on their promise to educate the leaders of the future and help build tomorrow's business world. Furthermore, through a critical perspective on the SDGs themselves, some chapters might also assist in redesigning management education into a sector that could inspire and assist others, including politics and the business world, to move beyond the SDGs only having discursive impact and to start using them as leverage for transformative impact (Biermann et al., 2022). The thought-provoking ideas, vivid stories (including personal accounts and experiences), and appealing and engaged forecasts that are included, turn this book into a catalyst for taking stock and reflecting through introspection, through celebrating successes and learning from failures (retrospection) and through looking forward (prospection). Together, these perspectives might prove valuable in inspiring a future of management education and leadership development that truly demonstrates its relevance to sustainable development of wider society.

Set-up and contents

The remainder of this book is organised around three themes. Part 1 – Visions and responses (Chapters 1–4) – contains chapters that provide perspectives on the roles and responsibilities of management education within the context of the world's most pressing sustainability challenges, as well as (reflections on) strategies that business schools and other providers of management education have followed to address the SDGs. Part 2 – Critical and personal reflections (Chapters 5–7) – brings together critical views on business schools' role in society and how management education has addressed sustainability thus far. This part also includes critical reflections on the SDGs themselves and potential consequences of the imperfections of this framework for management education. Finally, Part 3 – Creative pedagogies and assessments (Chapters 8–11) – contains descriptions of new and original tools, methods, and learning strategies that management educators across our globe have used in practice, and that may inspire others to adopt and adapt these for their own context and purposes.

Chapter 1, by Simon Smith, Hugues Séraphin, and Karen Cripps, explores and discusses RME as a paradox. It contemplates whether it is actually irresponsible to deliver RME. The theory of Organisational Ambidexterity, a theory pertaining to paradox, is applied as a lens to critically reflect on progress with respect to the PRME and the achievement of the SDGs. This chapter discusses tensions that are hindering the impact of the PRME and the SDGs and presents ambidextrous approaches as a potential solution for (responsible) management educators and business schools to move forward, especially in relation to a deeper embedding of competencies for Education for Sustainable Development (ESD).

In Chapter 2, Joanna Carey and James Hunt point out that we need to explore a variety of educational approaches to help develop leaders who are able to create and manage a sustainable world that is aligned with the SDGs. They describe their experiences from a co-taught interdisciplinary elective course on business-environment interactions offered to undergraduate business majors. The chapter shows how they used a systems thinking framework for integrating earth science and management disciplines, which are quite divergent in many respects but share a bias towards the development of cognitive and analytic competencies. Therefore, they explore the important opportunities that emerge from the emotional experiences generated by addressing sustainability challenges and how these facilitate the development of a more holistic approach to sustainability leadership. As such, this chapter explores the development of empathy as a critical leadership competency and presents lessons learned that can be of help in a variety of educational contexts aimed at developing the leadership capabilities necessary to address the current grand challenges facing society.

Chapter 3 addresses RME courses and why they are fundamental to increasing students' awareness of environmental and social challenges, and to promote leadership that aligns with the SDGs. However, the authors, Muhammed Atif and Enrico Fontana, conclude that these courses are often characterised by a pedagogical-didactical approach that fails to address the importance of emotions and how to manage them. Therefore, this chapter presents an overview of the literature on emotions in the context of teaching and learning and, against this backdrop, then explains how managing emotions can help improve the quality of RME courses. By offering some initial thoughts on how to manage emotions in the classroom, the authors hope to encourage discussions among scholars and managers interested in advancing the SDGs.

The final chapter of Part 1, Chapter 4, by Alex Hope, addresses the challenge to develop effective RME that truly equips future leaders with the capabilities needed to address the SDGs and engage in responsible management practice. This chapter presents a blueprint for integrating RME and sustainability leadership into business and management programmes. This blueprint was developed during work to deliver a new suite of undergraduate business programmes recently launched at a large UK public university, which were designed from the bottom up with the SDGs and responsible leadership in mind. The author hopes that this blueprint may act as a catalyst for other responsible management educators seeking to develop study programmes that incorporate RME, the SDGs, and related content, also by sharing some insights on how to overcome institutional challenges and barriers to implementation.

Part 2 kicks off with Chapter 5, in which Elaine Berkery and Nuala Ryan put forward that full and effective participation, as well as equal opportunities for women in leadership positions and at all levels of decision making in political, economic, and public life, can and, more importantly, should be addressed by business schools and other providers of management education. In fact, they state that business schools are in a unique position to influence social change, providing guidance on how to empower women in the workplace, marketplace, and community, by preparing future graduates to enter the workforce ready to challenge and eliminate inequalities experienced by women globally. Guided by the results of a cohort study over a 10-year period at a PRME champion business school, they discuss the roles and responsibilities of business schools in creating an environment that allows learners to acquire the knowledge and skills needed to promote gender equality through teaching of topical areas like implicit bias, second-generation bias, and the double blind phenomenon. The chapter could serve as a useful guideline to inform business schools' engagement with stakeholders, such as learners, policy makers, and organisations in general.

In Chapter 6, Guénola Abord-Hugon Nonet, Afrodita Dobreva, and Lucas Meijs question whether business schools are capable of reversing their co-dependent relationship as obedient business servants who, so far, have often blindly followed the corporate path. Will business schools be able to shift their focus away from generating blind followers and confederates of destructive industry practices and take the lead in shaping a new (and very much needed) generation of business leaders that are able to achieve sustainability targets? In order to answer this question, this chapter examines current educational practices and compares the current (and outdated) model to a new approach to education that seeks to encourage students from the perspective of developing head, heart, hands and soul. The authors argue that the multidisciplinary nature of business schools does indeed equip them to take a leading role in this shift. However, to do so, they must redefine their position in relation to the broader context. This chapter concludes that, as is the case for the relationship between business and the community, the first step for a business school should be to shift the focus away from the individual student and towards an embedded view of the student within multiple contexts of wellbeing: individual, collective, and planetary.

Ranjit Voola's learnings from his journey to find his calling as an SDG-marketing scholar, as presented in Chapter 7, conclude Part 2 of this book. In this chapter, Ranjit contends that scholars who reflect on their calling are more likely to contribute to transformational RME because RME anchored in the SDGs requires a scholarly determination that challenges the underlying assumptions of business-as-usual. As an illustration, he describes his own journey of finding his calling, guided by the Narrative Model of Authoring an Identity as a Called Professional by Bloom, Colbert, and Nielsen. This description includes a reflection on lived experiences such as the sacrifice demonstrated by Ranjit's parents as doctors in an Indian Christian missionary non-profit hospital, the kindness shown by his living kidney donor, and his desire to do his best to tackle gender inequality, as the father of two daughters. It also includes a reflection on crafting personal authenticity by proactively reflecting on and constructing a compelling narrative for becoming an SDG-marketing scholar. Finally, by detailing how he created innovative SDG curricula and a call for marketing scholars to engage with SDG research, proactively and strategically, Ranjit hopes to encourage other scholars to reflect on their calling and engage in transformational RME.

In the first chapter of Part 3, Chapter 8, Ruth Areli García-León concludes that there is no consensus (yet) on the best way to integrate sustainable development topics in the business and management school curriculum nor on how they should be taught. Therefore, the author concludes, it is necessary to develop new pedagogical-didactical tools to address these topics within management courses. This chapter contributes to this by presenting a new pedagogy based on using news articles as a tool to include sustainable development issues in management course content. This proposal is grounded in the educational social constructivist theory of learning, the collaborative learning approach, and the author's personal experience of more than eight years of using news items as a pedagogical-didactical tool. The chapter details how to prepare classroom activities, as well as the steps to follow during classroom teaching, also based on two real-life examples. The chapter concludes with recommendations for obtaining different final outcomes, insights on the importance of the instructor as a designer of the activity, and highlighting the advantages of applying this tool.

Chapter 9, by Mirjam Minderman, describes how Appreciative Inquiry (AI) can be used in support of RME and furthering the SDGs through management education. RME provides current and future leaders with the knowledge, skills, and attitude to develop pathways towards a sustainable future. An essential part of this education is creating the awareness that incremental change and a focus on eco-efficiency are not enough, and that transformation is imperative for dealing with the world's challenges as summarised by the SDGs. Yet, the author argues, management education has traditionally been shaped with concepts that are at odds with transformation, such as risk management, control, and problem analysis. This chapter suggests AI for strengthening management education with transformative methods and pedagogies. First, AI is explained. Then its application in RME is discussed and illustrated with the example of AIM2Flourish in the fulltime MBA program of TIAS School for Business and Society (the Netherlands). This combination of theory and practice leads to several considerations and lessons learned about how AI can strengthen RME and contribute to shaping sustainability leadership.

Sarah Williams and David Murphy explore, in Chapter 10, how leaders in business and other organisations from 180 different countries are engaging with teaching and learning on the SDGs through an authentic assessment approach that is aligned to the PRME. The vehicle for this is the online MBA module 'Local-Global Challenges in Ethics, Responsibility and Sustainability,' which uses the SDGs as a sustainability management education framework. The authors report that in the academic years 2020–2021 and 2021–2022, more than 1,000 leaders studying for one of eight specialist MBAs, delivered by the University of Cumbria in partnership with Robert Kennedy College (Switzerland), have made practical commitments to address selected SDGs. With the students predominantly at senior manager or CEO level, the quality of the organisational action plans developed through the teaching, and their potential for making a difference, has been outstanding. At the same time, the academic learning process continues to develop and refine the teaching of the SDGs within an authentic and responsible management education and assessment context. This innovative SDG-focused teaching and learning initiative is described in full detail, as inspiration for management educators seeking to advance PRME implementation and management education's contribution to realising the SDGs.

In the final chapter of this book, Chapter 11, Lauren Verheijen describes how higher education has done well in establishing itself as the supplier of business talents with stable markers of success that indicate when a student is ready for the *real world*. However, Lauren argues, the role of education is evolving, especially in relation to sustainable development, and this more and more requires education to be holistic, transformative, and learner-centred. This approach demands new forms of meaningful assessment that emphasise learning over metrics. Therefore, this chapter explores learning as conceived in RME and ESD, and the related function of assessment, to articulate a research and practice agenda focused on exploring new forms of assessment for management education that is truly relevant to sustainable development of wider society.

References

Biermann, F., Hickmann, T., Sénit, C.-A., Beisheim, M., Berstein, S., Chasek, P., Grob, L., Kim, R.E., Kotzé, L.J., Nilsson, M., Llanos, A.O., Okereke, C., Pradhan, P., Raven, R., Sun, Y., Vijge, M.J., van Vuuren, D. and Wicke, B. (2022). 'Scientific evidence on the political impact of the Sustainable Development Goals', *Nature Sustainability*, 20 June 2022. Online at: 10.1038/s41893-022-00909-5 Accessed: 27/06/2022.

Dooley, L., Sheats, J., Hamilton, O., Chapman, D. and Karlin, B. (2021). *Climate Change and Youth Mental Health: Psychological Impacts, Resilience Resources, and Future Directions*. Los Angeles: See Change Institute.

Hickman, C., Marks, E., Pihkala, P., Clayton, S., Lewandowski, R.E., Mayall, E.E., Wray, B., Mellor, C. and van Susteren, L. (2021). 'Climate anxiety in children and young people and their beliefs about government responses to climate change', *The Lancet – Planetary Health*, 5(12), pp. E863–E873.

Høgdal, C., Rasche, A., Schoeneborn, D. and Scotti, L. (2019). 'Exploring the hidden curriculum in responsible management education', *Academy of Management Proceedings*, 2019(1).

Kelly, O., Illingworth, S., Butera, F., Steinberger, J., Blaise, M., Dawson, V., Huynen, M., Martens, P., Bailey, S., Savage, G., White, P., Schuitema, G. and Cowman, S. (2022). *Tertiary Education in a Warming World, Reflections from the Field*. Dublin: University College Dublin Press.

Moratis, L. and Melissen, F. (2022a). 'The future of business schools: Existential innovation of obsolescence?', *EFMD Global Focus*, 2(16), pp. 28–35.

Moratis, L. and Melissen, F. (2022b). 'Bolstering responsible management education through the sustainable development goals: Three perspectives', *Management Learning*, 53(2), pp. 212–222.

Moratis, L., Melissen, F. and Idowu, S. (eds.), 2018). *Sustainable business models: Principles, promise, practice*. Berlin: Springer.

Springett, D. (2005). ''Education for sustainability' in the business studies curriculum: a call for a critical agenda', *Business Strategy and the Environment*, 14(3), pp. 146–159.

Stewart, I.S., Hurth, V. and Sterling, S. (2022). 'Editorial: Re-Purposing Universities for Sustainable Human Progress', *Frontiers in Sustainability*, 3: 859393.

Teerikangas, S., Painter, M. and Matser, I. (2022). *Transforming business education for sustainability: The case for paradigm shifts in pedagogy and theory*, April 2022. Online at: https://www.abis-global.org/news/transforming-business-education-for-sustainability Accessed: 26/07/2022.

United Nations (n.d.). *Sustainable Development Goals: Take Action for the Sustainable Development Goals*. Online at: https://www.un.org/sustainabledevelopment/sustainable-development-goals/ Accessed: 27/06/2022.

Weybrecht, G. (2017). 'From challenge to opportunity – Management education's crucial role in sustainability and the Sustainable Development Goals – An overview and framework', *The International Journal of Management Education*, 15(2B), pp. 84–92.

Part I

Visions and responses

1 The responsible management education paradox: Applying the conceptual lens of Organisational Ambidexterity

Simon M. Smith, Hugues Séraphin, and Karen Cripps

Introduction

In this chapter, the core focus considers one overriding critical reflective question for responsible management educators:

> Are we *irresponsible* in delivering responsible management education (RME)?

Crucially, we are discussing this question to draw out significant realities within responsible management education (RME). For example, we will discuss shortcomings in the delivery of the Principles for Responsible Management Education (PRME) and the achievement of Sustainable Development Goals (SDGs). Yet, it is of course crucial that RME works, has meaningful and lasting impact, and contributes to achieving the SDGs.

The aims and objectives of this chapter are three-fold. First, we want to take a step back and honestly and critically reflect on where we are up to within the RME journey (with a primary focus on PRME and the SDGs). Second, we want to conceptualise and frame within a theory pertaining to paradox why there are key tensions and barriers affecting the delivery of PRME and achievement of the SDGs. Finally, we want to instil hope and possibilities for moving forward and overcoming such tensions and barriers.

The critical perspectives offered and discussed here provide additional depth and contrast some of the perspectives already presented in other chapters. This then presents further contemplations within the leadership of the SDGs and also draws out much needed critical reflection within RME.

For some, the overarching question will make the 'blood boil' and question 'what on earth' we are trying to achieve in this writing. For others, it may fall in line with reflective questions already being asked. Regardless of where you are in the spectrum on this, we will certainly first explain the premise for such a controversial question. The chapter then outlines PRME and paints a picture of where we are in the journey of RME and the achievement of the SDGs. Following this, the theory of organisation

DOI: 10.4324/9781003244905-3

ambidexterity, a theory pertaining to paradox, is introduced. With this theory, greater meaning is provided within critical reflections and the difficulties of implementing and delivering on PRME and the SDGs. A discussion of other relevant areas is explored, namely the 'Alpha' Framework and a competencies approach. Finally, suggestions for ways forward are offered in an attempt to leave a more inspirational message for action to reinvigorate and reenergise responsible management educators for the challenge ahead, primarily focusing on approaches towards educational competencies.

We think it is wise to provide a note of caution to the reader of this chapter. We, as authors, present a critical debate around PRME and the achievement of the SDGs. However, this is not to say we are anti-PRME or anti-SDGs. In fact, we are strong advocates of the need for models like PRME and the SDGs to succeed. We *want* them to succeed. Importantly, we recognise and discuss the difficulties around the journey to potential success, but with a view to generating action and solutions – this is a crucial element within our message portrayed. The theory of Organisational Ambidexterity presented provides an alternative lens to contemplate action and solutions that could be crucial in moving forward to greater success in achieving the SDGs.

The paradoxical premise

When providing an oxymoron like 'Are we *irresponsible* in delivering RME?,' it is perhaps essential to set out our intentions and meaning early on. In short, we believe the delivery of RME is *paradoxical* by nature. This paradox can be portrayed by a classic position versus a more modern-day position. For example, the traditional argument by Friedman (1962, 1970) outlines 'There is one and only one social responsibility of business – to use its resources and engage in activities designed to increase its profits.' The other end of this dichotomy, and arguably a more modern perspective, is a responsible management position that balances sustainability (e.g., resources, the environment, climate change), responsibility (for all stakeholders) and moral dilemmas (ethics) (Laasch and Conaway, 2015). In short, we argue the two are mutually exclusive. We will later evolve this debate through the conceptual lens of Organisational Ambidexterity and other related research. For now, we want you to keep in mind that we are attributing this paradoxical positioning as one reason for potential shortcomings in the delivery of PRME and the achievement of the SDGs. Crucially, such a critical position is seldom discussed within the literature. We feel it is essential to bringing necessary criticality with a view of increasing SDG impact moving into the coming years.

PRME

This discussion begins with PRME and an outline of what we aspire to in RME. PRME is a United Nations-supported initiative designed to enhance the profile of sustainability in business and management schools around the world, and inspire future leaders to balance economic and sustainability goals (and this includes links to the SDGs) (PRME, 2021). On the surface of the definition here, we can already see conflict emerge through this 'balancing' of economic and sustainability goals. For example, how far would organisations (intentionally referring to an organisation as an entity here) really go to sacrifice economic goals in favour of sustainability goals?

Despite the initial conflict, it is pertinent to start with the positives. PRME is certainly engendering change within higher education. Within a UK context, the authors of this chapter have both worked/are working within a PRME Champion business school (note: since August 2021, the first author now works in a university that is a PRME Signatory, but had worked in a PRME Champion business school where the other authors currently reside). In our careers, this means we have seen curriculum and module contents change significantly to provide much greater focus on sustainability. We see more academics than ever (including ourselves) producing research and publications around sustainability. We would argue that students are gaining values-based skills and toolkits to take into the workplace after graduation. Thus, we can evidence educational impact quite well, even though one might argue this is anecdotal evidence.

Critically reflecting on PRME

The above shows a good start. But is this enough? Is RME transcending into SDG achievement? Is all as it seems within the delivery of RME? Can change be measured through PRME providers?

Séraphin et al.'s (2021b) research highlights that PRME uptake in European higher education providers is not at a level where it can make extensive inroads and necessary changes into the curriculums of a large demographic of institutions. Their research also highlights that there does not appear to be a correlation between PRME institutions who deliver tourism education and then the performance of where the destinations these institutions are based (particularly in terms of environmental sustainability). Thus, the argument can be made that PRME does not yet appear to be transcending from education into business practice (at least not in local/regional form anyway). Of course, this study is limited to the field of tourism, although the nature of this industry has allowed for some metric comparisons to be made in this way and contemplate the measurement of PRME post-education.

Related to the study above, Séraphin et al. (2022) conducted a global study analysing PRME adoption and making comparisons with the Travel and Tourism Competitiveness Index from the Travel and Tourism Competitiveness Report 2019. Again, limitations were highlighted between PRME uptake and sustainability transitioning into the tourism industry within the same destinations. As a more focused example, Séraphin et al.'s (2021a) research conducted with students at Kedge Business School (Marseille, France) also reveals limitations between RME within a PRME institution and related/transitioning impact on practice outside of the educational context. What we can take from these studies is that more needs to be done and the journey is far from complete.

Beyond the positive messages being derived via PRME, the evidence to support educational transition into practice is still required and still building. Thus, the connections to furthering the achievement of the SDGs is perhaps lacking at this point. But, as a symbol of hope and a beacon of theoretical light, PRME currently gives us one of our best models of practice. The challenge is moving that rhetoric into reality and impact. The following sections around Organisational Ambidexterity will consider this dichotomy and contemplate how we can attempt to move further into reality and impact. Crucially, it is positioning the conversation through an alternative lens that hopefully gives rise and scope to considering different approaches that will ultimately help to further achieve the SDGs (as well as other necessary agendas in organisations).

What is Organisational Ambidexterity?

Organisational Ambidexterity is a theory pertaining to paradox. In other words, because of its opposing and conflicting positions, it allows a discussion around potential paradox from two extreme points of consideration. Then, when you contemplate maximising organisational performance or practice from these two positions, it should provide alternative approaches in theory (see Table 1.1 for theoretical examples). It is worth noting that this theory was not primarily designed for RME. Indeed, we are mapping the theory/lens to this subject domain. The theory, importantly, is robust enough to allow for that mapping.

Organisational Ambidexterity is built around two conceptual opposing positions: *exploitation* and *exploration* (Birkinshaw and Gupta, 2013; O'Reilly and Tushman, 2013; Raisch et al., 2009; Stokes et al., 2015; Stokes et al., 2019). One end of this spectrum relates to *exploitative approaches* that are generally focused on what is known (underpinned by convergent thinking) and centred on existing customers and markets. The other end of this spectrum relates to *explorative approaches* that are generally focused on moving beyond that existing knowledge into new knowledge through embracing aspects like innovation, experimentation, flexibility, and divergent thinking. With these polar opposites, Organisational Ambidexterity can assist in presenting a complicated and potentially paradoxical juxtaposition through this dichotomous framing.

To help visualise the framing above, Table 1.1 presents those basic conventions relating to Organisational Ambidexterity. In addition, this table helps to make other connections. For example, *exploitation* can be related in some part to theoretical aspects within McDonaldization (Ritzer, 2008), cost

Table 1.1 Overview of Organisational Ambidexterity

Organisational Ambidexterity: the extremes	Exploitation	Exploration
Common associations	Existing customers and/or markets Efficiency Refinement Expanding what is generally *known* to the organisation	Focus on new knowledge and movements away from existing knowledge Experimentation Flexibility Innovation Divergent thinking
Theoretical links	McDonaldization (Ritzer, 2008; Smith, 2016) through: Efficiency, Calculability, Predictability, and Control Cost leadership or cost focus through Porter's Generic Strategies (Porter, 1980, 1985, 2004; Smith, 2016) Transactional Leadership (Hater & Bass, 1988; Smith, 2016)	A focus on differentiation or differentiation focus through Porter's Generic Strategies (Porter, 1980, 1985, 2004; Smith 2016) Transformational Leadership (Hater & Bass, 1988; Smith, 2016)
Organisational examples	McDonalds IKEA Ryanair Primark	Apple BMW Google Toyota
Examples of ambidextrous organisations (i.e., both exploitative and explorative)	Netflix Amazon Xiaomi Phantom Geak Tencent	

leadership within Porter's Generic Strategies (1980, 1985, 2004), and Transactional Leadership (Hater and Bass, 1988). The emphasis here is the mastery through which such efficiency, cost leadership, and so on is achieved. For *exploration*, the obvious counter-theory is again related to Porter's Generic Strategies, whereby the emphasis is on mastery through differentiation, as well as Transformational Leadership (Hater and Bass, 1988). Organisational examples are then connected that are perhaps best known within those theories. Then, to go one step further, we identify what could arguably be presented as successful ambidextrous organisations.

To expand here though, we present Netflix as an ambidextrous organisation (e.g., Kohli and Mier, 2021). As a subscription-based streaming service for films and TV, they are a global organisation that maintains relatively low subscription rates for customers which keeps competition at bay (*exploitation*). The main difficulty for new competition comes at the hands of innovation and investment in new products, notably new films and TV (*exploration*). While this is a somewhat simplified example, it could be argued that Netflix could quite easily raise their prices for goods and services with all those premium products attached. Yet, they appear to hold back. One reason could be that they make so much through global subscription and having over 200 million customers. Another reason could centre around ambidextrous practice. In other words, through maintaining lower subscription rates but maximising investment in new products and services, it truly makes Netflix very difficult to compete with. This is an organisation that started out in the early guise of being a DVD rental service via mail. Innovative, but ultimately the business approach did not cut it. Yet, they have gone on to utilise technology and globalisation (e.g., economies of scale) in particular to achieve ambidexterity (whether done consciously or not). Thus, it proves that an ambidextrous organisation can be achieved and there are examples to compare and aspire to.

Plenty of literature (e.g., Raisch et al., 2009) will discuss how to 'balance' *exploitative* and *explorative* business practices. However, we will work from the argument that the polar opposites identified through exploitation and exploration can be reconsidered and positioned to work 'paradoxically in tandem' (Smith, 2016, p. 12), which is to maximise each end of the spectrum contained within the paradox. Although this may sound counterintuitive and arguably impossible, we argue that organisations must consider responsible management and sustainability in this way for any chance to succeed through PRME or the SDGs. This is akin to accepting a paradox and using it constructively (Poole and Van de Ven, 1989). In essence, we cannot merely balance profit versus planet; they need to be (and arguably are) mutually exclusive and we need to maximise both ends of this particular spectrum. Instead of being stunted by the nature of the paradox, the understanding and positioning around it creates a line of strategic thinking to move forward by tackling those polar opposites simultaneously, but without compromise at either end – it hence may be the only way to generate the purposeful change required. That general context here surrounds the difficulty of implementation and delivery of responsible management principles, including the SDGs and PRME (i.e., values orientated; new knowledge and practice) versus more traditional business approaches (i.e., profit orientated; existing knowledge).

Although we presented the example of Netflix earlier as an ambidextrous organisation, that example sits within, arguably, more normative business practice, such as 'people versus profit' and surrounding organisational conversations. For this chapter moving forwards, the focus will look more like 'people versus profit versus planet.' The dichotomy almost becomes a trichotomy when layering in RME in addition to those normative business practices. This adds weight to the complexity of delivery and potential for success for the SDGs. We delve further into this in the following section.

Applying the conceptual lens of Organisational Ambidexterity to RME

In this section, we are going to focus on a number of tensions within RME. These tensions will highlight through an Organisational Ambidexterity lens why it is so challenging to achieve the SDGs through PRME. The paradoxical elements outlined will serve to highlight why an ambidextrous approach could be required for greater impact in the delivery of PRME and greater success for the SDGs. As Hahn et al. (2018, p. 235) highlight, a paradoxical perspective within sustainable development will embrace the tensions to be discussed 'to simultaneously accommodate competing yet interrelated economic, environmental, and social concerns.' Indeed, Moratis and Melissen (2022) argue that when we address the SDGs, this automatically comes with trade-offs, tensions and paradoxes. Following this section, we move into discussing the hidden curriculum and the part it plays for executing (or not) RME. Subsequently, we discuss a competencies focus for RME and how this could act as a catalyst for greater impact moving forward.

Tension 1: Shareholders versus stakeholders versus sustainable development

There is a traditional positioning whereby shareholders sit in potential opposition to other stakeholders. Stakeholder theory effectively highlights how many potential relationships could be intertwined into business, including governmental bodies, political groups, trade associations, trade unions, communities, financiers, suppliers, employees, customers, and even competitors (Freeman, 2015). We could consider profit orientation and maximisation (*exploitation*) versus the considering of all other stakeholders where it is potentially costly to address them all (*explorative*). This is challenging enough and comes with many complications due to the vast and diverse nature of those stakeholder relationships. Yet, to go further and deal with something such as climate change, becoming carbon neutral, and other sustainable development aspects, we arguably need to go beyond just visualising stakeholders and reacting to their presence, because there are aspects like the natural environment to consider and generally going much deeper into issues raised (i.e., like the SDGs outline).

To truly achieve the SDGs then, organisations may need to radically alter their business practices, and this is likely to be costly in the first instance. Thus, perhaps organisations will just maintain this paradoxical situation and status quo, which we can perhaps label as profit- and shareholder-driven (*exploitative*) versus sustainable development action- and stakeholder-driven (*explorative*). Quite rightly, the former could be seen as the simpler and more secure option for a business, so could go a long way in explaining why organisations are slow to react and reluctant to make necessary changes. To effectively achieve the SDGs, however, the need for *explorative* approaches is theoretically clear; organisations need to be doing considerably more and embracing this need for change. If such change is resisted, contributions to the SDGs could be minimalist, tokenistic and fall considerably short of what is required.

So how can the above be done simultaneously, 'paradoxically in tandem' (Smith, 2016, p. 12)? One approach commonly suggested is finding cost efficiency through sustainable practices. This is arguably applying *exploitation*, because of the efficiency element, but also requires *exploration* to generate the new practices needed. This is perhaps where we are currently falling short in achieving the SDGs. If we can build this ambidextrous approach in more organisations, then arguably profit orientation and the SDGs can be simultaneously achieved? One aspect of this tension is clear. If the majority of organisations persist in resisting the application of necessary *explorative* practices, and therefore persist in being slow to change, this will only lead to limited achievement of the SDGs. But how can such change be achieved, at the rate that is required to meet the SDGs by 2030, within a fundamentally capitalist paradigm?

Tension 2: Transactional leadership versus transformational leadership versus responsible leadership

Leadership is another great area to highlight tension and potential paradox. To build that discussion here, we will highlight some very basic connections to leadership theory. The discussion could go a lot deeper, but we only want to introduce the debate to reflect on the subject matter within this chapter.

Transactional Leadership is commonly characterised through rewards in accordance to contracts and efforts exerted, and an avoidance of new direction when old practice fulfils performance goals (*exploitative*) (Hater and Bass, 1988; Smith, 2016). In contrast, Transformational Leadership is commonly characterised through an ability to instil pride, faith, respect and a sense of mission; an ability to delegate, teach, and coach; and an encouragement to think and act in new and creative ways (*explorative*) (Hater and Bass, 1988; Smith, 2016). This is perhaps the common tension often discussed in leadership literature. However, these are somewhat internalised and focused upon the organisation being worked for.

There is certainly greater emphasis on elements external to the organisation when considering responsible leadership, which can bring in areas of ethics, values, an emphasis on all stakeholders, serving and caring for others, trust and emotional intelligence (Maak and Pless, 2006; Pless, 2007; Tronto, 1993; Voegtlin et al., 2012). Thus, although *explorative* practices may clearly be needed here to focus on sustainable development, it is important to realise it is potentially an extra dimension of leadership capability. This intensifies the tension and the potential for paradox and even highlights further the need for practice that embraces various aspects of leadership approaches. The link between responsible leadership and achieving the SDGs becomes clear here: if PRME and the SDGs are externalised, it could become difficult for managers/leaders to even consider, never mind operationalise, relevant action to respond to these challenges.

Tension 3: Traditional education versus RME

A capitalism–related tension needs to be highlighted here as it has such a profound impact upon RME. If society accepts that we live in and prosper around a capitalist economy, then profit sits at the heart of this (Hirsch, 2021). Arguably then, to be effective at business in society, we need to be effectively trained in universities on profiteering and profit maximising. Society almost dictates this. As a result, the tension comes why trying to radically alter the minds of future business leaders (*explorative*) and bring in something potentially counterintuitive to that profit-focused training (*exploitative*), which is RME. General dimensions might include sustainability (triple bottom line), responsibility (stakeholder value) and ethics (moral excellence) (Laasch and Conaway, 2015). Despite criticisms that business schools need to become more socially responsible and grow beyond criticisms that they are 'brainwashing institutions educating their graduates only in relatively narrow shareholder value ideology' (Matten and Moon, 2004, p. 323), the tension and potential paradox will remain if society is generally built in such a capitalistic manner. This tension is further discussed through the hidden curriculum section that follows.

As academic educators, as the opening question highlights, we could be irresponsible in delivering RME if we are not successfully preparing graduates for a profit-focused capitalistic society. This is a real source of potential paradox/tension and one that is not discussed and explored enough amongst academics. Worse still, could it potentially mean that RME teachings become potentially *tokenistic* if graduates revert to business practices more akin to those traditional capitalistic teachings? In other words, it is all very well hearing about the importance of the SDGs and responsible management, but it would be devastating for impact if little action were to follow.

The difficulty of implementing and delivering on responsible management principles

The tensions identified and discussed in the previous section perhaps highlight the absence of an 'Alpha' (leader) in the RME system. Indeed, an inadequate structure for an organisation and an absence of positive synergy amongst members of a system are barriers to the sustainability of this system (Sun et al., 2013; Todd et al., 2017).

The 'Alpha' framework is used to discuss interactions amongst members of a system (Ek and Larson, 2017). This framework stipulates that a system must be spearheaded by an 'Alpha,' taking the role to make decisions for the entire group (Mech, 1999), as this person or organisation has been identified as the most capable to lead, but with the support of others (Mirjalili et al., 2014). Amongst these are the 'Beta,' who have a secondary role as part of its remits is to reinforce instructions from the 'Alpha,' as well as advising and providing feedback. The 'Beta' is/are the second in line if the 'Alpha' is not capable of performing relevant duties. The 'Omega' is at the bottom of the hierarchy as they are only required to obey orders, and serve as a scapegoat to vent frustrations and tensions. All the others below the 'Omega' are referred as 'Delta.' They are subordinates and do not have any specific role (Mirjalili et al., 2014).

With the above said, it is also worth mentioning the fact that the 'Alpha,' known to be strong, authoritative, and well-accomplished individuals or lead organisations, are also being perceived as weak, as their strengths are also their weaknesses (Ludeman and Erlandson, 2006). The concept of the 'Alpha' is ambidextrous by nature, because, and linking a Janusian thinking approach, there is a need to contemplate and consider simultaneously opposing operational strategies and implementations (Rothenberg, 1996; Sanchez and Adams, 2008; Vo-Thanh et al., 2020). This is almost a *sine qua non* condition for success. The ambidextrous 'Alpha' can be seen as both a hero who can save a group, but also as a villain who can harm this group (Mirjalili et al., 2014; Mkono et al., 2020). This is all the more important for complex systems, as these types of systems can lead to innovation (Rouard and Schegg, 2019) and, more importantly, improvement (Fragnière and Simon, 2019).

The context of RME is, based on previous discussions, a complex system that could benefit from ambidextrous approaches. Thus, for RME delivery it is important to determine the role ('Alpha,' 'Beta,' 'Omega,' and 'Delta') of each party involved in the system. Based on the tensions previously discussed, an 'Alpha' is certainly needed, but there is also an important role for an 'Omega.' At the moment, the related 'Alpha' role within RME institutions is not really performing effectively enough due to the fact that there is a disconnection between academia and industry when it comes to research related to sustainability and outcomes expected (Belmonte-Urena et al., 2021). This create tensions (like those previously mentioned). Graduates could arguably play the role of the 'Omega,' providing they manage to demonstrate their ability to simultaneously help an organisation to grow and offer sustainable and responsible strategies. For this to become effective as a transition from education to industry, it is also important to adopt a suitable type of structure for RME to work.

Organisations involved in collaboration schemes are organisations which have either a centralised structure based on hierarchy, an autonomous structure or a hybrid structure (Fragnière and Simon, 2019). Organisations based on a centralised structure are very efficient in terms of decision-making. However, when the hub of this centralised structure is negatively impacted by an issue, the entire network collapses and none of dependent satellites of the network can takeover. As for organisations based on an autonomous structure, the hub does not have a leading role and this makes these organisations difficult to manage. However, if the hub of the network collapses, a dependent satellite of the network can takeover. Finally, organisations based on hybrid structure are a mixture of the two previous one. This structure is quite dynamic, but also requires all satellites of the network to work very closely (Fragnière and Simon, 2019).

As ambidexterity has been underpinning much of the discussion in this chapter, a hybrid structure seems to be the most suitable when implementing and delivering RME. The centralised ('Alpha') role could be played by a leading PRME school (based on sustainability performance) in each country, which will play an advisory role to all other schools ('Delta') in the country. The schools will have some degree of autonomy in terms of how they implement PRME. However, because of the competitive nature of and between schools in terms of attracting students and positioning in leagues table, for instance. (Harker et al., 2016), this might be difficult to implement, even if a change in leadership approach is important for sustainability (Visser, 2016). Yet, when it comes to sustainability, and therefore RME, it appears that despite all stakeholders and shareholders being aware that change needs to happen, there is a reluctance to create radical changes in the way they operate (Mkono et al., 2020). This once again reveals ambidextrous/paradoxical tensions.

Competencies – an enabling tool for ambidextrous responsible management learning

By adopting a position that 'The purpose of business is to produce profitable solutions to the problems of people and planet, and not to profit from producing problems for people and planet' (Mayer and Roche, 2021, p.11), then, by extension, ambidextrous leaders are needed to address the goals of people *and* planet *and* profit. Paradoxically, transformational educational approaches also require transformational business approaches, since, in seeking innovative pedagogies, educators also need to focus on the employability competencies required by business. It would be irresponsible for business schools not to prepare graduates for workforce employability, while, at the same time, it can also be considered irresponsible for business schools not to prepare graduates to address the so-called 'wicked' problems of sustainability that businesses are, at the very least, answerable to. Thus, the following section considers how competencies can be embedded into education to equip graduates to seek profitable solutions (through exploitative efficiencies) to the problems of people and planet (through explorative innovative behaviours).

To analyse the potential impact of competencies as a tool for RME, it is helpful to first consider the application of competencies within an organisational context. While recognising there is extensive literature on varying definitions of competence versus competency/competencies, this chapter draws on early academic commentators such as Sparrow (1995) and leading practitioner bodies such as 'The Chartered Institute of Personnel and Development' (CIPD, 2020) in defining competencies as attitudes, skills and behaviours required for effective job performance. The subsequent section on the educational context will similarly define competencies as dimensions of Knowledge, Skills, and Attitudes/behaviours (KSA). Implications for responsible management analysis and action from an ambidexterity perspective will be considered across both organisational and educational competencies.

Organisational context

Competencies fall under the umbrella of contingency theories relating to performance management, whereby maximum performance is achieved when competencies are aligned with role requirements and organisational context (Boyatzis and Boyatzis, 2008). They are essentially talent management tools in recruiting, training, and evaluating performance. The CIPD (2020) advises that 'competency frameworks, when done well, can increase clarity around performance expectations and establish a clear link between individual and organizational performance.' The inherent paradoxes of competency frameworks are apparent here in that while they are descriptive tools in specifying desirable performance behaviours, at the same time, they are normative tools in terms of what people should do (Bolden et al., 2006). The suggestion that individual and organisational performance is benefitted 'when done well' can be juxtaposed with individual and organisational outcomes when they are not done well. Paradoxically, therefore, it might be said that while they are designed to benefit individual and organisational performance, they can potentially also constrain and inhibit effective behaviours. The same of course applies to their effective application in educational settings.

The multi-functional use of competency frameworks means they are applicable to Organisational Ambidexterity. This can serve as tools for both *exploitation* (for example, in selective recruitment processes or in defining the daily job roles in a realistic way) and *exploration* (for example, in performance development when they need to be applicable to as many people as possible or in defining the daily job roles as an aspirational guide for behaviour). There is a significant body of literature which details the limitations of competency frameworks effectively synthesised by Bolden and Gosling (2006) as being reductionist in a fragmented approach to what are often complex roles; generic without considering context; backward rather than forward looking; too focused on measurable behaviours rather than more subtle qualities; and mechanistic which results in a 'criteria compliance' (*exploitative*) rather than encouraging innovative and risk-taking behaviours that might not 'tick' within the competency 'box' (*explorative*).

Hollenbeck et al. (2006, p. 412) contend that although competency frameworks may appear to be reductionist and generic, they 'can be used and applied in complex ways' and that they 'are a useful attempt to help leaders learn a broader range of competencies and, in the process, learn how to use them differentially and effectively across different situations.' This view is helpful to inform an analysis of pedagogical approaches to embedding competencies for responsible management, in which they are flexibly and creatively applied, rather than restrictive and constraining to effective behaviours and learning. While it is straightforward to accept that they should not be used as a 'one size fits all' measuring instrument, whether in an organisational or educational context (in which they would be used exploitatively), it is perhaps less straightforward to ensure they are applied flexibly according to situational differences (i.e., *explorative*). The key, of course, is that they are both explorative and exploitative.

Embedding RME

University education represents a significant opportunity to influence society and business, and it is the purpose of PRME to shape the skills and behaviours of current and future business leaders. This section details some of the major areas of study into competencies for Education for Sustainable Development (ESD). This is an evolving field, which capture approaches, such as Rieckmann (2018), in informing educational pedagogy linking the SDGs to 12 ESD competencies (*A Rounder Sense of Purpose*, undated) through to the business discipline. For instance, building on Wiek et al. (2011), Laasch and Moosmayer (2016) provide a systematic literature review which underpins the competencies needed for the 'professionalisation' of responsible business management. This analyses competency literature according to KSA (Knowledge, Skills, Attitude) dimensions, which are also adopted in five competencies of the 'Competency Assessment for Responsible Leadership' (CARL, 2021; Muff et al., 2020).

At a broader level, UNESCO (2017, 2020) identified eight 'cross-cutting competencies for achieving the SDGs.' These link the competencies to the cognitive domain (Knowledge), behavioural domain (Skills) and socio-emotional domain (Attitudes). UNESCO's competencies have been adopted by The Quality Assurance Agency (QAA, 2021) which manages standards of higher education in the UK. The KSA dimensions provide a helpful framework for informing educators understanding of learning outcomes and activities. Table 1.2 compares the UNESCO (2017) competencies to those of the CARL framework. This is not intended as a definitive comparison and it is relevant to note that the CARL framework literature does not refer directly to UNESCO competencies. The purpose here is to demonstrate the alignment between mainstream sustainability and responsible management competencies.

As a result, we are calling for ambidextrous university education, which simultaneously develops graduates' commercial acumen as part of the more predictable (*exploitative*) expectations of a programme alongside main-streaming responsible management which can be seen as riskier (*explorative*). This represents a paradigm shift away from 'shoe-horning' the SDGs into modules, towards strategically embedding the principles from the top down, such as in programme revalidation design. The broader university context is fundamental in shaping students lived experiences and operationalising any definitions of sustainability/responsible management-focused competencies, in the same way as organisational contexts influence employee attitudes and behaviours. Therefore, competencies for sustainable education are useful in scrutiny of both formal learning and the 'hidden curriculum' (Blasco, 2011), which refers to the wider university experiences of campus life that can act to positively reinforce or undermine formal curriculum learning.

There is huge potential for graduates to enter the workforce with a mindset for transformative business action, filling the void identified by

Table 1.2 Comparison of competencies within sustainability frameworks (based on UNESCO (2017), CARL (2021) and Muff et al. (2020))

UNESCO/QAA Competencies for Achieving the SDGs	Competency Assessment for Responsible Leadership (CARL)
Systems thinking	Systems thinking
Normative	Ethics and values
Strategic	Change and Innovation
Collaboration	Stakeholder relations
Self-awareness	Self-awareness
Integrated problem-solving	
Anticipatory	
Critical thinking	

Gosling and Grodecki (2020, p. 251) that 'there is little to say that leaders should be willing to initiate transformative responses to injustice, ecocide and inequality. The world of management competences has yet to catch on to calls for radical changes to (or of) capitalism.' University is arguably the ideal base for developing students' competencies to develop the organisational competency frameworks needed for a new, ambidextrous responsible business paradigm. As set out by Redman et al. (2020), it is now necessary to consider how competencies can most effectively be assessed in educational contexts, linking to the same limitations of organisational contexts where Stokes and Oiry (2012) observe that competencies can be assessed in 'variable and unreliable' ways. The challenge for both business and education is to move from rhetoric to action.

Final reflections

It has been shown that while there is an understanding of the competencies required to address the so-called wicked problems of sustainability, it requires an urgent imperative for organisations to integrate responsible management competencies (capturing ethical, environmental, and social behaviours) into existing management competency frameworks. It is positive that competencies are being integrated into advice for 'Education for Sustainable Development 2030' as part of the SDGs, but if universities are to avoid the criticisms of businesses whereby frameworks are backwards rather than forward looking, it is vital for a common language of responsible management competencies to be developed between business and education. Within education, programmes need to consider paradoxical tensions in how responsible management competencies are featured across modules and programmes and use this to develop ambidextrous thinking, alongside how competencies are reinforced or possibly decoupled by the informal curriculum.

Returning to the initial question, 'Are we *irresponsible* in delivering RME?,' we hope the reader can see that the paradox and tensions explored make it a complicated answer. Yet, we strive for the answer to be a 'no' if we can tackle the paradox and tensions using Organisational Ambidexterity. By understanding the challenges under a different lens, we perhaps give ourselves a better chance of working towards effective change for the future that will support PRME and work towards greater achievement of the SDGs while maintaining some of the status quo related to society ideals, for instance a desire to make a significant profit in business. This offers greater depth of thought when considering the leadership of the SDGs, the role of business schools and this whole book overall. This chapter has explored RME under a different microscope/lens and this should build on the wealth of perspectives throughout the different chapters. We hope the journey through this chapter has been emotive, engaging, and forward thinking. It might have provoked some discomfort, but also a chance to self-reflect and be inspired. Responsible management educators are essential and important actors and it is crucial we are constantly pushing ourselves and our approaches to help businesses and students with their future working practices. Contemplating and embracing paradoxical practices could be an important way to assist in this development.

Where next?

Case studies demonstrating how responsible management competencies can most effectively be embedded into the formal and informal curriculum are needed, since to focus on the dimensions of KSA requires additional planning by educators, and additional focus by students. Such case examples should build on debates around the most effective ways of embedding competencies into *explorative* curriculums, within potentially *exploitative* contexts based on restrictive resourcing.

Research is needed into how embedding competencies into RME links to changes in business behaviours and attitudes. As stated at the beginning of this chapter, it would be devastating if educational inputs were not linked to positive industry impacts in effectively managing the paradox of people versus profit versus planet.

In terms of the paradoxical situations, we could argue there is a need to accept that such realities exist. Instead of trying to fix or resolve this, we could instead find practices that embrace the nature of paradox. Applying Organisational Ambidexterity, and even ambidextrous leadership approaches, could assist in finding workable solutions rather than being lost in the frustrations of complex paradoxical realities. For business schools and responsible management educators, applying critical reflection and then making effective change could be assisted by the lens of thinking offered here. In essence, we should not accept the norms and limitations of RME, but should seek to advance its delivery and impact.

References

Belmonte-Urena, L.J., Plaza-Ubeda, J.A., Vasquez-Brust, D. and Yakovleva, N. (2021). 'Circular economy, degrowth and green growth as pathways for research on sustainable development goals: A global analysis and future agenda,' *Ecological Economics*, 185(19).

Birkinshaw, J. and Gupta, K. (2013). 'Clarifying the distinctive contribution of ambidexterity to the field of organization studies,' *Academy of Management Perspectives*, 27(4), 287–298.

Blasco, M. (2011). 'Aligning the hidden curriculum of management education with PRME,' *Journal of Management Education*, 36(3), 364–388.

Bolden, R., Wood, M. and Gosling, J. (2006).' Is the NHS leadership qualities framework missing the wood for the trees?,' in Casebeer, A.L., Harrison, A., and Mark, A.L. (Eds.) *Innovations in health care - A reality check.* Palgrave Macmillan, pp. 17–29.

Boyatzis, R.E. and Boyatzis, R. (2008). 'Competencies in the 21st century,' *Journal of Management Development*, 27(1), 5–12.

CARL (2021). *CARL – The Competency Assessment for Responsible Leadership.* Available at: https://carl2030.org/ [Accessed 15/11/2021].

CIPD (2020). 'Chartered Institute of Personnel and Development,' *Competency Factsheet.* Available at: https://www.cipd.co.uk/knowledge/fundamentals/people/performance/competency-factsheet [Accessed 15/11/2021].

Ek, R. and Larson, M. (2017). 'Imagining the Alpha male of the tourism tribe,' *Anatolia*, 28(4), 540–552.

Fragnière, E. and Simon, M. (2019). 'Design de services et réseau d'acteurs Deux outils complémentaires pour une destination plus attractive,' *Espaces*, 347, 10–12

Freeman, R.E. (2015). 'Stakeholder theory,' In *Wiley encyclopedia of management.* John Wiley & Sons.

Friedman, M. (1962). *Capitalism and freedom.* Chicago, IL: Chicago University Press.

Friedman, F. (1970). *A friednzan doctrine.* New York Times, 13 Sept 17.

Gosling, J. and Grodecki, A. (2020). 'Competencies for responsible management (and Leadership) education and practice,' in Moosmayer, D., Laasch, O., Parkes, C., and Brown, K.G. (Eds.), *The SAGE handbook of responsible management learning and education.* SAGE Publications, pp. 245–264.

Hahn, T., Figge, F., Pinkse, J. and Preuss, L. (2018). 'A paradox perspective on corporate sustainability: Descriptive, instrumental, and normative aspects,' *Journal of Business Ethics*, 148, 235–248.

Harker, M.J., Caemmerer, B. and Hynes, N. (2016). 'Management education by the french grandes ecoles de commerce: Past, Present, and an Uncertain Future,' *Academy of Management Learning & Education*, 15(3).

Hater, J.J. and Bass, B.M. (1988). 'Superior's evaluations and subordinate's perceptions of transformational and transactional leadership,' *Journal of Applied Psychology*, 73(4), 695–702.

Hirsch, R. (2021). 'Risk and Trouble: Adam Smith on profit and the protagonists of capitalism,' *American Journal of Political Science*, 65(1), 166–179.

Hollenbeck, G.P., McCall, M.W. and Silzer, R.F. (2006). 'Leadership competency models,' *The Leadership Quarterly*, 17(4), 398–413.

Kohli, A. and Mier, J. (2021). *The Secret Ingredients in Netflix's Success Story.* Scheller News. Available at: https://www.scheller.gatech.edu/news-events/latest-news/2021/the-secret-ingredients-in-netflix-success-story.html [Accessed 05/11/2021].

Laasch, O. and Conaway, R. (2015). *Principles of responsible management: Glocal sustainability, responsibility and ethics.* Stamford: Cengage.

Laasch, O. and Moosmayer, D. (2016). *Responsible management competences: Building a portfolio for professional competence.* Academy of Management Annual Conference. Available at: https://www.researchgate.net/profile/Oliver-Laasch/publication/320790269_Responsible_Management_Competences_Building_a_Portfolio_for_Professional_Competence/links/5c734f5a458515831f6ccc95/Responsible-Management-Competences-Building-a-Portfolio-for-Professional-Competence.pdf [Accessed 15/11/2021].

Ludeman, K. and Erlandson, E. (2006). *Alpha male syndrome.* Boston, Massachusetts: Harvard Business School Press.

Maak, T. and Pless, N. (2006). *Responsible leadership.* New York: Routledge.

Matten, D. and Moon, J. (2004). 'Corporate social responsibility education in Europe,' *Journal of Business Ethics*, 54(4), 323–337.

Mayer, C. and Roche, B. (2021). *Putting purpose into practice: The economics of mutuality.* Oxford University Press.

Mech, D.L. (1999). 'Alpha status, dominance, and division of labour in wolf packs,' *Canadian Journal of Zoology*, 77(8), 1196–1203.

Mirjalili, S., Mirjalili, S.M. and Lewis, A. (2014). 'Grey wolf optimizer,' *Advances in Engineering Software*, 69, 46–61.

Mkono, M., Hughes, K. and Echentille, S. (2020). 'Hero or villain? Responses to Greta Thunberg's activism and the implications for travel and tourism,' *Journal of Sustainable Tourism*, 28(12), 2081–2098.

Moratis, L. and Melissen, F. (2022). 'Bolstering responsible management education through the sustainable development goals: Three perspectives,' *Management Learning*, 53(2), 212–222.

Muff, K., Liechti, A. and Dyllick, T. (2020). 'How to apply responsible leadership theory in practice: A competency tool to collaborate on the sustainable development goals,' *Corporate Social Responsibility and Environmental Management*, 27(5), 2254–2274.

O'Reilly, C.A. and Tushman, M.L. (2013). 'Organizational ambidexterity: Past, present, and future,' *Academy of Management Perspectives*, 27(4), 324–338.

Poole, M.S. and Van de Ven, A.H. (1989). 'Using paradox to build management and organization theories,' *Academy of Management Review*, 14(4).

Porter, M.E. (1980). *Competitive strategy: Techniques for analyzing industries and competitors.* New York: Free Press.

Porter, M.E. (1985). *The competitive advantage: Creating and sustaining superior performance.* New York: Free Press.

Porter, M.E. (2004). *Competitive strategy.* New York: Free Press.

Pless, N.M. (2007). 'Understanding responsible leadership: Role identity and motivational drivers,' *Journal of Business Ethics*, 74, 437–456.

QAA. (2021). 'The Quality Assurance Agency for Higher Education and Advance HE,' *Education for sustainable development guidance* https://www.qaa.ac.uk/quality-code/education-for-sustainable-development [Accessed 06/05/2022].

Raisch, S., Birkinshaw, J., Probst, G. and Tushman, M.L. (2009). 'Organizational ambidexterity: Balancing exploitation and exploration for sustained performance,' *Organization Science*, 20(4), 685–695.

Redman, A., Wiek, A. and Barth, M. (2020). 'Current practice of assessing students' sustainability competencies: a review of tools,' *Sustainability Science*, 16(1), 117–135.

Rieckmann, M. (2018). 'Learning to transform the world: key competencies in ESD,' In *Issues and Trends in Education for Sustainable Development* United Nations Educational, Scientific and Cultural Organization https://en.unesco.org/sites/default/files/issues_0.pdf.

Ritzer, G. (2008). *The McDonaldization of society 5.* London: Sage.

Rothenberg, A. (1996). 'The Janusian process in scientific creativity,' *Creativity Research Journal*, 9(2), 207–231.

Rouard, A. and Schegg, R. (2019). 'Construire une destination via la mise en réseau des acteurs Le projet européen Transfrontour,' *Espaces*, 347, 6–9.

Sanchez, P.M. and Adams, K.M. (2008). 'The Janus-faced character of tourism in Cuba,' *Annals of Tourism Research*, 35(1), 27–46.

Séraphin, H., Smith, S.M., Ghidouche, F. and Nechoud, L. (2022). 'The principles of responsible management education and responsible tourism strategies: Success, failure or trauma for generation Z?,' in Séraphin, H. (eds.) *Children in Sustainable and Responsible Tourism*. Emerald Publishing Limited.

Séraphin, H., Smith, S.M. and Yahiaoui, D. (2021a). 'Investigating the perception and attitude of business school students toward overtourism at *Marseille Calanques National Park*,' In Mandic, A. and Petric, L. (eds.) *Mediterranean protected areas in the era of overtourism: Challenges and solutions*. Cham: Springer.

Séraphin, H., Yallop, A.C., Smith, S.M. and Modica, G. (2021b). 'The implementation of the principles for responsible management education within tourism higher education institutions: A comparative analysis of european union countries,' *International Journal of Management Education*, 19(3).

Smith, S.M. (2016). 'Management and organization – the 21st century global and international context,' in Stokes, P., Moore, N., Smith, S.M., Rowland, C. and Scott, P. (Eds.), *Organizational management: Approaches and solutions*. London: Kogan Page, pp. 1–26.

Sparrow, P. (1995). 'Organizational competencies: A valid approach for the future?,' *International Journal of Selection and Assessment*, 3, 168–197.

Stokes, P., Moore, N., Moss, D., Mathews, M., Smith, S.M. and Yi-Peng, L. (2015). 'The micro-dynamics of intra-organizational and individual behaviour and their role in organizational ambidexterity boundaries,' *Human Resource Management*, 54(1), 63–86.

Stokes, P. and Oiry, E. (2012). 'An evaluation of the use of competencies in human resource development – a historical and contemporary recontextualisation,' *EuroMed Journal of Business*, 7(1), 4–23.

Stokes, P., Smith, S.M., Wall, T., Moore, N., Rowland, C., Ward, T. and Cronshaw, C. (2019). 'Resilience and the (Micro-)Dynamics of organizational ambidexterity: Implications for strategic HRM,' *International Journal of Human Resource Management*, 30(8), 1287–1322.

Sun, Y.Y., Rodriguez, A., Wu, J.H. and Chuang, S.T. (2013). 'Why hotel rooms were not full during a hallmark sporting event: The 2009 World Games experience,' *Tourism Management*, 36, 469–479.

Todd, L., Leask, A. and Ensor, J. (2017). 'Understanding primary stakeholders' multiple roles in hallmark event,' *Tourism Management*, 59, 494–509.

Tronto, J. (1993). *Moral boundaries: A political argument for an ethic of care*. New York, NY: Routledge.

UNESCO. (2017). *Education for Sustainable Development Goals: Learning Objectives*. United Nations Educational, Scientific and Cultural Organization. Available at: https://www.unesco.de/sites/default/files/2018-08/unesco_education_for_sustainable_development_goals.pdf [Accessed 15/11/2021].

UNESCO. (2020). *Education for sustainable development: A road map*. United Nations Educational, Scientific and Cultural Organization. Available at: https://unesdoc.unesco.org/ark:/48223/pf0000374802 [Accessed 15/11/2021].

Visser, W. (ed.) (2016). *The world guide to sustainable enterprise*. Sheffield: Greenleaf Publishing.

Voegtlin, C., Patzer, M. and Scherer, A.G. (2012). 'Responsible leadership in global business: A new approach to leadership and its multi-level outcomes,' *Journal of Business Ethics*, 105, 1–16.

Vo-Thanh, T., Séraphin, H., Okumus, F. and Koseoglu, M.A. (2020). 'Organizational ambidexterity in tourism research: A systematic review,' *Tourism Analysis*, 25(1), 137–152.

Wiek, A., Withycombe, L. and Redman, C.L. (2011). 'Key competencies in sustainability: a reference framework for academic program development,' *Sustainability Science*, 6(2), 203–218.

2 Emotional competency in the interdisciplinary classroom: A systems thinking perspective

Joanna C. Carey and James Hunt

Introduction

There is consensus that higher education must help prepare students to address grand social and environmental challenges, as exemplified by the UN's Sustainable Development Goals (SDGs). Leadership and political will are essential in addressing the SDGs (United Nations, 2016) and as such, leadership development should be a critical component of sustainability education. We need leaders who have both the emotional and intellectual maturity to deal with the complexity of sustainability challenges, leaders who can create empathetic and fact-based arguments.

Traditionally, education in sustainability has focused largely on building students' cognitive understanding of sustainability-related issues (Montiel et al., 2018). Shrivastava (2010), however, has argued for a more holistic approach to management education for sustainability, incorporating emotional and spiritual perspectives, in addition to the cognitive. An important goal of such an approach is to help build a passion for change, which is thought to be a key component of leadership effectiveness. However, we ask, do students really need help building a passion for sustainability?

Evidence suggests that many Gen Z and Millenial Americans are already passionate about sustainability; survey findings from the Pew Research Center point to a very high level of commitment for taking action on climate change from this age group. Students frequently describe business and government as doing too little to deal with sustainability-related issues, especially climate change, and in turn, they are willing to take action – even if such actions negatively impact their financial wellbeing (Tyson et al., 2021). Such evidence, and our own anecdotal experience, suggests that emotions are running high among students concerned about sustainability.

Is that a problem? The answer is likely yes, and no. As stated above, passion is a major driver of leadership action (Shrivastava, 2010). At the same time, powerful emotions by themselves are not always helpful to a leader. Research on emotional intelligence and leadership development, suggests that leaders need to be able to harness their emotions without being overwhelmed by them (Goleman and Boyatzis, 2017). The central

DOI: 10.4324/9781003244905-4

question we raise here is: *how can we help our passionately committed students further their development as sustainability leaders in light of the inherent emotional nature of the challenges before us?*

We recently completed a two-year launch of an interdisciplinary co-taught elective course, *Unintended Consequences: At the interface of Business and the Environment*, taught by an earth science professor and a management professor. All enrolled students were business majors, many of whom demonstrated a passion for sustainability. We designed our course using a systems thinking framework (Meadows, 2008) as a way to unite the disciplines and examine sustainability-related problems from multiple perspectives. We quickly learned that, in addition to divergent disciplinary perspectives, we also had to address the divergence between the cognitive and the emotional challenges provoked by the issues and students' concerns.

Below we provide a brief review of sustainability leadership development in order to provide broader context for our observations and suggestions. We then describe the course, including details of reflective writing assignments in which students discussed sustainability from a personal perspective. These assignments provided the students and faculty a view of the emotional and cognitive challenges associated with sustainability leadership. We explore the themes that emerged from student written reflections and then discuss lessons learned from our experience that may be useful to other educators. Our experiences points to a number of pedagogical approaches that may help students integrate their commitment to change in a way that promotes their effectiveness as leaders.

Evolving perspectives on sustainability leadership

Who is a sustainability leader? What role do they play? What skills are required?

Simply put, sustainability leaders are those who take up the cause of sustainability in an effort to address long-term needs of individuals, social systems, and the environment (Ferdig, 2007). Such leaders may be formal or informal, in that they may or may not have an organisationally defined leadership role. The sustainability leader does not need one to be to be the most knowledgeable or most capable regarding the issue at hand; the leader can be anyone who advocates for change and engages others in the process.

However, taking an advocacy position is not necessarily easy or even effective from a change agent perspective. For example, a study of graduates of a sustainability-informed construction program found that they did not feel prepared to advocate for change, and when they did so, they were not successful, despite having a solid technical knowledge of the sustainability issues in their industry (Thomas et al., 2020). The array of structural factors in their workplace (e.g., norms, roles, traditions and the market) likely make it difficult for even knowledgeable graduates to effect change. These authors suggest that 'their educational institutions would need to develop curriculum to help students *resist* the opposing influences of the workplace (e.g., market/end user, clients and colleagues)' (Thomas et al., 2020, p. 1211; italics is ours).

Such interpretations of sustainability leadership (Ferdig, 2007; Thomas et al., 2020) take an individual agency perspective on the part of the sustainability leader. The leader advocates and when necessary, resists. Such an individualistic perspective has been described by some scholars as 'heroic' (Bradford and Cohen, 2007). The notion of the heroic leader is deeply embedded in Western culture and is widespread in the media, past and present. Such heroic imagery implies that leaders can make change happen on their own, if they are sufficiently skilled and courageous (Heizmann and Liu, 2017). This perspective has also supported a management development industry that focuses on building individual level competencies, such as influence, team building, and conflict management.

The heroic mental model of leadership puts responsibility on the shoulders of the individuals who care, resulting in the linear assumption that *we need a hero who can save us.* Individual agency begets assumptions of individual agency. Not only does this reflect a linear – and perhaps inaccurate – model of leadership and change, it creates the potential for blame, guilt, and anger. As educators, we find reoccurring instances of student anger regarding society's failure to respond effectively to social and environmental needs. While we often share that anger, we question the productivity of this limiting, emotionally driven idea of leadership.

Leadership scholarship has evolved considerably over the past several decades to encompass a social view of leadership, one with less of a focus on individual agency and more on collective agency (Raelin, 2016, Bradford and Cohen, 2007, Pearce et al., 2013). In this view, leaders are relationship builders, bringing people together around a shared vision. That shared vision cannot be the leader's alone, but reflects the aspirations of all of those involved. Leaders and followers are not necessarily bound by organisational structures, but rather by aspirations. Leaders are implicitly in the business of finding shared visions among people who may not necessarily be allies outright.

Linking the collective agency leadership model with systems thinking

Collective models of leadership acknowledge that change takes place in the context of complex systems, a notion quite familiar to systems thinkers. However, differing systems frameworks yield very different approaches to sustainability leadership, and the distinction between individual and collective agency leadership is mirrored in the distinction between the functional and the complex adaptive systems frameworks (Porter and Cordoba, 2009).

The functional perspective relies on a comprehensive traditional system model. That model holds that system components, and the relationships between those components, are knowable and can be fully described. Causality is largely linear in nature. Functionalist framework learning goals include identifying system components and their relationships, as well as how to change these components and relationships to improve system functioning. The heroic leader applies the technical skills that have a predictable impact on the system. The leader should be able to apply recognised solutions and 'fix' system problems.

Alternatively, the complex adaptive system framework sees systems as densely connected, self-organising, and dynamic over time. System evolution is not necessarily coordinated by a top-down plan, but rather by the experience of the system and its response. System change is not necessarily predictable, particularly over extended periods of time. In order to participate in the system's evolution, one must identify key stakeholders, their perspectives, and leverage points for change. In this framework, the leader is one of many. Collaboration with key stakeholders, including those with whom one disagrees, is therefore essential. The skills of the individual are important, but the leader cannot act in isolation.

The complex system perspective for sustainability leadership development is consistent with the skill requirements articulated by many corporate leaders. In a survey of 194 executives from companies that are signatories to the United Nations Global Compact, the following knowledge and skill sets appeared among the top 11 desired items, out of 26 options (Gitsham and Clark, 2012):

- Ability to make decisions when facing considerable complexity and ambiguity
- Ability to be flexible and responsive in the face of change
- Ability to engage in effective dialogue and partnerships with a wide variety of organisational stakeholders, including people with different perspectives and world views.

While these skills were desired, executives felt that they were lacking in potential sustainability leaders (Gitsham and Clark, 2012). These perspectives suggest that traditional models of leadership may not be as effective as shared leadership.

The role of empathy in sustainability leadership

The complex system perspective for sustainability leadership thus challenges traditional individualistic models of leadership. In addition, discussions of sustainability are often accompanied by emotional responses (Montiel et al., 2018). Sustainability problems, such as climate change, can be frightening to those engaged with the issue, and the solutions can be equally – if not more – frightening to those impacted by proposed fixes. The potential for emotional and practical gridlock can be sufficiently great to discourage active participation. For that reason, trying to remove emotion from a discussion of sustainability to focus solely on the 'rational' is problematic, if not impossible.

Both emotion and cognition play important roles in shaping how complex systems adapt to sustainability-related challenges (Chapman et al., 2017; Meadows, 2008). Emotions are not simple levers, but rather system components that are changeable as a system evolves. Effectively participating in a system's evolution requires careful attention to emotions. For example, research examining the relative roles of fear and anger versus hope and optimism in motivating people to take action on climate change demonstrate the complex – and sometimes counterintuitive – relationships between system elements (Thomas et al., 2009; O'Neill and Nicholson-Cole 2009; Chapman et al., 2017).

It is for these reasons that we argue that empathy is critical to the development and success of sustainability leaders. Empathy here refers to the ability to thoughtfully consider, understand, and validate both the feelings and perspective of others (Goleman, 2017). Empathy is likely to be essential to establishing effective collaborations, particularly those with whom one may disagree (Bradford and Cohen, 2007).

Our challenge as educators becomes how to teach the value of understanding other's points of view. Can we teach students to understand the feelings and perspectives of other stakeholders in a constantly evolving complex system? Promising pedagogies on this topic involve active learning rather than traditional instruction (MacVaugh and Norton, 2012), coupled with reflection on oneself and the system with which one is involved (Ayers et al., 2020). In the following sections, we will explore how we addressed these issues in our course.

The course: Unintended consequences – At the interface of business and the environment

Our course on unintended consequences grew from our shared interests in the impact of business activity on the environment. The title speaks to a focus on the long-term, unforeseen (or poorly understood) consequences of business decisions on the environment. Could such consequences have been foreseen? Are there tools that could warn decision-makers of such risks? Can the factors that shape such decisions be understood? While this was not a leadership development course per se, our systems-oriented curriculum, coupled with the interdisciplinary orientation of the faculty, continually raised the question of how stakeholders might find common ground on divisive topics relating to business-environment interactions.

A foundation in systems thinking

To address such questions and link two distinct academic disciplines (earth science and management), we used a systems thinking framework

(Meadows, 2008). Systems thinking provides a vehicle for integrating and understanding the complex interdisciplinary decisions that business leaders face, decisions that may be impactful over an extended period of time. System thinking also provides the tools to understand an individual's place in larger systems, providing useful context for students to recognise the challenges of attempting to effect change. Our course goals were to help students learn to:

• Apply systems thinking to a business opportunity in order to better understand the short and long term implications of that opportunity for a variety of stakeholders
• Apply scientific concepts and the scientific method to assess the potential environmental impact of business behaviour over time
• Use scientific concepts and methods to understand how to mitigate problematic consequences of certain economically driven behaviour, particularly those associated with ecological degradation.

We relied upon a number of systems thinking concepts throughout: how systems are defined and interact, the dynamic nature of systems through their stocks and flows over time, the role of feedbacks in system dynamics, and common system traps, such as the tragedy of the commons (Meadows, 2008; Ostrom, 2008). We addressed feedback delays, which are often critical barriers to effective business decision making. We also examined systems thinking topics that relate to both to business and the environment, such as system resilience, hierarchy, and boundaries (Meadows, 2008).

Our goal was to create an immersive educational experience by exposing students to rich stories, particularly those in which conflicts between various system components were present. Narratives structured as stories have been found to facilitate emotional arousal and engagement, especially on the topic of climate change (Morris et al., 2019). We pulled our narratives from a series of contemporary and historical cases that lie at the intersection of business and the natural environment. For example, we spent considerable effort exploring the ecological impact of river damming to power textile mills in New England during the 18th and 19th century. In doing so, we examined the forces that promoted the damming of rivers during the industrial revolution, alongside the naiveté over the damages caused by such behaviour.

Importantly, we used a flipped classroom approach to explore student-chosen cases, in which students presented their analysis and system diagrams of the business and environmental systems involved in each case, as well as lead a class discussion pertaining to the case (Mazur, 2013). These case studies were chosen from current events, which frequently portray two adversarial perspectives on environmental issues as they relate to economic activity – the environment versus the economy. The students reported feeling torn between the two worlds – one that cared about the environment and the other that valued financial well-being and corporate success. In reality, the sustainability of ecological and economic conditions is intertwined and often interdependent. The exploration of these ideas through a systems thinking lens allowed us to illuminate these connections between economic and environmental sustainability, and created opportunities for students to reflect on their ties to both.

In addition to the flipped class, we also assigned a group project in which students explored the interactions between a specific business system and a natural ecosystem of their choice. Our discussion and assessment of the student projects relied heavily on the importance of taking multiple perspectives on the issues in question. Reductionist analyses were discouraged, with the intent of a thorough cognitive exploration of the systems that included the emotional aspects of the conflict. Finally – and perhaps most importantly – we assigned two self-reflection papers that asked students to consider their own assumptions and their individual role in larger systems. Reflection papers gave us, as instructors, critical feedback that allowed us to adapt our teaching to address common emotions and gaps in understanding.

While the activities and assignments were cognitively oriented, student-chosen cases and topic areas had significant emotional meaning to the students. The reflection papers were particularly insightful at elucidating student perceptions, thought processes, and intense emotional reactions relating to a variety of sustainability-related topics; these insights presented challenges for students in fully grasping the complexity of the systems at play in sustainability crises and, in turn, are the focus of our effort described in this text. The prompts for these papers were as follows:

Reflection paper 1 prompt: Cannot see the forest for the trees

When we compare reductionist versus systems theory approaches to solving problems, one of the central issues becomes our focal point – do we focus on the interconnectedness and function of a system, or do we focus on individual elements of a system? The objective of this paper is to consider your own individual assumptions about the proper relationship between businesses and the environment. What factors in your life have shaped those assumptions? How do those assumptions impact your decision-making and analysis in a business context? In other words, how do your assumptions shape your ability to see the whole? Can you see the forest for the trees?

Reflection paper 2 prompt: Boom, bust, and you

Business sustainability in many respects is closely related to environmental and social sustainability. Throughout the course we have seen repeated examples of business boom and bust, and the impact of those cycles on the social and environmental world.[1] Knowing the rapid movement of the business world that is a function of technological and social change, as well as the capital system within which we live, how do you manage your own career, your own business decisions? For example, would you start a business that you foresee becoming obsolete in the future? Think of yourself as a system. What other systems are likely to drive you? What are your alternatives in managing those system relationships?

Emerging themes on business-environment interactions from reflective writing

Reflective pedagogies are designed to help students integrate the technical and the emotional aspects of their development (Ayers et al., 2020). Our students' reflections were strongly influenced by their personal, familial, and cultural experiences, resulting in a wide variety of responses to the assignment prompts. However, we did identify several recurring themes regarding the emotional perspectives from which students view sustainability issues. These themes shed light on the challenges people experience when trying to understand their place in a complex system. In particular, they contrast the individual or heroic perspective versus a perspective offering potential collaboration.

The individual perspective brings with it feelings of anger and guilt. The individual is aligned against the system. As one student said:

> 'Businesses should prioritize finding substitutes and alternatives to plastic waste that do not contribute to negative impacts on the environment throughout their lifecycle. Because of this, I try not to forgive businesses even more than I try not to forgive myself. We are all part of this complex system, however businesses hold a bigger role and have more control over the system than consumers.'

Similarly, another student, who is an avid skier, indicated that, as a skier, they did not see the 'forest for the trees' until taking coursework in sustainability. This more enlightened view of mind brought with it a greater sense of personal responsibility:

> 'Ski areas are not the only one's lagging behind, though, because individuals visiting ski resorts are also causing environmental damage in the process. I'm extremely guilty of causing unnecessary pollution due to ski-related travel.'

Of course, seasoned systems thinking teachers are used to such linear simplifications of what is actually a complex systems problem. Their personal involvement in behaviors that they see as being unsustainable is broadly experienced as a failing:

> 'I want to make an eco-friendly purchase, I have found myself purchasing the cheapest option. It can be hard to balance my financial

needs with my desire for sustainable products. It is necessary that I constantly remind myself of the global issues and impacts that businesses have on the environment so that I do not lose sight of the bigger picture.'

While personal responsibility and sacrifice are laudable and can be personally fulfilling, it will likely have a minimal impact on the sustainability problems we confront. Such linear assumptions that have significant emotional meaning are common. Compare the desire for self-improvement above to a desire for corporate behaviour change here:

'Every industry produces waste and the companies do not take responsibility for the harm they are creating for the environment. Companies need to realize their role in the destruction of our planet, especially before people stop purchasing their products.'

The 'us versus them' perspective based on anger and blame is difficult to miss here. Guilt and blame, though completely understandable, do not help us empathically view system participants in a way that facilitates collaboration. While this linear perspective was common, we also heard about the potential for empathy-based collaboration. A more dispassionate and empathic perspective can facilitate a better understanding of the relationship among system stakeholders. The possibilities for collaboration were particularly evident when students found business models that seemed to reflect collaboration in action. Contrast that perspective with the following, again from our skier:

'I spent roughly 10 days in (interning in a large ski resort management company) and it shocked me to learn about the incredible steps they were taking to limit their effect on our climate. Because of these steps, [the company] is a company I would want to work for.'

How should faculty address individualistic and linear assumptions? We found it useful to repeatedly ask students to reflect on their own perceptions of sustainability-related challenges, and their assumptions of the conflict between business and the environment. The adversarial approach inherent in a linear perspective seems very unlikely to help solve large-scale sustainability problems. While we cannot discount the very real bad actors in the business community who degrade environmental and social capital for the sake of financial success, a systems thinking approach that identifies and recognises the perspectives of all stakeholders is an essential component of finding solutions to sustainability-related problems. We found pedagogies related to reflective writing and analysis that considers both the cognitive and emotional aspects of complex systems to be an effective method for teaching these tools.

Lessons learned

There is tremendous value in helping students reflect on the emotional nature of sustainability work. Our goal is not therapeutic, but rather reflective. Our aim is to help students articulate the wide variety of emotional responses to sustainability challenges as a means of better understanding their roles in various systems. Validating emotional and personal reactions is not just a compassionate act; the ability to reflect on one's emotional reactions is an essential leadership competency. Here we offer suggestions to help other educators address this competency.

Inclusivity facilitates emotional explorations intrinsic to sustainability challenges

An inclusive classroom culture is essential in facilitating the emotional growth and exploration we observed in the classroom. As instructors, we deliberately shared appropriate personal aspects of our own reactions and stories as they related to the class material in order to cultivate a 'safe' or 'brave' atmosphere (Oleson, 2021). In doing so, we created a classroom culture that validated the importance of personal emotion and experience.

We also encouraged a sense of personal agency through the class assignments. We asked students to choose their own cases to increase the breadth of content and variety of perspectives into our course discussions (Oleson, 2021). Student-chosen cases also increased student interest and motivation in the content; a student's interest in skiing was leveraged to examine a much more expansive topic than only skiing *per se*.

Finally, we set clear guidelines for respectful and thoughtful dialogue in the classroom. This is particularly important when teaching a diverse student body. In our case, over half of our students were from outside the United States. While most of our students in this elective course were interested in sustainability, their perspectives and viewpoints varied widely. Sustainability challenges look very different depending on the socio-economic situation of one's home. Career ambitions among students also varied, with a few students hoping to become environmental or social activists and many others targeting a more traditional business career. Let us stress that the diversity in our classroom was a very important positive resource from which we could all learn. The different cultural and socio-economic perspectives brought to the in-class discussions created on-going opportunities to learn and empathise.

After completing a first draft of each reflection paper, we asked students to engage in the peer review process. The peer reviews of the personal reflection paper gave the students the opportunity to understand perspectives other than their own, which aids inclusivity and increases awareness of a range of stakeholder viewpoints. The peer review process also had several additional benefits, including: (1) provide constructive feedback to classmates before they turn in their final paper with the hopes of improving work quality; (2) learn from their peers by reading their work, considering their approach, and using that experience to reflect on their own work; (3) foster communication and connection among peers in the classroom.

In the classroom we encouraged, rather than suppressed, emotional responses (Chapman et al., 2017), all the while asking students to support their arguments with fact-based analysis. Our intent was to encourage students to think about how they might engage with a sustainability problem as a passionate collaborator, not just as observer. As such, the final course grade was heavily weighted towards student participation and leadership (10% of the final grade).

Modelling empathy and collaboration through guest speakers

We invited several guest speakers into the classroom who provided the students with examples of application of topics outside of class. These guest speakers represented a range of practitioner roles and activities, from a river restoration specialist who removes dams, to an artist who works with communities impacted by contaminated groundwater supplies, to an energy engineer who engages with foreign and domestic communities on the renewable energy transition.

The three guest speakers were not environmental advocates *per se*, but rather advocates for well-functioning social systems that respected and valued both environmental and economic conditions. They positioned their work in the context of having to influence others in a constructive way and collaborate with individuals with whom they may disagree. They recognised that other stakeholders have different points of view, demonstrating a knowledge of the systems impacting their sustainability challenge – be it river restoration, clean drinking water, or renewable energy transitions. Students found these guest speakers inspiring in their ability to role model collaborative behaviours.

The value and tension of interdisciplinary teaching

The ability to integrate cognitive and emotional perspectives on sustainability problems appears to be a key competency with regard to mobilising, assessing, and comprehending systems, dealing with conflict, and managing change. Such integration is challenging within our own professional practices, and is amplified when integrating disciplines. At times during the semester, tensions surfaced between common mental models of business and science, as well as the practical challenges of collaboration across disciplinary boundaries. For example, a barrier to collaboration across disciplinary lines is simply a lack of knowledge of the other's field of study, particularly if shared goals are not apparent. One of the greatest benefits of co-teaching with both instructors continually together in the classroom is the opportunity to role model effective collaboration between two very different disciplines. As Meadows points out, 'Interdisciplinary communications works only if there is a real problem to be solved, and if the representatives from the various disciplines are more committed to solving the problem than to being academically correct. They will have to go into learning mode' (2008, p. 183). We definitely went into learning mode while teaching this class, trying our best to model empathy and collaboration in the classroom.

Despite budgetary pressures that make such collaborative teaching opportunities scarce (Carey et al., 2021), they are worth the effort and expense. Nevertheless, interdisciplinary interactions can be created with the resources one has available, such as via guest speaker pairs with differing perspectives. In this case, we suggest that faculty focus not only on different cognitive perspectives, but also to the tensions between those perspectives as a gateway to exploring collaborative challenges and opportunities.

Meeting the moment – our class in the context of the Covid-19 pandemic

World events provided potent content for exploration during our course. We taught the course during the fall semesters of 2019 and 2020. As such, our second offering occurred during the heart of the Covid-19 pandemic. The pandemic provided a robust example of a large-scale disturbance to our interconnected global system of nations and people, exemplifying many of the system dynamics covered during class (e.g., system resilience, bounded rationality, and policy resistance). Many of the flipped classroom exercises and group projects addressed the sustainability aspects of the pandemic (e.g., shifts in fossil fuel usage, impacts of reduced travel, waste associated with personal protective equipment). Moreover, because our students were online during 2020, several of them experienced immediate impacts of climate change depending on their location; several students in the Western US described the impact of wildfires near their home, solidifying the immediacy of the climate change threat. Finally, we also addressed lessons the pandemic provided us in how to tackle another global public health crisis – climate change, specifically demonstrating how leadership impacts the outcome of a system disturbance.

While we remained concerned about our students' level of stress during the pandemic, we maintained our expectations of academic rigor as we worked towards integration across disciplinary lines. There are several different ways in which faculty can construe their roles as educators. To simplify, we can see ourselves as imparting information and building skills or we can see ourselves as helping students develop (Greenberg et al., 2007). The latter interpretation draws our attention to the importance of learning to develop 'psychological capital,' a concept encompassing, hope, self-efficacy, resilience, and optimism in the face of significant challenges (Luthans and Youssef-Morgan, 2017). We hope that making sense out of significant world events in a supportive context that values emotional and cognitive-based understanding furthers the development of psychological capital and empathy.

Conclusion

Meeting the SDGs will be a challenge, resulting in large-scale system disturbances that will no doubt provoke a variety of emotional responses – from fear and anger, to relief and hope. Engaging with such reactions in a collaborative environment is essential, and requires the ability to understand the perspective and concerns of others. As such, the ability to empathise is equally important as the ability to cognitively analyse a sustainability challenge.

Leadership requires passion and empathy grounded in a comprehensive knowledge of the topic at hand. Future sustainability leaders need to be able to make fact-based arguments while being empathic. The interdisciplinary classroom, which brings together different perspectives in both harmony and conflict, offers the potential for an integrated systems-based approach to understanding the cognition and emotional aspects of sustainability challenges. Emotional reactions can be understood from a systemic standpoint, facilitating student learning about system functioning and their own roles in a system. Doing so requires a classroom culture that encourages the exploration of emotions in a sustainability context, as well as active student engagement with others around those concerns.

Our experience described here comes from an elective course, drawing individuals with a sincere interest in sustainability. We did not explore these issues through a survey or required courses, in which the willingness to be such an active participant may or may not be present. Likewise, such exploration requires a level of comfort on the part of faculty. Given that many of us were not trained to explore emotional, interdisciplinary aspects inherent in our subject matter, faculty development for such work should be encouraged. The benefits of such trainings would benefit students and faculty alike, as our experience highlights that sustainability leadership is a fertile ground for interdisciplinary action and scholarship. The connections between system adaptation, the sciences of our world, economic sustainability, and our emotional experience are ripe for study, and are critical to the UN's SDG efforts.

Note

1 In class we studied the systems aspect of the boom and bust cycles, how destructive they can be to social justice and to the environment and, yet, how difficult it was for businesses to resist a boom.

References

Ayers, J., Bryant, J. and Missimer, M. (2020). 'The use of reflective pedagogies in sustainability leadership education – a case study,' *Sustainability*, 12, p. 6726.

Bradford and Cohen, A. (2007). *Power up: Transforming organizations through shared leadership*. New York: Wiley.

Carey, J.C., Beitelspacher, L.S., Tosti-Kharas, J. and Swanson, E. (2021). 'A resource-efficient modular course design for co-teaching integrated sustainability in higher education: Developing the next generation of entrepreneurial leaders,' *Entrepreneurship Education and Pedagogy*, 4(2), pp. 169–193.

Chapman, D.A., Lickel, B. and Markowitz, E.M. (2017). 'Reassessing emotion in climate change communication,' *Nature Climate Change*, 7(12), pp. 850–852.

Ferdig, J. (2007). 'Sustainability leadership: Co-creating a sustainable future,' *Journal of Change Management*, 7(1), pp. 25–35.

Gitsham, M. and Clark, T. (2012). 'Market demand for sustainability in management education,' *International Journal of Sustainability in Higher Education*, 12(30), pp. 291–303.

Goleman, D. (2017). 'What is empathy?,' in Goleman, D., McKee, A. and Waytz, A. (eds.) *Empathy*. Cambridge, MA: Harvard Business School Publishing.

Goleman, D. and Boyatzis, R. (2017). 'Emotional intelligence has 12 elements. Which do you need to work on?,' *Harvard Business Review Digital Article*. Retrieved September 9, 2021 from https://hbsp.harvard.edu/product/H03F4A-PDF-ENG?Ntt=emotional%20intelligence%20has%2012%20elements.

Greenberg, D., Clair, J. and MacLean, T. (2007). 'Enacting the role of management professor: Lessons from Athena, prometheus, and Asclepius,' *Academy of Management Learning and Education*, 6(4), pp. 439–457.

Heizmann, H. and Liu, H. (2017). 'Becoming green, becoming leaders: Identity narratives in sustainability leadership development,' *Management Learning*, 49(11), pp. 40–58.

Luthans, F. and Youssef-Morgan, C. (2017/March). 'Psychological capital: An evidenced-based positive approach,' *Annual Review of Organizational Psychology and Organizational Behavior*, 4, 339–366.

Mazur, Eric. (2013). *Peer instruction: A user's manual*. New York City: Pearson.

MacVaugh, J. and Norton, M. (2012). 'Introducing sustainability into business education contexts using active learning,' *International Journal of Sustainabilitly in Higher Education*, 13(1), pp. 72–87.

Meadows, D.H. (2008). *Thinking in systems: A primer*. White River Junction, VT: Chelsea Green publishing.

Montiel, I., Antolin-Lopez, R. and Gallo, P. (2018). 'Emotions and sustainability: A literary genre-based framework for environmental sustainability management education,' *Academy of Management Learning and Education*, 17(2), pp. 155–183.

Morris, B.S., Chrysochou, P., Christensen, J.D., Orquin, J.L., Barraza, J., Zak, P.J. and Mitkidis, P. (2019). 'Stories vs. facts: Triggering emotion and action-taking on climate change,' *Climatic change*, 154(1), pp. 19–36.

O'Neill, S. and Nicholson-Cole, S. (2009). '"Fear won't do it" promoting positive engagement with climate change through visual and iconic representations,' *Science communication*, 30(3), pp. 355–379.

Oleson, Kathryn C. (2021). *Promoting inclusive classroom dynamics in higher education: a research-based pedagogical guide for faculty*. Sterling, VA: Stylus Publishing.

Ostrom, E. (2008). 'Tragedy of the commons,' *The new palgrave dictionary of economics*, 2.

Pearce, C., Manz, C. and Akanno, S., (2013). 'Searching for the holy grail of management development and sustainability,' *Journal of Management Development*, 32(3), pp. 247–257.

Porter, T. and Cordoba, J., (2009). 'Three views of systems theories and their implications for sustainability education,' *Journal of Management Education*, 33(3), pp. 323–347.

Raelin, J., (2016). 'Imagine there are no leaders: Reframing leadership as collaborative agency,' *Leadership*, 12(2), pp. 131–188.

Shrivastava, P. (2010). 'Pedgagoy of passion for sustainability,' *Academy of Management Learning and Education*. 9(3), pp. 443– 455.

Thomas, E.F., McGarty, C. and Mavor, K.I. (2009). 'Transforming "apathy into movement": The role of prosocial emotions in motivating action for social change,' *Personality and Social Psychology Review*, 13(4), pp. 310–333.

Thomas, I., Holdsworth, S. and Sandri, O. (2020). 'Graduate ability to show workplace sustainability leadership: Demonstration of an assessment tool,' *Sustainability Science*, 15, pp. 1211–1221.

Tyson, A., Kennedy, B. and Funk, C. (2010). 'Gen Z, millennials stand out for climate change activism, social media engagement with issue,' Retrieved on September 6, 2021 from https://www.pewresearch.org/science/2021/05/26/gen-z-millennials-stand-out-for-climate-change-activism-social-media-engagement-with-issue/.

Tyson, A., Kennedy, B. & Funk, C. (2021). 'Gen Z, millennials stand out for climate change activism, social media engagement with issue,' Pew Research Center, May.

United Nations (2016). 'A "Theory of Change" for the UN development system to function "as a system" for relevance, strategic position and results,' Summary Paper Version 1.0 26 January 2016. Retrieved on January 7, 2021 from https://www.un.org/ecosoc/sites/www.un.org.ecosoc/files/files/en/qcpr/theory-of-change-summary-paper.pdf.

3 Managing emotions in responsible management education courses and promoting the leadership of the Sustainable Development Goals

Muhammad Atif and Enrico Fontana

Introduction

The key objectives of introducing responsible management education (RME) courses in universities is to increase students' awareness of environmental and social challenges, to promote the leadership of the United Nations Sustainable Development Goals[1] (SDGs), and to develop responsible leaders of tomorrow (Chankseliani and McCowan, 2021; Høgdal, et al., 2021).

A number of scholars have however showed concerns about RME courses' pedagogical approach, which often fosters knowledge through analytical and reason-oriented frameworks (Audebrand, 2010; Shrivastava, 2010). These scholars have called for the need of crafting more comprehensive approaches to teaching and learning about environmental and social challenges that address the importance of emotions and how to manage them (Hagenauer and Volet, 2014; Moratis and Melissen, 2021). Emotions can be defined as pungent, instinctive, and intuitive feelings often provoked through social interaction (Linnenbrink and Pintrich, 2002; Pekrun et al., 2002), and their management in university courses can be valuable to promote SDG leadership among students, ultimately improving the quality of teaching and learning (Gates, 2000; Riley 2011; Taxer and Frenzel, 2015).

While the urgency of tackling environmental and social challenges could not be more obvious, in this chapter we add to these calls and argue that managing emotions in the context of RME courses will be increasingly fundamental to promote SDG leadership, to improve students' educational experience, and help them become more ethical decision-makers in their professional life.

Against this background, this chapter provides an overview of the literature on emotions and on how to manage them. While focusing on teachers and students, we include several of our own experiences with managing emotions when teaching RME courses such as corporate social responsibility (CSR) and sustainability management.

DOI: 10.4324/9781003244905-5

This chapter concludes with key takeaways on how managing emotions can ultimately bring awareness of environmental and social challenges and promote SDG leadership. We recognise that integrating the management of emotions in RME courses is an ambitious project. It requires developing new materials and techniques, but also adjusting current university curricula. By offering some initial thoughts on how to accomplish this project, we hope to encourage new discussions among scholars and managers interested in advancing the United Nations agenda 2030.

Managing emotions: from elementary and secondary schools to universities

Emotions are frequently expressed in everyday life, yet their meaning is subject to countless interpretations. They have been defined in multiple ways and have been studied at length by social scientists, especially within the domains of psychology, philosophy, sociology, anthropology, and organisation science (Oatley, 2000; Izard, 2010).

Emotions are generally considered as pungent, instinctive, and intuitive feelings often resulting from a social interaction (Linnenbrink and Pintrich, 2002; Pekrun et al., 2002). Most researchers broadly agree that emotions can be either positive or negative. They originate from a combination of opposite physiological factors, especially through perception and over the course of an event (Scherer, 2000; Ellsworth and Scherer 2003). In other words, emotions are constituted by internal as well as situational components. Their internal components are based on intuition and are an integral part of an individual's cognitive scheme. Situational components instead are outcomes of social construction, that is, the encounters with other individuals in everyday life (Mansfield and Dobozy, 2015). They also have implications that are not restricted to the level of the individual who experiences them. Research by Zeelenberg and Breugelmans (2022) on the psychology of greed, for instance, highlights how negative emotions can have advantageous and disadvantageous consequences that extend to the level of society.

Much research exists on managing emotions when teaching and learning in elementary and secondary schools (Camino and Knight 2009; Riley 2011). This body of knowledge indicates that teachers experience a multitude of positive and negative emotions and how these emotions impact their performance, satisfaction, wellbeing, and relations with students (Hagenauer and Volet, 2014; Stupnisky et al., 2019). Although these studies concentrate on teachers as educators, they highlight how teachers' emotions are often a by-product of their relations with students (Hargreaves, 2005). Managing emotions in elementary and secondary schools has been credited with developing a higher quality environment in terms of better courses and higher learning capacity (Pekrun and Linnenbrink-Garcia, 2014).

Universities are however characterised by different social dynamics and offer an educational experience that is hardly comparable with those of elementary and secondary schools. Such a divide has led researchers to voice the need to study the management of emotions in university courses more extensively and as a separate phenomenon, especially to understand how managing emotions can heighten the quality of teaching and learning (Hagenauer and Volet, 2014; Moratis and Melissen, 2021).

The importance of managing emotions in universities has been long downplayed in favour of more reason-oriented approaches. This derives from the broad assumption that emotions are connected with 'irrationality,' 'impulsiveness,' and 'immaturity' (Sutton and Wheatley, 2003). Although expressing emotions may be considered inappropriate in some circumstances, scholars increasingly recognise that managing emotions can be fundamental to improving students' educational experience in universities (Mega et al., 2014; Pekrun et al., 2002; Postareff and Lindblom-Ylänne, 2011; Woods, 2010). Emotions can also improve the relation between teachers and students and create a more congenial environment in the classroom (Pekrun and Linnenbrink-Garcia, 2014). This is particularly relevant in the context of RME courses where students' satisfaction and higher awareness of environmental and social challenges is arguably necessary to promote SDG leadership.

In the next sections, we provide a brief overview of the literature on teachers' and students' emotions and the management of emotions in universities.

Teachers' emotions in universities

Teachers in universities develop emotions through their interaction with students in the classroom and on campus (Hargreaves, 2005; Riley, 2011; Sutton et al., 2009; Zembylas, 2005). They also develop emotions because of the growing difficulty to balance teaching and research activities, to reconcile professional and private life, and the growing standards to obtain a tenured position (Cipriano and Buller, 2012; Stupnisky et al., 2019).

While teachers' positive emotions include enjoyment, pride, and hope; negative emotions frequently range from anger to anxiety and frustration with students (Sutton, 2007; Sutton and Harper, 2009; Sutton and Wheatley, 2003; Taxer and Frenzel, 2015). We identify a short-term and a long-term element of teachers' emotions in the classroom that we believe are particularly important in the context of RME and to promote SDG leadership: (1) transmissibility and (2) motivation.

1 *Transmissibility.* Teachers' emotions are contagious and easily spread among students (Frenzel et al., 2009). While transmitting their emotions to students in different occasions, teachers generate short-term moods and feelings. In their experimental study conducted in multiple countries, for instance, Mendzheritskaya and Hansen (2019) show how teachers' anger makes students angry and unsatisfied. Although teachers'

emotions are themselves influenced by their interaction with students, teachers often bring their emotions into the classroom from outside. Think for instance of a teacher who experiences joy after receiving particularly positive news from a co-worker right before starting her teaching session. Her joy is likely to be noticeable in the classroom and spread to the students.

2   *Motivation.* Teachers' emotions can shape the long-term motivation of the students. They influence how students view a subject and how much they like a course (Hagenauer and Volet, 2014; Rumenapp, 2016). When students' attitude, behaviour or performance exceeds teachers' expectations, teachers are likely to experience positive emotions that motivate students to perform even better (Hagenauer and Volet, 2014). Think, for instance, of a teacher who discovers that some of her students are highly interested in an environmental problem discussed in class and achieve high marks on an exam. This event is likely to increase the teacher's positive emotions, thereby increasing the students' appreciation of the course and long-term motivation to learn more about a subject.

Students' emotions in universities

Students are likely to experience different emotions, especially in the context of RMEwhere they become aware of environmental and social challenges and engage in group activities with their peers to discuss solutions. A key example of that is the feeling of anxiety that often emerges from debating SDG 13 (Climate action) in the classroom, and especially the effects of climate change on the natural world. According to a recent survey run by Hickman et al. (2021)[2], children and young adults are increasingly experiencing sadness, anxiety, anger, powerlessness, helplessness and guilt when asked about climate change and feel that government responses are insufficient. These emotions can clearly be discouraging, but they can also motivate change and promote SDG leadership.

Although there might be numerous reasons at the individual level that explain why students are more inclined to perceive certain emotions rather than others (e.g., age, social class, family background, gender), we elaborate on three important variables that influence university students' emotions in the classroom and that we think are relevant in the context of RME and to promote SDG leadership: (1) feelings of control, (2) event predictability, and (3) group influence.

1   *Feelings of control.* According to control value theory, individuals perceive positive or negative emotions depending on whether they feel that an event is relevant to them and under their control (Pekrun, 2006). What we mean by feelings of control is that, when students experience an event that is relevant to their interest but do not consider

it to be under their control, they are likely to experience negative emotions. Take for instance the case of a student who absolutely needs a high grade on the final exam to graduate, but who is also very insecure about her preparation. The student probably feels that graduating is a very important event for her, but she is likely to experience anxiety or stress because she feels she has little control over whether she can really obtain a high grade and graduate. That same final exam is likely to provoke different emotions among students depending on whether they need a high grade to graduate and feelings about their preparation for the final exam.

2   *Event predictability*. According to control value theory, students' emotions are likely to be susceptible to the predictability of an event, that is, the information they have about the possible occurrence of that event. This information includes the possible behaviour of their classmates and their teacher. What we label as event predictability often depends on the familiarity of students with a specific event. Think about a student who is expected to present in front of the teacher and her classmates on a specific day. She might experience distress after discovering that one of her teammates, who is expected to present with her, decided not to show up for class. However, she might not necessarily experience the same level of distress if her teammate has a reputation of skipping classes and she is aware of that. Clearly, the availability of information makes some events more predictable than others.

3   *Group influence*. Students' emotions vary depending on their interests, their attention span, but also their group dynamics. What we label here as group influence is the impact of classmates' learning characteristics and behaviour on students' willingness and ability and to learn (Ayoko et al., 2012, Bakhtiar et al., 2018; Jiang et al., 2016). Think about a student who experiences joy because she is assigned to a group project whose scope aligns to her personal interest. Although she might be particularly motivated to work on it, she may reconsider the value of the project if her teammates are disengaged and find the project to be uninteresting. In turn, she might start experiencing frustration because her teammates do not share her enthusiasm.

Managing emotions in the classroom

Managing emotions in the classroom is a process of modifying, magnifying, filtering, and moderating the emotions experienced by teachers and students. Teachers manage their emotions as part of their job, to improve their wellbeing but also to improve the educational experience of their students. The teacher's role is particularly important in managing their students' emotions, thereby ensuring that they do not negatively affect the environment of the classroom. Further, teachers can promote positive emotions thus enhancing students' interest in CSR and sustainability contents and encouraging SDG leadership. In his autobiographic account, Gates (2000) for instance explains how he manages his emotions and his students' emotions for his own job satisfaction as well as to develop students' trust and appreciation. Against this backdrop, the management of emotions in the classroom can be leveraged upon to successfully implement RME courses and to create an awareness of environmental and social challenges. In the next subsections we provide an overview of the different approaches that teachers can adopt to manage their emotions and their students' emotions, especially in the context of RME.

Teachers' management of their emotions

Although teachers can adopt different verbal and non-verbal communication such as words, phrases, facial expressions, and body gestures (Gross, 1998; Koole, 2009), managing emotions is not only about controlling how emotions are expressed. Zhang and Zhu's (2008) empirical study shows that, when university teachers solely try to conceal their feelings, they risk burning out. Hence, managing emotions also requires teachers to be aware of their susceptibility to emotions and to avoid potentially disruptive emotions before they are generated. Take, for instance, the example of a teacher who is likely to blush every time she feels embarrassed because she cannot answer a specific question. She can manage her emotions not only by using different facial expressions that might cover her embarrassment, but also to grow awareness of her emotional reaction, and try to avoid the situations that make her embarrassed.

Extant literature points to ways in which teachers can manage their own emotions. We synthetise three main approaches that are particularly valuable in the context of RME courses and to promote SDG leadership: (1) situation modification, (2) attention diversion, and (3) situation reappraising (Fried, 2011; Gross, 1998; 2002; Koole, 2009).

1   *Situation modification* means that the teacher tries to alter the context that triggers her emotions. This includes avoiding seeing certain people, places, or objects that would negatively impact their emotions. Take, for example, the case of a teacher who is aware of the fact she is easily irritated by noise, which naturally rises during students' groupwork. She might try to modify the situation and lower the risk of experiencing negative emotions by reserving different rooms in advance for her students' groupwork to avoid a noisy class, or even take a break outside the classroom as the students discuss together in groups. The teacher could also walk away from the group of students who are less cooperative or to walk to another group and could discuss with the disruptive group outside the classroom. Finally, the teacher could also change the nature of the activity and ask students to work individually and quietly to avoid a noisy class.

2   *Attention diversion* implies that the teacher alters her emotions by orienting her attention towards different sources of information that are likely to create positive emotions and lower her negative emotions. Take, for example, the case of a teacher who gets easily irritated by the talkative students in the classroom, but also happens to have a strong passion for music. She might recurrently try to think about her passion of music as a means of diverting her attention from the noise of the students and avoiding negative emotions.

3   *Situation reappraising* means that the teacher tries to reinterpret her perception of a current situation to increase her positive emotions or reduce her negative emotions. Think, for example, about a teacher who is a strong advocate for social justice, and he overheard some racist comments from his students during a group activity. Rather than letting his negative emotions emerge, he might want to give the benefit of the doubt to the student and try to convince himself that he did not hear the comments correctly before singling out the student. To reduce negative emotions while teaching, teachers can change the way they consider a particular situation. The students who criticise the teacher or his approach may be considered as an opportunity to improve thus thinking of the positive the aspects of criticism.

We provide below an example of how we adopted a 'situation modification' approach in one of our RME courses to manage emotions. Hence, we tried to increase the interest of students on an important environmental challenge and to promote SDG leadership, with particular attention to SDG 13.

A discussion with MBA students on plastic pollution in Thailand – SDG 13

It has always been rather easy to teach RME courses in Thailand. Many of the MBA students I had the opportunity to teach were part of volunteer groups for the environment, within and outside the university. They were particularly vocal in class when discussing environmental challenges, especially climate change and SDG 13. Although these challenges can bring a lot of frustration, they made me hopeful to see so much engagement.

During one particular class on sustainable supply chains, I was talking with approximately 40 students about plastic pollution, which is a particularly a big issue in Thailand and has negative repercussions on climate action. We started to discuss multinational corporations around the world and how they can solve the problem of plastic by making biodegradable products. One student raised his hand and, speaking on behalf of his group, argued that: 'They just want to innovate to make us buy more, but the problem of plastics will not disappear.' A section of the students in the class then started to shake their heads. Their discontent quickly spread among all the other students. Some started to whisper: 'Multinational corporations from the Global North, really? They are doing nothing.' Others smiled mockingly and looked at me with disillusionment.

Although I was initially delighted to hear these critical comments, my positivity quickly turned into anxiety as I recognised that I could not provide a clear answer to the students. I felt I was losing control of the class. In fact, there is no clear solution to the problem of plastic and many of the solutions of the multinational corporations that we were discussing in the context of addressing SDG 13 were, in my view as well, of limited value. In a natural reaction of my feelings, my face became pale. This was immediately recognised by some students. At that point, I felt I had to do something because I could not just try to hide my feelings anymore. So, I decided to tell them that: 'Yes, exactly. This is what I wanted you to see. As long as we continue to operate in a regime of shareholder capitalism, businesses will always try to gain personal benefits, especially when coming here from other countries. It is very complex to create shared value. However, as MBA students and potential social entrepreneurs, how can you become leaders of change and solve this problem here in Thailand?' I decided on the spot to divide the students in groups and make them work on solutions. At that point, I managed to shift the conversations away from the multinational corporations. The students started to share knowledge about how to tackle the problem of plastic by structuring activities of recycling locally. This turned the students' discontent into curiosity and confidence. While putting them in the lead, I also regained my emotional balance and defused my own tensions. I later realised how moving from feelings of disillusionment to curiosity really drove students' leadership and engagement to the problem of plastic and SDG 13. Many students contacted me again after the class and the problem of plastic remained a matter of discussion for days.

Teachers' management of students' emotions

Students' emotions are part of their learning process and part of campus life. Teachers can manage students' emotions to improve their learning performance and the environment in the class (Järvenoja et al., 2019). Despite the importance, managing students' emotions in the classroom is difficult and often represents a main source of stress for teachers. Students' emotions are also not just individual, but are closely linked with those of their classmates as part of their learning environment (Ayoko et al., 2012; Bakhtiar et al., 2018; Jiang et al., 2016). Hence, the main challenge for teachers in the context of RME consists of managing the emotions of all students together.

This translates into identifying or even using *emotionally charged situations* to improve students' educational experience (Bakhtiar et al., 2018; Näykki et al., 2014), including increasing their interest in specific environmental and social challenges and promoting SDG leadership.

Using emotionally charged situations. When properly managed, emotionally charged situations can be particularly valuable to improve the students' educational experience. However, they can be challenging for teachers because they are attached with negative emotions that may make students lose interest in the problems being discussed and even lose their trust in the teacher's capabilities. Teachers can create emotionally charged situations or they can identify and evaluate them as they emerge naturally during classroom discussions. An important element of emotionally charged situations is to ensure that teachers can move away from further discussions that may provoke additional negative emotions, while being able to create positive emotions. Shifting from negative to positive emotions through the use of emotionally charged situations can improve the students' mood and environment of the classroom. It can be used on purpose to increase the attention of the students towards particular environmental and social challenges.

Research suggests that multiple situational events in the classroom can help foster student's long-term interest (Renninger and Hidi, 2011; Rotgans and Schmidt, 2017). Hence, emotionally charged situations can also serve as a trigger to foster the interest of their students in the problems being discussed. This is moderated by the teachers' expertise and experience (Quinlan, 2019), their ability to explain complex concepts in an accessible manner (Rotgans and Schmidt, 2011b) and their enthusiasm (Clayson and Sheffet, 2006). Teachers' agreeableness, openness, empathy, and body language have a particularly positive impact on students' interests when discussing sensitive issues such as social and environmental challenges (Dohn et al., 2009; Rotgans and Schmidt, 2011b).

We provide two examples below of how we managed emotionally charged situations in our RME courses, thereby promoting SDG leadership. In the first example, we briefly show how we combined images of corporate irresponsibility and responsibility to shift students' emotions. Hence, we promoted SDG leadership by trying to increase the students' interest in the subject of CSR. In the second example, we show how we deliberately created an emotionally charged situation and tried to promote SDG leadership by trying to make the students reflect further about an important social problem in society.

A discussion with undergraduate students on companies and corporate social responsibility in France – SDG 12

When teaching CSR, I emphasise that companies must be profitable, competitive, and efficient. They should also care about and be conscious of their impact on the environment and society as a means to advance the SDGs. Most of the time, students agree on the importance of these aspects. However, it occurs that some students express genuine scepticism. Some express resentment and even anger about corporations when it comes to responsible production and consumption – SDG 12 (Responsible consumption and production). Indeed, the corporate image is marred by stories of power, abuse, ecological scandals, and tax evasion. On those occasions, negative emotions fill the classroom as students contest the profit-seeking orientation of companies and their CSR activities. Exchanges between students are heated, especially when they exhibit opposite belief systems. Although emotions naturally emerge during discussions, emotionally charged situations such as these need to be managed so that they can support students' educational experience. Every time this happens, I want to spark emotion of discontent by providing the students with clear images of irresponsibility and make sure they do not forget them. One of the examples that never fails to shake them is that of Rana Plaza, a factory in Bangladesh that collapsed in 2013 with poor health and safety conditions due to the complacency of international brands. I discuss in detail the aftermath of the disaster: mass protests, worldwide criticism of brands, but also how that criticism helped raise awareness and create change.

After that, I use images of good companies and how they are creating value for social and environmental stakeholders to defuse strong negative emotions in the classroom. Examples of engaged companies such as Patagonia, Schneider, and Tom Shoes help create positive emotions and ignite new debates among students. My objective is to arouse emotions by using different images and create strong convictions about CSR. Triggering and defusing an emotionally charged situation helps the students reach this conviction. In particular, when the students start with negative emotions and then shift to positive emotions, I see how their interest towards CSR is not only restored but is significantly reinforced, ultimately encouraging SDG leadership. It often remains with the students long after the session.

A brief discussion with undergraduate students on sexual harassment in France – SDG 5

Sexual harassment, whether verbal or physical, is one of the most pressing societal issues today. A recent survey from France shows that 87% of sexual assaults occur in public transportation. 48% of women publicly admit having changed their clothing style because of fears of being harassed. Some also admit thinking about avoiding public transportation when coming back from an evening out (Rapport gouvernemental, 2019).

During one of my RME courses, I wanted to create an emotionally charged situation to make students internalise the importance of this social problem. I knew in advance that this was going to provoke different emotions among the students. I started with a question: 'Do you think that we live in a male-dominated society?' Male students loudly said no. However, one of the female students admitted that: 'Yes, we are living in a male-dominated society and my male classmates face much fewer problems than we do.' At this point, most of the male students started nodding their heads in disagreement. This immediately created an emotionally charged situation, which was characterised by reciprocal (within the groups of female students and the groups of the male students) and contradictory (between girls and boys) feelings.

To create an emotional balance, but also to use this situation to emphasise the problem, I told all the students: 'Well, let's do a quick survey in the class. I will ask the female and male students a question each.' I started with the male students and asked if any of them had ever faced a situation whereby they felt unsafe or uneasy in public transportation. No one raised their hand. When I asked the same question to the female students, almost all of them raised their hands.

This was quite astonishing for the male students. Despite the initial denial, they almost unanimously expressed their surprise over the reaction of the female students. One of the males, after the class, said to me that he did not realise how much and how often females have to face the inappropriate behaviours of others on public transport. Creating an emotionally charged situation can be particularly effective in making students reflect about challenges, such as gender discrimination, male-female equality, and women empowerment which represent the core of SDG 5 (Gender equality).

Conclusion

Our purpose with this chapter was to shine a spotlight on emotions and how teachers in universities and business schools can manage their own emotions and the emotions of their students to improve the quality of teaching and learning (Riley, 2011; Sutton et al., 2009; Gates, 2000; Taxer and Frenzel, 2015). Hence, we highlighted how emotions can be particularly important when discussing social and environmental challenges in the context of RME, which aims to promote SDG leadership and help students become more ethical decision-makers in their professional life.

Figure 3.1 provides a brief summary of the key features of teachers' and student's emotions, as well as the different approaches to manage emotions in the context of RME courses, as discussed in the chapter.

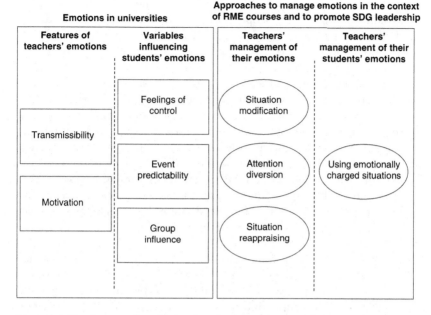

Figure 3.1 Key features of teachers' and student's emotions and the management thereof.

In this section, we conclude with key takeaways for scholars and managers interested in advancing Agenda 2030 and achieving the SDGs. We hope that these takeaways can spark debate on the importance of managing emotions in universities, especially in improving RME and promoting SDG leadership.

1 *Teachers' emotions.* Teachers naturally experience opposite emotions in the classroom. It is particularly relevant for teachers to understand their emotions for two main reasons. On the one hand, teachers' emotions easily spread to the students, who are likely to reflect similar feelings. On the other hand, they influence the level of motivation of their students towards the problems being discussed, thereby shaping the learning environment in the classroom and students' willingness to learn.

2 *Students' emotions.* Students experience opposite emotions as part of their educational experience. However, their emotions are often influenced by different variables. These include how students feel about specific situations (e.g., their preparation before an exam), the predictability of events in the classroom (e.g., the information they have about unexpected occurrences), and the classmates with whom they work in the classroom (e.g., the level of interest of their classmates to specific problems or during groupwork).

3 *Teachers' management of their own emotions.* Teachers need to both understand how susceptible they are to emotions and regulate their emotions to prevent undesirable situations in the classroom. They can

do that by altering the context that drives their negative emotions (e.g., avoiding seeing certain people, places, or objects), by trying to divert their own attention (e.g., to thoughts that are likely to provoke positive emotions for them), or by reappraising the situation (e.g., trying to change their perceptions about whether an event really happened).

4   *Teachers' management of their students' emotions.* Teachers can take advantage of emotionally charged situations in the classroom to improve the educational experience of their students. They can do so by triggering emotions in the classroom (e.g., by exposing the students to negative images of irresponsible behaviours of companies) and then turn those negative emotions into positive emotions (e.g., by exposing the students to positive images of CSR in creating social and environmental change). Shifting between different emotional states can help students become more interested in the problems being discussed and internalise the lessons in the long-term.

RME courses are essential to increase students' awareness of environmental and social challenges, and to promote the SDGs. A comprehensive peda-gogical approach coupling analytical and reason-oriented learning with emotional experiences cannot only improve the quality, but also effectiveness of such courses.

Notes

1 In this chapter, we term 'SDG leadership' as the efforts of students to accomplish the goals of the United Nations' Agenda 2030 (UN 2022 – https://www.un.org/youthenvoy/becomeyoungleader/).

2 The results of Hickman et al.'s (2021) study are derived from 10,000 children and young people (aged 16–25 years) surveyed in Australia, Brazil, Finland, France, India, Nigeria, Philippines, Portugal, the United Kingdom and the United States.

References

Audebrand, L.K. (2010). 'Sustainability in strategic management education: The quest for new root metaphors,' *Academy of Management Learning & Education*, 9(3), pp. 413–428.

Ayoko, O., Konrad, A. and Boyle, M. (2012). 'Online work: Managing conflict and emo-tions for performance in virtual teams,' *European Management Journal*, 30(2), pp. 156–174.

Badad, E. (2007). ''Teachers' Nonverbal behavior and its effects on students,' in Smart, J.C. (ed.) *Higher Education: Handbook of Theory and Research*. Vol. XXII, Dordrecht: Springer, pp. 219–279.

Bakhtiar, A., Webster, E.A. and Hadwin, A.F. (2018). 'Regulation and socio-emotional interactions in a positive and a negative group climate,' *Metacognition and Learning*, 13(1), pp. 57–90.

Chankseliani, M. and McCowan, T. (2021). 'Higher education and the sustainable development goals,' *High Educ*, 81, pp. 1–8 (2021).

Cipriano, R.E. and Buller, J.L. (2012). 'Rating faculty collegiality,' *Change: The Magazine of Higher Learning*, 44(2), pp. 45–48.

Clayson, D.E. and Sheffet, M.J. (2006). 'Personality and the student evaluation of teaching,' *Journal of Marketing Education*, 28, pp. 149–160.

Dohn, N.B., Madsen, P.T. and Malte, H. (2009). 'The situational interest of undergraduate students in zoophysiology,' *Advances in Physiology Education*, 33(3).

Ellsworth, P.C. and Scherer, K.R. (2003). 'Appraisal Processes in Emotion,' in Davidson, R.J., Scherer, K.R. and Hill Goldsmith, H. (eds.) *Handbook of affective sciences*. Oxford: University Press, pp. 572–595.

Frenzel, A.C., Goetz, T., Stephens, E.J. and Jacob, B. (2009). 'Antecedents and effects of teachers' Emotional experiences: An integrated perspective and empirical test,' in Schutz, P.A. and Zembylas, M. (eds.) *Advances in teacher emotion research*. Heidelberg: Springer, pp. 129–151.

Fried, L. (2011). 'Teaching teachers about emotion regulation in the classroom,' *Australian Journal of Teacher Education*, 36(3).

Gates, G.S. (2000). 'The socialization of feelings in undergraduate education: A study of emotional management,' *College Student Journal*, 34(4), pp. 485–504.

Goetz, T., Sticca, F., Pekrun, R., Murayama, K. and Elliot, A. (2016). 'Intraindividual relations between achievement goals and discrete achievement emotions: An experience sampling approach,' *Learning and Instruction*, 41, pp. 115–125.

Gross, J.J. (1998). 'The emerging field of emotion regulation: An integrative review,' *Review of General Psychology*, 2(3), pp. 271–299.

Gross, J.J. (2002). 'Emotion regulation: Affective, Cognitive, and Social consequences,' *Psychophysiology*, 39(3), pp. 281–291.

Hadwin, A.F., Bakhtiar, A. and Miller, M. (2018). 'Challenges in online collaboration: Effects of scripting shared task perceptions,' *International Journal of Computer-Supported Collaborative Learning*, 13(3), pp. 301–329.

Hagenauer, G. and Volet, S. (2014). "I don't think I could, you know, just teach without any emotion': Exploring the nature and origin of university teachers' emotions,' *Research Papers in Education*, 29(2), pp. 240–262.

Hargreaves, A. (2005). 'The emotions of teaching and educational change,' in Hargreaves, A.. (eds.) *Extending educational change: International handbook of educational change*. Dordrecht: Springer, pp. 278–295.

Hickman, C., Marks, E., Pihkala, P., Clayton, S., Lewandowski, R.E., Mayall, E.E., Wray, B., Mellor, C., van Susteren, L. (Dec 1 2021). 'Climate anxiety in children and young people and their beliefs about government responses to climate change: a global survey,' *The Lancet Planetary Health*, 5(12), pp. e863–e873.

Høgdal, C., Rasche, A. and Schoeneborn, D. (2021). 'Exploring student perceptions of the hidden curriculum in responsible management education,' *J Bus Ethics*, 168, pp. 173–193.

Izard, C.E. (2010). 'The many meanings/aspects of emotion: Definitions, functions, activation, and regulation,' *Emotion Review*, 2(4), pp. 363–370.

Järvenoja, H., Näykki, P. and Törmänen, T. (2019). Emotional regulation in collaborative learning: When do higher education students activate group level regulation in the face of challenges? *Studies in Higher Education*, 44(10), pp. 1747–1757.

Jiang, J., Vauras, M., Volet, S. and Wang, Y. (2016). 'Teachers' emotions and emotional regulation strategies: Self- and students' Perceptions,' *Teaching and Teacher Education*, 54, pp. 22–31.

Koole, S. (2009). 'The psychology of emotion regulation: An integrative review,' *Cognition & Emotion*, 23, pp. 4–41.

Linnenbrink, E.A. and Pintrich, P.R. (2002). 'Achievement goal theory and affect: An asymmetrical bidirectional model,' *Educational Psychologist*, 37(2), pp. 69–78.

Mansfield, F.L. and Dobozy, E. (2015). 'Teacher emotion research: Inntroducing a cenceptual model to guide future research,' *Issues in Educational Research*, 25(4), pp. 415–441.

Mega, C., Ronconi, L. and de Beni, R. (2014). 'What makes a good student? How emotions, self-regulated learning, and motivation contribute to academic achievement,' *Journal of Educational Psychology*, 106(1), pp. 121–131.

Mendzheritskaya, J. and Hansen, M. (2019). 'The role of emotions in higher education teaching and learning processes,' *Studies in Higher Education*, 44(10).

Moratis, L. and Melissen, F. (2021). 'Bolstering responsible management education through the sustainable development goals: Three perspectives,' *Management Learning*. February 2021.

Näykki, P., Järvelä, S., Kirschner, P. and Järvenoja, H. (2014). 'Socio-Emotional conflict in collaborative learning-a process-oriented case study in a higher education context,' *International Journal of Educational Research*, 68, pp. 1–14.

Näykki, P., Isohätälä, J., Järvelä, S., Pöysä-Tarhonen, J. and Häkkinen, P. (2017). 'Facilitating socio-cognitive and socio-emotional monitoring in collaborative learning with a regulation macro script – an exploratory study,' *International Journal of Computer-Supported Collaborative Learning*, 12(3), pp. 251–279.

Oatley, K. (2000). 'Emotion: Theories,' in Kazdin, A.E. (Ed.), *Encyclopedia of psychology*. Vol. 3. New York: Oxford University Press, pp. 167–171.

Pekrun, R., Goetz, T., Titz, W. and Perry, R.P. (2002). 'Academic emotions in students' Self-Regulated learning and achievement: A program of quantitative and qualitative research,' *Educational Psychologist*, 37(2), pp. 91–105.

Pekrun, R., Elliot, A. and Maier, M. (2006). 'Achievement goals and discrete achievement emotions: A theoretical model and prospective test,' *Journal of Educational Psychology*, 98(3), pp. 583–597.

Pekrun, R. (2006). 'The control-value theory of achievement emotions: Assumptions, corollaries, and implications for educational research and practice,' *Educational Psychology Review*, 18(4), pp. 315–341.

Pekrun, R. and Bühner, M. (2014). 'Self-Report measures of academic emotions,' in Pekrun, R. and Linnenbrink-Garcia, L. (eds.) *International handbook of emotions in education*. New York: Taylor & Francis, pp. 561–579.

Pekrun, R. and Linnenbrink-Garcia, L. (2014, eds.) *International handbook of emotions in education*. New York: Routledge.

Postareff, L. and Lindblom-Ylänne, S. (2011). 'Emotions and confidence within teaching in higher education,' *Studies in Higher Education*, 36(7), pp. 799–813.

Rumenapp, J.C. (2016). 'Analyzing discourse analysis: Teachers' views of classroom discourse and student identity,' *Linguistics and Education*, 35, pp. 26–36.

Rapport annuel sur l'état des lieux du sexisme en France. (2019). Rapport N°2020-02-25 STER 42, Gouvernement française.

Renninger, K.A. and Hidi, S. (2011). 'Revisiting the conceptualization, measurement, and generation of interest,' *Educational Psychologist*, 46(3), pp. 168–184.

Renninger, K.A. and Hidi, S. (2016). *The power of interest for motivation and engagement*. New York, NY: Routledge.

Riley, P. (2011). *Attachment theory and the teacher–student relationship*. London: Routledge.

Rotgans, J.I. and Schmidt, H.G. (2011a). 'Situational interest and academic achievement in the active-learning classroom,' *Learning and Instruction*, 21(1), pp. 58–67.

Rotgans, J.I. and Schmidt, H.G. (2011b). 'The role of teachers in facilitating situational interest in an active-learning classroom,' *Teaching and Teacher Education*, 27(1), pp. 37–42. Studies in higher education 11.

Rotgans, J.I. and Schmidt, H.G. (2017). 'Interest development: Arousing situational interest affects the growth trajectory of individual interest,' *Contemporary Educational Psychology*, 49, pp. 175–184.

Schutz, P.A., Cross, D.I., Hong, J.Y. and Osbon, J.N. (2007). 'Chapter 13 - Teacher identities, beliefs, and goals related to emotions in the classroom,' in Schutz, P.A. and Pekrun, R. (eds.) *Educational psychology, emotion in education*. Academic Press, 2007, pp. 223–241.

Scherer, K.R. (2000). 'Emotions as episodes of subsystem synchronization driven by nonlinear appraisal process,' in M.D. Lewis and I. Granic (eds.) *Emotion, development, and self-organization: Dynamic systems approaches to emotional development*. New York: Cambridge University Press, pp. 70–99.

Shuman, V. and Scherer, K.R. (2014). 'Concepts and structures of emotions,' in Pekrun, R. and Linnenbrink-Garcia, L. (eds.) *International handbook of emotions in education*. New York: Routledge, pp. 13–35.

Shrivastava, P. (2010). 'Pedagogy of passion for sustainability,' *Academy of Management Learning & Education*, 9(3), pp. 443–455.

Stupnisky, R.H., Hall, N.C. and Pekrun, R. (2019). 'The emotions of pretenure faculty: Implications for teaching and research success,' *The Review of Higher Education*, 40(4), pp. 1489–1526.

Sutton, R.E. and Wheatley, K.F. (2003). 'Teachers' emotions and teaching: A review of the literature and directions for future research,' *Educational Psychology Review*, 15(4), pp. 327–358.

Sutton, R.E. (2007). 'Teachers' anger, frustration, and self-regulation,' in Schutz, P.A. and Pekrun, R. (eds.) *Emotion in education*. Amsterdam: Elsevier, pp. 259–274.

Sutton, R.E. and Harper, E. (2009). 'Teachers' emotion regulation,' in Saha, L.J. and Dworkin, A.G. (eds.) *International handbook of research on teachers and teaching*. US: Springer, pp. 389–401.

Taxer, J.L. and Frenzel, A.C. (2015). 'Facets of teachers' emotional lives: A quantitative investigation of teachers' genuine, faked, and hidden emotions,' *Teaching and Teacher Education*, 49, 78–88.

Walker, H.L., Gough, S., Bakker, E.F., Knight, L.A. and McBain, D. (2009). 'Greening operations management,' *Journal of Management Education*, 33(3), pp. 348–371. 55.

Widmeyer, W.N. and Loy, J.W. (1988). 'When You're Hot, You're Hot! Warm-Cold effects in first impressions of persons and teaching effectiveness,' *Journal of Educational Psychology*, 80, pp. 118–121.

Woods, C. (2010). 'Employee wellbeing in higher education workplace: A role for emotion scholarship,' *Higher education*, 60, pp. 171–185.

Zeelenberg, M. and Breugelmans, S.M. (2022). 'The good, bad and ugly of dispositional greed,' *Current Opinion in Psychology*, 46, p. 101323.

Zhang, Q. and Zhu, W. (2008). 'Exploring emotion in teaching: Emotional labor, burnout, and satisfaction in chinese higher education,' *Communication Education*, 57, pp. 105–122.

Zembylas, M. (2005). 'Teaching with Emotion,' *A Postmodern Enactment*. Greenwich, CT: Age Publishing.

4 Shaping sustainability leadership from the start: Educating for sustainable development in undergraduate business and management programmes

Alex Hope

Introduction

Corporate scandals, the global credit crisis, environmental issues and increased income and wealth inequality have increased public scrutiny of the role of business in society.

Unsurprisingly, as bad management and poor leadership have been blamed for damaging society, business schools have been found culpable for poorly educating business leaders and managers for many years (Amann et al., 2011). As the training grounds for the managers and executives of the future, business schools have come under scrutiny with regard to their role in instilling ethical and responsible management values (Adler, 2002). Traditionally, business education has been delivered in a way that emphasises the economic impacts rather than relational and societal influences (Ghoshal, 2005; Pfeffer and Fong, 2004). As a result, it is not surprising that some business leaders behave in a socially irresponsible manner and perpetuate the profit over society paradigm despite the role of business managers is a crucial social activity (Khurana and Nohria, 2008). There is then a need for the transformation of management education to meet the increasing demand for responsible business. As Solitander et al. (2011) suggest, the role of business school education will prove to be central to the development of responsible managers of the future.

Multiple pressures and drivers are conspiring to drive business schools to seek to re-orientate their activities towards responsible management education (RME) and incorporate sustainability leadership and sustainable development topics within learning and teaching activities. In addition to the societal pressures described above, it is becoming increasingly important in professional and educational accreditation (Lamoreaux and Bonner, 2009; Persons, 2012). Evidence suggests that students themselves are seeking out business courses that promise to help them develop their skills in responsible and ethical management (Young and Nagpal, 2013) reflecting the fact that

DOI: 10.4324/9781003244905-6

effective corporate social responsibility (CSR) strategies are increasingly recognised as good business practice (Ducassy, 2013). In addition, it has been suggested that there is a strong moral case for management educators to shape their students and thus social and human development (Chung, 2016).

Business education can and should be seen as a force for good; a potential solution to societal challenges and as a method through which to transform business and managerial conduct (Painter-Morland, 2015). Indeed, universities play a critical role in preparing managers and leaders. There is now broad agreement that there is a need to integrate sustainability into university missions, strategy, facilities and operations and business practices, as well as into the curriculum, research and enterprise strategies and beyond (Barlett and Chase, 2013; Dmochowski et al., 2016; Rusinko, 2010). Indeed, higher education institutions such as business schools are essential to achieving the SDGs as they are able to equip the next generation of leaders and managers with the skills, knowledge, and understanding to address sustainability challenges and opportunities and undertake research that advances the sustainable development agenda (Chineme et al., 2019; Miotto et al., 2020; Mori Junior et al., 2019).

This chapter sets out a blueprint for integrating RME and sustainability issues into business and management programmes. It begins by setting out the challenge that business schools face in developing education programmes for responsible leadership before setting the context within which the approach was developed. It then articulates a five-stage model of sustainability integration designed to act as a guide for management educators seeking to develop a programme of curriculum change themselves. Each stage is then addressed in turn setting out some of the literature which supports the approach, highlighting some of the key resources available to management educators to assist them in their efforts. It concludes with some key messages and suggestions for other responsible management educators and business school leadership teams seeking to develop educational programmes which address the SDGs and develop sustainability leaders.

The RME challenge

The challenge that business schools face is how to develop effective management education that equips future leaders with capabilities for sustainable development and responsible management practice. This drive to reform business and management education has led to the development of a range of models and initiatives designed to do just that. The most well-established initiative arguably is the United Nations Principles for Responsible Management Education (PRME) which arose in 2007 as an urgent call to modify business education in light of changing ideas about corporate citizenship, CSR, and sustainability (Alcaraz & Thiruvattal, 2010). Out of this initiative, authors have presented ways in which to institutionalise RME (Beddewela et al., 2017; Burchell et al., 2014; Maloni et al., 2012; Wersun, 2017), methods of embedding ethics and societal views of business in management curricula (Fougère et al., 2013; Kelley and Nahser, 2014; Laasch and Conaway, 2016; Molthan-Hill, 2017) and pedagogical approaches to teaching sustainability-related issues (Hope et al., 2020; McLaughlin and Prothero, 2017).

The scale of the challenge, and the opportunity, cannot be understated. Business and administration subjects are by far the most popular degrees in many countries as students seek a course of study with a direct route to employment. In the UK there are more students, both home and international, taking a business programme than those taking mathematics, computing, or engineering combined (HESA, 2021). Internationally the picture is similar with business being the most popular major in the US (NCES, 2017), the EU (Eurostat, 2020), India, and China where business and management-related majors account for almost half of degrees studied (Liu, 2019). With so many young people studying business-related courses, the majority at undergraduate level, it is critical that business and management educators embed the SDGs and related content into teaching and learning from the start of student's higher education journey. The SDGs themselves mandate their inclusion in higher education curricula within their targets and indicators. For example, SDG 13 (Climate Action) includes target 13.3 to *'Improve education, awareness-raising and human and institutional capacity on climate change mitigation, adaptation, impact reduction and early warning'* measured by indicator 13.3.1, the *'Number of countries that have integrated mitigation, adaptation, impact reduction and early warning into primary, secondary and tertiary curricula'* (UN DSDG, n.d.). This is the context within which the SDG blueprint was developed as a group of management educators in a large UK business school began to develop an initiative designed to overhaul its undergraduate programme provision with the aim of incorporating RME and the SDGs.

Blueprint for RME and SDG integration

Getting started in integrating RME and the SDGs into a course, programme, school, or university can seem overwhelming. However, many business schools will already have some degree of sustainability education, and many more have worked to formalise their RME strategies. In addition to this there is now a wealth of knowledge, information, resources, and networks that can assist institutions in maximising the opportunities and navigating some of the challenges. The blueprint was developed from the author's own experience in undertaking a sustainability integration project, alongside an analysis of the common approaches reported throughout the literature on the integration of education for sustainable development, RME, and sustainability more generally. The blueprint (as depicted in Figure 4.1) can be broken down into five stages on a continuous cycle, all designed to deal with different parts of the integration challenge. These stages are not intended to be prescriptive or exhaustive; rather, they reflect the activities most described within sustainability integration projects. Each will be discussed in turn.

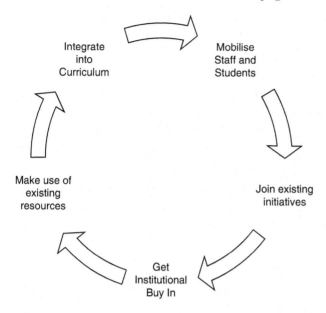

Figure 4.1 Blueprint for sustainability integration in management education.

Stage 1: Mobilise students and staff

When seeking to incorporate sustainable policies and practices to support sustainability, campus stakeholder engagement, in particular with students, is key (Brulé, 2016; Butt et al., 2014; Grady-Benson and Sarathy, 2016; Xypaki, 2015). As Shriberg and Harris (2012) state, active involvement and leadership of students are essential to achieving the deep organisational transformations necessary for integrating sustainability into higher education through the bottom–up pressure they offer. They offer a unique influence driven from the bottom up in their ability to operate outside traditional decision-making systems and their capability to pressure their universities in ways that employees simply cannot (Helferty and Clarke, 2009). There are several ways in which this can be achieved both formal and informal, but it is useful to review some of the organisations who engage university students with sustainability issues and operate on many campuses.

Enactus

Enactus are a global non-profit and community of student, academic and business leaders committed to using the power of entrepreneurial action to transform lives (Enactus, 2021). Research has indicated that Enactus projects which focus on the SDGs are an effective way to engage undergraduate students with sustainability issues (Dalibozhko and Krakovetskaya, 2018). In return these students can help to raise awareness of sustainability issues amongst faculty and institutional leadership, raising the importance of universities in engaging themselves.

Oikos international

Oikos international was established more than 30 years ago as a global community of student change agents. Operating in over 20 countries and 50 cities worldwide, its aim is to organise on campuses to raise awareness for sustainability and transform their own education (Oikos International, 2021). Oikos members see education as one of the key systems that needs to change in order to help society move towards addressing the challenges articulated by the SDGs (Braunschweig et al., 2021). As such, institutions with an Oikos International Chapter, or students involved in the movement, have access to both powerful student advocates and often a willing resource.

Students organising for sustainability (SOS)

SOS is a student-led charitable organisation that focuses on promoting lifelong learning and work on sustainability across all forms of education, including early years, universities, and workplace learning. It is active internationally in 76 countries reaching over 3.5 million students (SOS International, 2019). They work closely with regional student organisations such as the National Union of Students (NUS) in the UK and act as a support crew in facilitating, encouraging, and mentoring students with regard to sustainability (SOS UK, 2022). They also administer their SDG Curriculum Mapping student-led audit programme through which students are trained and supported by SOS UK staff to undertake an SDG audit in their own institution (SOS UK, 2020).

Every university will likely find students who are willing to engage with sustainability integration projects. However, having more formal support both internally and external to the organisation helps to ensure long-term engagement and critical mass.

Regarding staff engagement, many institutions will also likely find that there is a willing and engaged core of academic and professional service staff willing to assist with efforts to embed RME and the SDGs into higher education practice. Faculty members are a key driving force for embedding sustainability and responsible management as reported by a number of researchers (see for example Beddewela et al., 2017; Cowton and Cummins, 2003; Fukukawa et al., 2013; Matten and Moon, 2004). These authors emphasise the importance of engaging passionate and enthusiastic faculty to lead change in their schools and departments. They are also key to assisting in the diffusion of RME and the SDGs throughout the taught curriculum. Whilst harnessing pockets of engaged staff is clearly an important step in gaining support for embedding sustainability into a higher education institutions activity, success is more likely when more formal help, support and guidance is available.

Stage 2: Join existing initiatives

When it comes to embedding the SDGs and engaging in RME there are several initiatives, groups and other networks which can be of use.

PRME

The United Nations Principles of Responsible Management Education (PRME) acts as a platform to raise the profile of sustainability in business schools around the world helping to equip business students with the understanding of sustainability issues articulated by the SDGs. PRME is a voluntary initiative with over 800 signatories worldwide making it the largest organised relationship between the United Nations and management-related higher education institutions. PRME has long been recognised as a key framework for the improvement and adaptation of the curriculum and teaching methods as well as well as in the research of business schools (Alcaraz and Thiruvattal, 2010). The power of PRME comes from its networks which support the implementation of the SDGs at the global, regional, and thematic level. There are 14 regional PRME Chapters who help to advance the SDGs within a particular geographic context whilst the PRME Working Groups represent 8 issue-area collaborations of faculty, industry experts, business leaders and students who explore a range of topics and their implications for RME. PRME Champions are a select group of high-performing institutions that have radically transformed their curricula and research around the six principles of PRME. Through becoming part of the PRME network business schools gain access to a wealth of published resources on RME and SDG implementation, but also the broader network of individuals working on the implementation of RME and SDGs within business schools. This network acts as an invaluable support mechanism to assist newer members in overcoming challenges within their own school contexts.

Global Compact

The United Nations Global Compact (GC) is aimed predominantly at business organisations supporting them to do business responsibly by aligning their strategies and operations with its 10 principles on human rights, labour, environment, and anti-corruption. It also encourages companies to take strategic actions to advance broader societal goals, such as the SDGs, with an emphasis on collaboration and innovation. Whilst not designed to offer support on embedding the SDGs into university education and research, GC represents over 15,000 signatories in over 160 countries and can help business schools with access to organisations leading on sustainability issues. This can be useful in helping to bring topics alive to students through real-life case studies, guest lectures, internships, and other industry-focused activities.

BITC

Business in the Community (BITC) is a British business-community outreach charity promoting responsible business, CSR, and corporate responsibility internationally and is the largest and longest established business-led membership organisation dedicated to responsible business. It was founded by HRH The Prince of Wales 40 years ago with the aim of helping business organisations to continually improve their responsible business practice, leveraging the collective impact for the benefit of communities. Like GC, the BITC is not focussed specifically on the higher education sector. However, many universities in the UK and Ireland are institutional members, enabling them, and their students, to access BITC's wealth of responsible business resources whilst also affording them access to the wider network of organisations working on sustainability challenges.

The SDG Accord

The SDG Accord was founded and launched in 2017 by the Environmental Association for Universities and Colleges (EAUC), with the support of over 60 endorsing sustainability networks and partners (United Nations, n.d.). Its role is to inspire, celebrate, and advance the critical role that education has in delivering the SDGs and the value it brings to governments, business and wider society (SDG Accord, 2022). The SDG Accord is also a commitment that educational institutions making to one another to do more to deliver the SDGs, to annually report on progress, and to do so in ways which share the learning with each other both nationally and internationally. This provides an invaluable source of information for educators and institutions looking to enhance their sustainability activity.

Accrediting bodies

Accrediting bodies such as the Association for the Advancement of Collegiate Schools of Business (AACSB), European Foundation for Management Development (EFMD)'s European Quality Improvement System (EQUIS), the Association of Masters of Business Administration (AMBA) and others are an important driver of business school behaviour as they require schools to align their curriculum and practices to their standards (Storey et al., 2017). In the UK, higher education-focused agencies and professional, statutory and regulatory bodies, such as the Quality Assurance Agency (QAA), Higher Education Academy (HEA) and Higher Education Funding Council for England (HEFCE), call for 'sustainable development to be central to higher education' (HEFCE, 2014, p. 2). They ask that 'educators work with students to foster their knowledge, understanding and skill in the area of sustainable development' (QAA/HEA, 2014, p. 4). The aim of such institutions is to promote continuous improvement and, as such, they can assist in an organisation's journey towards embedding sustainability and the SDGs into their activities.

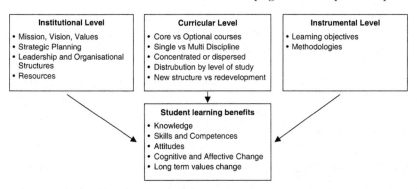

Figure 4.2 Integrating ethics, CSR, and sustainability in management education (adapted from Setó-Pamies and Papaoikonomou, 2016).

Stage 3: Get institutional buy-in

To be effective, higher education institutions need to be fully committed to support and implement projects that integrate RME and the SDGs into their strategy, operations, and daily practice. Many authors have opined that integration at the institutional level is the first order of action (see for example Beddewela et al., 2017; Bunch, 2019; Ryan and Tilbury, 2013; Setó-Pamies and Papaoikonomou, 2016; Wersun, 2017; Wright, 2002). This required strong internal support and pressure from faculty leadership (Maloni et al., 2012; Walck, 2009). Setó-Pamies and Papaoikonomou (2016) developed a model for integrating ethics, CSR and sustainability into management education which begins with a focus on institutional level actions. They emphasise the importance of embedding RME and the SDGs into schools' mission, vision and values, its strategic plan, considered within its leadership and organisational structure, and ensuring the appropriate allocation of resources. Figure 4.2 illustrates an adaptation of this model which seeks to demonstrate the importance of considering sustainability integration across multiple levels.

Whilst early engagement with university, faculty, and school leadership is essential, it can be useful to have built some bottom-up support from faculty and students first to provide a little more pressure and demonstrate that there is some demand for change from school stakeholders. Early engagement with some of the previously mentioned initiatives and networks is also useful to demonstrate to leadership the legitimacy of the endeavour and that many other leading higher education institutions are already engaged.

Stage 4: Make use of existing resources

One of the challenges that faculty often report when seeking to embed RME and the SDGs into curricula is a lack knowledge about specific sustainability-related topics, and a lack of time to be able to develop specific teaching resources (Doherty et al., 2015). Here, it can be useful to introduce colleagues to the many resources that have grown over the last decade or so specifically designed to assist educators in the teaching of sustainability. There are some resources which act as blueprints to help develop a holistic approach to embedding sustainability into school programmes and courses, some of which may be used in specific teaching contexts, and a growing range of textbooks covering every business school topic.

PRME Champions Blueprint

In 2020, a group of PRME Champion Schools developed a blueprint for SDG integration into the business school curriculum, research, and partnerships (Wersun et al. 2020). This blueprint has two main aims. Firstly, to provide concepts and frameworks to support business schools as they integrate the SDGs into their curricula, research, and partnerships. Secondly, it aims to provide a practical focus by offering examples of approaches already adopted by business schools. It acts as a comprehensive resource for those looking to get started with RME and SDG integration as well as a wealth of ideas and evidence for those at a more advanced stage.

PRME Curriculum Tree

The PRME Curriculum Tree is a conceptual framework that integrates the PRME principles into business school curriculum design (Hope, 2018). The framework is built on the premise that sustainability and responsible management topics can function to build a bridge across disciplines and integrate the business curriculum as a whole by promoting holistic understanding and systemic thinking. The key to the framework is that it seeks to integrate and complement existing curricular structures that have evolved within business schools over many years. As such, business school academics can use the framework to inform the development of curriculum and approaches to teaching that promote RME.

SDG Compass

The SDG Compass provides a five-step process for organisations to follow to ensure that they make a positive contribution to the global sustainable development agenda. These steps are to: understand the SDGs, define priorities, set goals, integrate sustainability into core business, and to report and communicate on performance in relation to sustainable development (GRI, 2015). The process can be utilised by higher education institutions as a guide for assessing their contribution towards the SDGs and developing a strategic plan for integration as described by Gough and Longhurst (2018) who used it in their practice at the University of West of England.

Giving Voice to Values

Giving Voice to Values (GVV) is a pedagogy and curriculum for values-driven leadership development designed for use in business education as well as the workplace (Gentile, 2017). Initiated in 2010 with support from The Aspen Institute Business & Society Program and Yale School of Management, its purpose was to transform the pedagogy and curriculum for values-driven leadership and business ethics around the globe. GVV has been adopted worldwide at over 600 universities, schools of business, and firms as a way to present a normative decision-making structure that is complementary to familiar constructs of business decision-making (Arce and Gentile, 2015).

The Sustainability Literacy Test

Sustainability literacy is the 'knowledge, skills and mindsets that allow individuals to become deeply committed to build a sustainable future and that help them to make informed and effective decisions to this end' (Sulitest, 2016). It is important that students and faculty possess a basic understanding of the current global challenges and their responsibility in resolving them. The aim of the Sustainability Literacy Test (Sulitest) is to provide higher education institutions with an internationally re-cognised and locally relevant tool to measure and improve sustainability literacy (Décamps et al., 2017). It can be used as a training and assessment tool to raise awareness amongst students, staff, and other stakeholders on the way to producing sustainability-literate graduates as future decision-makers.

Carbon Literacy Training

Carbon literacy is defined as 'an awareness of the carbon dioxide costs and impacts of everyday activities and the ability and motivation to reduce emissions on an individual, community and organisational basis' (The Carbon Literacy Trust, 2018). Carbon Literacy Training for Educators, Communities, Organizations and Students (CLT-ECOS) is a virtual train-the-trainer developed and upscaled by Nottingham Business School in collaboration with GC and the PRME Working Group on Climate Change (Molthan-Hill, 2021). Its aim is to empower people to embed high-impact climate solutions in their personal, professional and community life. The free, open-source Carbon Literacy Toolkit enables anyone with training experience and knowledge of climate change to teach university staff and students from all departments and disciplines. The course consists of four two-hour virtual interactive sessions made up of presentations, activity resources, and a comprehensive trainer manual which can be adapted for the local context.

Textbooks

In recent years there has been an increasing number of sustainability related textbooks relevant to management learning. These textbooks are distinct from those discipline-specific books focussing on sustainability issues in areas such as strategy, marketing, and accounting. Instead, they may be used as core texts for undergraduate business programmes providing a holistic overview of RME and SDG-related topics. *The Business Student's Guide to Sustainable Management: Principles and Practice* (Molthan-Hill, 2017) is a core textbook for business undergraduates providing a full introduction to sustainable management. The textbook covers all subject areas relevant to business students and the second edition features fully updated chapters on how to integrate the SDGs into accounting, marketing, HR and other subjects in management and business studies. Similarly, *Principles of Management: Practicing Ethics, Responsibility, Sustainability* (Laasch, 2021) provides an introduction to management through an ethical and sustainable lens in order to develop responsible managers and leaders. The textbook includes coverage of the SDGs and can be used for introductory management courses as well as courses that cover business ethics, business and society, CSR, sustainability and responsible management.

Stage 5: Integrate into the curriculum

Once staff, students, and leadership teams are mobilised and bought into a project to incorporate sustainability teaching into the curricula, support gathered from existing initiatives and some useful resources gathered, work can begin on a curriculum change programme.

Develop a baseline

It is likely that most business and management schools will already have many courses which include sustainability teaching and content that deals with RME and the SDGs. Therefore, it is useful to map existing practice and develop a benchmark for what teaching is taking place, against which SDG(s) and where in the curriculum. Several universities have adopted such an approach already, providing a framework which others can use in their own practice. In the UK, the University of the West of England (Gough and Longhurst, 2018), Nottingham Trent University (Willats et al., 2018), Winchester University (Shiel et al., 2020) and Northumbria

University (Northumbria Univeristy, 2020) have all been through the process and published the results. Some universities, such as Nottingham Trent University, have sought to embed the SDGs across the entire taught curriculum. They utilised a university-wide system to integrate the SDGs into their core curriculum since 2016 (Willats et al., 2018). The 'Curriculum Refresh' project was used to assess the sustainability content of the more than 640 courses and encourage educators to explore how their disciplines can integrate the SDGs into their curriculum and how they can collaborate for the SDGs. A similar approach has been adopted at the National University of Kaohsiung in Taiwan who explored the sustainability status of the course offerings and to understand the interdisciplinary capacity in pursuing the SDGs across the entire curriculum (Chang and Lien, 2020).

In the case of the author's institution, Northumbria University, the mapping exercise revealed that whilst most of the SDGs were taught to some degree within a typical business and management programme, there were clusters that had more coverage (SDG 8 (Decent work and economic growth), SDG 9 (Industry, innovation, and infrastructure), SDG 12 (Responsible consumption and production) and SDG 16 (Peace, justice, and strong institutions)) and others which had very little (SDG 2 (Zero Hunger), SDG 6 (Clean water and sanitation)). This provides some intelligence as to where to focus attention.

Curriculum design

Consideration needs to be given as to how to integrate RME and the SDGs into curriculum. Traditionally, sustainability teaching has been 'bolted' onto existing curricula through elective modules/subjects, detached from the core curriculum of business schools (Louw, 2015). However, increasingly educators have realised that such content should be incorporated into core curricula, specialist modules and as extramural activities (Beddewela et al., 2017). Such an approach ensures that all students are exposed to broad sustainability issues through core modules and courses, but are also able to specialise and contextualise their knowledge within the specific discipline they are studying through specialist modules and electives. This approach ensures that there is a 'golden thread' of sustainability issues diffused and interlinked throughout an educational programme (Sunley and Leigh, 2017). Consideration also needs to be given as to how the SDGs and sustainability-related content are incorporated into specific modules and courses. There is an argument that to be effective, business and management schools need to look beyond formal curricular content and pay close attention to the implicit dimensions of the learning environment (Blasco, 2012). As Blasco (2012) recommends, an SDG-focused curriculum should not be hidden, but should be loudly publicised.

Pedagogy

When seeking to teach RME and the SDGs, it is important to note that it is not enough to just include sustainability content; the way in which it is taught is vitally important too (Sunley and Leigh, 2017). Approaches such as problem-based, inquiry-based, experiential, and collaborative learning methods, contribute to higher-order learning, which facilitate 'how to think' rather than 'what to think' within the framework of sustainability (Savage et al., 2015). Indeed, an experiential learning approach to university teaching has long been established as an effective pedagogy for student learning (Boud et al., 1993; Moon, 2013) and one which is often used in sustainability education for its ability to provide a deep and student-centred learning type of environment which is important for good learning (Chan, 2016). Thomas (2009) suggests that sustainability teaching approaches should focus on the processes of learning rather than the accumulation of knowledge. This represents a shift from the traditional knowledge-focused and lecture-style teaching to a more process-based and student-focused approach to learning. Through this method, the learning experience is more personalised and nurtures a sense of environmental and social responsibility, and produces a capacity for enacting change (Thomas, 2009). Experiential learning can also deliver lifelong, key skills such as critical thinking, teamwork, creativity, problem-solving, leadership and communication (Bradley-Levine et al., 2010; Chan, 2016; Delaney and Kelleher, 2008; Savery, 2006) – all skills that are essential in solving sustainability challenges.

Embedding in practice

To ensure that sustainability issues are embedded into all activities in such a way that they are maintained over time, regardless of changes to staff or structures, it is essential that efforts are formally included in faculty and/or university strategy as well as relevant documentation. At Newcastle Business School, programme design is governed by a 'Programme Specification' which is used to set out all the relevant attributes of the course and is used as a quality assurance document, approved by relevant university committees. Each programme was mapped against the SDGs to ensure appropriate coverage throughout the collection of core modules as demonstrated in Figure 4.3. This step is an essential quality check and one which can be used as evidence to demonstrate the formal integration of the SDGs into a programme of study. It also signifies to both staff and students that the SDGs and sustainability issues are core considerations within a programme rather than peripheral issues which help to raise the profile of sustainability teaching in general.

Module Number	Module Title	Sustainable Development Goals (SDGs)																
		1	2	3	4	5	6	7	8	9	10	11	12	13	14	15	16	17
	Level 4																	
MK9414	Introduction to Marketing												X					
AF4038	Financial Decision Making								X		X							
HRXXXX	People, Management and Organisations			X		X			X	X	X						X	X
BM9403	Business Analysis for Decision Making																	
HRXXXX	Business, Economy and Society	X	X		X		X	X		X		X	X	X	X	X		
HRXXXX	Preparing for Professional Practice			X					X		X							
	Level 5																	
MK9414	Progressing Professional Practice			X					X		X							
MK9414	Resourcing and Development for Diversity			X		X					X		X					
MK9414	HR Analytics and the Labour Market	X				X			X	X								
MK9414	Employment Law					X			X	X							X	X
MK9414	Reward and Performance					X			X								X	
MK9414	Management Research and Analysis				X													
	Level 6																	
HRXXX	Strategic Leadership and Change																	X
HRXXX	Transforming Self and Organisations					X			X	X								X
HRXXX	HRM Dissertation																	
NX9629	Undergraduate Consultancy Project																	
NX9624	Management Enquiry																	
HRXXX	Critical HRD																	

Sustainable Development Goals List		
GOAL 1: No Poverty	GOAL 7: Affordable and Clean Energy	GOAL 13: Climate Action
GOAL 2: Zero Hunger	GOAL 8: Decent Work and Economic Growth	GOAL 14: Life Below Water
GOAL 3: Good Health and Well-being	GOAL 9: Industry, Innovation and Infrastructure	GOAL 15: Life on Land
GOAL 4: Quality Education	GOAL 10: Reduced Inequality	GOAL 16: Peace and Justice Strong Institutions
GOAL 5: Gender Equality	GOAL 11: Sustainable Cities and Communities	GOAL 17: Partnerships to achieve the Goal
GOAL 6: Clean Water and Sanitation	GOAL 12: Responsible Consumption and Production	

Figure 4.3 SDG Programme Specification mapping.

Conclusion

This chapter set out to articulate a blueprint for integrating RME and the SDGs into undergraduate business and management programmes in order to develop sustainable leaders and managers. Drawing on the extant literature and the experience gained from running a curriculum change project, the blueprint demonstrates and evidence-led approach that others may adopt to improve the formal integration of RME and the SDGs into their own programmes of study. It sets out a five-stage approach that management educators and/or business school leaders seeking to implement similar initiatives can adopt in order to increase the chance of success:

- Stage 1: Mobilise students and staff
- Stage 2: Join existing initiatives
- Stage 3: Get institutional buy-in
- Stage 4: Make us of existing resources
- Stage 5: Integrate into the curriculum

The blueprint represents just one experience of embedding RME and the SDGs into business and management education and is not designed to be exhaustive. There are many more considerations not discussed here, such as how to incorporate appropriate RME and SDG research and other activities into the curriculum or the importance of offering extramural activities outside of the formal curriculum to bring sustainability issues out of the classroom and into a real-world context. As Beddewela et al. (2017) point out, it is important to remember that there is a broader need for business and management schools to move beyond focussing merely on modifications to the taught curriculum, but also to attain systemic changes to research, pedagogy, and organisational strategies.

References

Adler, P.S. (2002). 'Corporate scandals: It's time for reflection in business schools,' *The Academy of Management Executive*, 16(3), pp. 148–149.

Alcaraz, J.M. and Thiruvattal, E. (2010). 'An interview with manuel escudero the united nations' Principles for responsible management education: A global call for sustainability,' *Academy of Management Learning & Education*, 9(3), pp. 542–550.

Amann, W., Pirson, M., Dierksmeier, C., Von Kimakowitz, E. and Spitzeck, H. (2011). *Business Schools Under Fire: Humanistic Management Education as the Way Forward.* Palgrave Macmillan.

Arce, D.G. and Gentile, M.C. (2015). 'Giving voice to values as a leverage point in business ethics education,' *Journal of Business Ethics: JBE*, 131(3), pp. 535–542.

Barlett, P.F. and Chase, G.W. (2013). *Sustainability in higher education: Stories and strategies for transformation.* MIT Press.

Beddewela, E., Warin, C., Hesselden, F. and Coslet, A. (2017). 'Embedding responsible management education--Staff, student and institutional perspectives,' *The International Journal of Management Education*, 15(2), pp. 263–279.

Blasco, M. (2012). 'Aligning the Hidden Curriculum of Management Education With PRME: An Inquiry-Based Framework,' *Journal of Management Education*, 36(3), pp. 364–388.

Boud, D., Cohen, R. and Walker, D. (1993). *Using experience for learning.* McGraw-Hill Education (UK).

Bradley-Levine, J., Berghoff, B., Seybold, J., Sever, R., Blackwell, S. and Smiley, A. (2010). 'What teachers and administrators "need to know" about project-based learning implementation,' *Annual Meeting of the American Educational Research Association. Denver, CO.* http://www.dr-hatfield.com/science_rules/articles/WHAT%20TEACHERS%20AND%20ADMINISTRATORS%20NEED%20TO%20KNOW%20ABOUT.pdf

Braunschweig, O., Longworth, G. and Proctor, J.C. (2021). 'Oikos international and the decade of action,' in *Responsible management education.* Routledge, pp. 386–400.

Brulé, E. (2016). 'Voices from the margins: The regulation of student activism in the new corporate university,' *Studies in Social Justice*, 9(2), pp. 159–175.

Bunch, K.J. (2019). 'The state of undergraduate business education: a perfect storm or climate change?' *Academy of Management Learning & Education.* 10.5465/amle.2017.0044

Burchell, J., Kennedy, S. and Murray, A. (2014). 'Responsible management education in UK business schools: Critically examining the role of the United Nations principles for responsible management education as a driver for change,' *Management Learning.* 10.1177/1350507614549117

Butt, L., More, E. and Avery, G.C. (2014). 'The myth of the 'green student': student involvement in Australian university sustainability programmes,' *Studies in Higher Education*, 39(5), pp. 786–804.

Chan, C.K.Y. (2016). 'Facilitators' perspectives of the factors that affect the effectiveness of problem-based learning process,' *Innovations in Education and Teaching International*, 53(1), pp. 25–34.

Chang, Y.-C. and Lien, H.-L. (2020). 'Mapping course sustainability by embedding the SDGs inventory into the university curriculum: A case study from national university of kaohsiung in taiwan,' *Sustainability: Science Practice and Policy*, 12(10), pp. 4274.

Chineme, A., Herremans, I. and Wills, S. (2019). 'Building leadership competencies for the SDGs through community/university experiential learning,' *Journal of Sustainability Research*, 1(2). https://pdfs.semanticscholar.org/c95f/4754b01d0cfc15b87c40360df056ab0d4b55.pdf

Chung, K. (2016). 'Moral muteness of faculty in management education,' *The International Journal of Management Education*, 14(3), pp. 228–239.

Cowton, C.J. and Cummins, J. (2003). 'Teaching Business ethics in UK higher education: progress and prospects,' *Teaching Business Ethics*, 7(1), pp. 37–54.

Dalibozhko, A. and Krakovetskaya, I. (2018). 'Youth entrepreneurial projects for the sustainable development of global community: evidence from Enactus program,' *SHS Web of Conferences*, 57, 01009.

Décamps, A., Barbat, G., Carteron, J.-C., Hands, V. and Parkes, C. (2017). 'Sulitest: A collaborative initiative to support and assess sustainability literacy in higher education,' *The International Journal of Management Education*, 15(2, Part B), pp. 138–152.

Delaney, K. and Kelleher, J.B. (2008). *Real-World process design for mechanical engineering students: A case study of PBL in DIT.* https://arrow.dit.ie/engschmeccon/16/

Dmochowski, J.E., Garofalo, D., Fisher, S., Greene, A. and Gambogi, D. (2016). 'Integrating sustainability across the university curriculum,' *International Journal of Sustainability in Higher Education*, 17(5), null.

Doherty, B., Meehan, J. and Richards, A. (2015). 'The business case and barriers for responsible management education in business schools,' *International Journal of Management & Enterprise Development*, 34(1), pp. 34–60.

Ducassy, I. (2013). 'Does corporate social responsibility pay off in times of crisis? An alternate perspective on the relationship between financial and corporate social performance,' *Corporate Social Responsibility and Environmental Management*, 20(3), pp. 157–167.

Enactus. (2021). *What is Enactus?* Enactus UK. http://enactusuk.org/

Eurostat. (2020). *Tertiary education statistics.* Eurostat Statistics Explained. https://ec.europa.eu/eurostat/statistics-explained/index.php?title=Tertiary_education_statistics

Fougère, M., Solitander, N. and Young, S. (2013). 'Exploring and exposing values in management education: Problematizing final vocabularies in order to enhance moral imagination,' *Journal of Business Ethics: JBE*, 120(2), pp. 175–187.

Fukukawa, K., Spicer, D. and Fairbrass, J. (2013). 'Sustainable change: Education for sustainable development in the business school,' *Journal of Corporate.* http://www.ingentaconnect.com/content/glbj/jcc/2013/00002013/00000049/art00007

Gentile, M.C. (2017). 'Giving voice to values: A global partnership with UNGC PRME to transform management education,' *The International Journal of Management Education*, 15(2, Part B), pp. 121–125.

Ghoshal, S. (2005). 'Bad management theories are destroying good management practices,' *Academy of Management Learning & Education*, 4(1), pp. 75–91.

Gough, G. and Longhurst, J. (2018). 'Monitoring progress towards implementing sustainability and representing the UN Sustainable Development Goals (SDGs) in the Curriculum at UWE Bristol,' in Leal Filho, W. (Ed.), *Implementing sustainability in the curriculum of universities: Approaches, methods and projects*. Springer International Publishing, pp. 279–289.

Grady-Benson, J. and Sarathy, B. (2016). 'Fossil fuel divestment in US higher education: student-led organising for climate justice,' *Local Environment*, 21(6), pp. 661–681.

GRI. (2015). *SDG Compass: The guide for business action on the SDGs*. Global Reporting Initiative. http://sdgcompass.org/wp-content/uploads/2015/12/019104_SDG_Compass_Guide_2015.pdf

HEFCE. (2014). *Sustainable development in higher education: HEFCE's role to date and a framework for its future actions*. Higher Education Funding Council for England.

Helferty, A. and Clarke, A. (2009). 'Student-led campus climate change initiatives in Canada,' *International Journal of Sustainability in Higher Education*, 10(3), pp. 287–300.

HESA. (2021). *What do HE students study?: Personal characteristics*. HESA Student Analysis. https://www.hesa.ac.uk/data-and-analysis/students/what-study/characteristics

Hope, A., Croney, P. and Myers, J. (2020). 'Experiential learning for responsible management education,' in Moosmayer, D., Laasch, O., Parkes, C. and Brown, K.G. (Eds.), *The SAGE handbook of responsible management learning and education*. SAGE, pp. 265–279.

Hope, A.J. (2018). 'The PRME curriculum tree: A framework for responsible management education in undergraduate business degree programmes,' in *Redefining success: Integrating sustainability into management education*. London: Routledge.

Kelley, S. and Nahser, R. (2014). 'Developing sustainable strategies: Foundations, method, and pedagogy,' *Journal of Business Ethics: JBE*, 123(4), pp. 631–644.

Khurana, R. and Nohria, N. (2008). 'It's time to make management a true profession,' *Harvard Business Review*, 86(10), pp. 70–77, 140.

Laasch, O. (2021). *Principles of management: Practicing ethics, responsibility, sustainability* (Second edition). SAGE Publications Ltd.

Laasch, O. and Conaway, R. (2016). *Responsible business: The textbook for management learning, competence and innovation*. Routledge.

Lamoreaux, M.G. and Bonner, P. (2009). 'Preparing for the next opportunity,' *Journal of Accountancy*, 208(5), p. 28.

Liu, X. (2019, October 1). *What are the most popular college majors in the world and why? The answers may surprise you!* Youth Time EU. https://youth-time.eu/what-are-the-most-popular-college-majors-in-the-world-and-why-the-answers-may-surprise-you/

Louw, J. (2015). '"Paradigm Change" or no real change at all? A critical reading of the U.N. principles for responsible management education,' *Journal of Management Education*, 39(2), pp. 184–208.

Maloni, M.J., Smith, S.D. and Napshin, S. (2012). 'a methodology for building faculty support for the united nations principles for responsible management education,' *Journal of Management Education*, 36(3), pp. 312–336.

Matten, D. and Moon, J. (2004). 'Corporate social responsibility,' *Journal of Business Ethics: JBE*, 54(4), pp. 323–337.

McLaughlin, C. and Prothero, A. (2017). 'Embedding a societal view of business among first-year undergraduates,' in *Inspirational Guide for the Implementation of PRME*. Routledge, pp. 103–109.

Miotto, G., Blanco-González, A. and Díez-Martín, F. (2020). 'Top business schools legitimacy quest through the sustainable development goals,' *Heliyon*, 6(11), p. e05395.

Molthan-Hill, P. (Ed.). (2017). *The Business Student's Guide to Sustainable Management: Principles and Practice*. London: Routledge.

Molthan-Hill, P. (2021, December). 'CLT-ECOS Carbon literacy training for educators, communities, organizations and students,' *Reimagine Education Conference*. Reimagine Education Conference 2021, Virtual. http://irep.ntu.ac.uk/id/eprint/44798/

Moon, J.A. (2013). *A handbook of reflective and experiential learning: Theory and practice*. Routledge.

Mori Junior, R., Fien, J. and Horne, R. (2019). 'Implementing the UN SDGs in universities: challenges, opportunities, and lessons learned,' *Sustainability: Science Practice and Policy*, 12(2), pp. 129–133.

NCES. (2017). *Digest of education statistics, 2017*. National Center for Education Statistics; National Center for Education Statistics. https://nces.ed.gov/programs/digest/d17/tables/dt17_318.40.asp?current=yes

Northumbria Univeristy. (2020). *Northumbria university sustainability annual report 2019- 2020*. Northumbria Univeristy. https://northumbria-cdn.azureedge.net/-/media/corporate-website/new-sitecore-gallery/services/campus-services/documents/pdf/sustainability-annual-report-2019-20-v1.pdf?modified=20201116095240

Oikos International. (2021). *About Us*. Oikos International. https://oikos-international.org/about_us/

Painter-Morland, M. (2015). 'Philosophical assumptions undermining responsible management education,' *International Journal of Management & Enterprise Development*, 34(1), pp. 61–75.

Persons, O. (2012). 'Incorporating corporate social responsibility and sustainability into a business course: A shared experience,' *Journal of Education for Business*, 87(2), pp. 63–72.

Pfeffer, J. and Fong, C.T. (2004). 'The business school "business": Some lessons from the US experience,' *The Journal of Management Studies*, 41(8), pp. 1501–1520.

QAA/HEA. (2014). *Education for sustainable development: guidance for UK higher education providers*. Quality Assurance Agency/Higher Education Academy.

Rusinko, C.A. (2010). 'Integrating sustainability in higher education: a generic matrix,' *International Journal of Sustainability in Higher Education*. http://www.emeraldinsight.com/journals.htm?articleid=1870727&show=abstract

Ryan, A. and Tilbury, D. (2013). 'Uncharted waters: voyages for Education for Sustainable Development in the higher education curriculum,' *The Curriculum Journal*, 24(2), pp. 272–294.

Savage, E., Tapics, T., Evarts, J., Wilson, J. and Tirone, S. (2015). 'Experiential learning for sustainability leadership in higher education,' *International Journal of Sustainability in Higher Education*, 16(5), null.

Savery, J.R. (2006). 'Overview of problem-based learning: definition and distinctions, The interdisciplinary,' *Journal of Problem-Based Learning*. http://citeseerx.ist.psu.edu/viewdoc/summary?doi=10.1.1.557.6406

SDG Accord. (2022). *SDG Accord*. The SDG Accord. https://www.sdgaccord.org/

Setó-Pamies, D. and Papaoikonomou, E. (2016). 'A Multi-level Perspective for the integration of ethics, corporate social responsibility and sustainability (ECSRS) in management education,' *Journal of Business Ethics: JBE*, 136(3), pp. 523–538.

Shiel, C., Smith, N. and Cantarello, E. (2020). 'Aligning campus strategy with the SDGs: An Institutional case study,' in Leal Filho, W., Salvia, A.L., Pretorius, R.W., Brandli, L.L., Manolas, E., Alves, F., Azeiteiro, U., Rogers, J., Shiel, C. and Do Paco, A. (Eds.), *Universities as living labs for sustainable development: Supporting the implementation of the sustainable development goals*. Springer International Publishing, pp. 11–27.

Shriberg, M. and Harris, K. (2012). 'Building sustainability change management and leadership skills in students: lessons learned from "Sustainability and the Campus" at the University of Michigan,' *Reports and Studies. IMO/FAO/Unesco-IOC/WMO/WHO/IAEA/UN/UNEP Joint Group of Experts on the Scientific Aspects of Marine Environmental Protection*, 2(2), pp. 154–164.

Solitander, N., Fougère, M., Sobczak, A. and Herlin, H. (2011). 'We are the champions: Organizational learning and change for responsible management education,' *Journal of Management Education*, 36(3), pp. 337–363.

SOS International. (2019). *Home*. Students Organizing for Sustainability International. https://sos.earth/

SOS UK. (2020). *SDG curriculum mapping overview*. Students Organising for Sustainability UK (SOS-UK). https://www.sos-uk.org/resources-file/sdg-curriculum-mapping-overview

SOS UK. (2022). *Working for environmental and social justice - About*. Students Organising for Sustainability. https://www.sos-uk.org/about

Storey, M., Killian, S. and O'Regan, P. (2017). 'Responsible management education: Mapping the field in the context of the SDGs,' *The International Journal of Management Education*, 15(2, Part B), pp. 93–103.

Sulitest. (2016). *What is Sustainability Literacy*. Sulitest.org. https://www.sulitest.org/en/vision-mission.html

Sunley, R. and Leigh, J. (2017). *Educating for responsible management: Putting theory into practice* (R. Sunley & J. Leigh, Eds.). Routledge.

The Carbon Literacy Trust. (2018, July 27). *What On Earth Is Carbon Literacy?* The Carbon Literacy Project. https://carbonliteracy.com/what-on-earth-is-carbon-literacy/

Thomas, I. (2009). 'Critical Thinking, Transformative Learning, Sustainable Education, and Problem-Based Learning in Universities,' *Journal of Transformative Education*, 7(3), pp. 245–264.

UN DSDG. (n.d.). *Goal 13*. United Nations Department of Economic and Social Affairs Sustainable Development. Retrieved July 29, 2021, from https://sdgs.un.org/goals/goal13

United Nations. (n.d.). *SDG Accord Action Network*. Sustainable Development Knowledge Platform. Retrieved January 24, 2022, from https://sustainabledevelopment.un.org/partnerships/sdgaccord

Walck, C. (2009). 'Integrating Sustainability Into Management Education: A Dean's Perspective,' *Journal of Management Education*, 33(3), pp. 384–390.

Wersun, A. (2017). 'Context and the institutionalisation of PRME: The case of the University for the Common Good,' *The International Journal of Management Education*, 15(2), pp. 249–262.

Wersun, A., Klatt, J., Azmat, F., Suri, H., Hauser, C., Bogie, J., Meaney, M. and Ivanov, N. (2020). *Blueprint for SDG integration into curriculum, research and partnerships*. United Nations Principles for Responsible Management Education (PRME). https://researchonline.gcu.ac.uk/en/publications/blueprint-for-sdg-integration-into-curriculum-research-and-partne-2

Willats, J., Erlandsson, L. and Molthan-Hill, P. (2018). 'A university wide approach to embedding the sustainable development goals in the curriculum—a case study from the Nottingham Trent University's Green Academy,' *Sustainability in the …* . https://link.springer.com/chapter/10.1007/978-3-319-70281-0_5

Wright, T.S.A. (2002). 'Definitions and frameworks for environmental sustainability in higher education,' *Higher Education Policy*, 15(2), pp. 105–120.

Xypaki, M. (2015). 'A practical example of integrating sustainable development into higher education: Green dragons, city university london students' union,' *Local Economy*, 30(3), pp. 316–329.

Young, S. and Nagpal, S. (2013). 'Meeting the growing demand for sustainability-focused management education: a case study of a PRME academic institution,' *Higher Education Research & Development*, 32(3), pp. 493–506.

Part II
Critical and personal reflections

5 Balancing the scales: Changing perceptions of gender stereotypes among students in a PRME champion business school

Elaine Berkery and Nuala Ryan

Introduction

Under the auspices of the United Nations (UN), the Principles for Responsible Management Education (PRME) initiative was launched in 2007 with the goal of inspiring and championing responsible management education (RME), research and thought leadership globally (Flynn et al., 2017). In so doing, a new vision for business school modules was envisioned, with principles for implementation guided by responsible attitudes towards corporate ethics, human rights, the environment, and – at the time – the UN Millennium Development Goals (MDGs). While two of the eight MDGs pertained specifically to women, namely Goal 3-Promote gender equality and empower women and Goal 5-Improve maternal health, Haynes and Murray (2017) demonstrate how unsustainable practices have a disproportionate effect on women and girls throughout the world. For example, although poverty affects the world's poor irrespective of gender, women, and girls endure the most challenges arising from economic, social, and environmental development in many parts of the world. Such challenges are evident through the feminisation of poverty, disease, and hunger; burden of unpaid work; adverse health and impacts from environmental degradation; vulnerability to conflicts and violence; lack of food security and land security; water and sanitisation issues; lack of political representation; and lack of education (United Nations Department of Economic and Social Affairs, 2010). This also suggests that issues of sustainability and gender (in)equality are inherently interrelated (Haynes and Murray, 2017). Following a high-level summit in September 2015 a new set of 17 Sustainable Development Goals (SDGs) were established. Within this set of goals, gender equality was designated a standalone goal through SDG 5. Again, Kilgour (2020) explains that while gender equality was designated a standalone goal, gender permeates all other goals, meaning all other goals must be viewed from a gender aware perspective. Doing so allows us to draw 'attention to gender dimensions of poverty, hunger, health, education, water and sanitation, employment, climate change, environmental degradation, urbanisation, conflict and

DOI: 10.4324/9781003244905-8

peace, and financing for development' (United Nations, 2018). Within this context Kilgour (2020) reiterates the need to recognise the structural reasons in developing our understanding of the concept of sustainability and understand why women suffer such pervasive inequalities, as well as the need to identify ways in which males benefit from the current system.

We begin hence our chapter with an overview and discussion of gender inequality in gender, before moving to investigate gender inequalities from three different perspectives: a business school, a student, and an organisational perspective. Our discussion then moves to gender role stereotypes and how these can influence gender equalities. For decades, gender role stereotypes and requisite managerial characteristics have led to the 'Think Manager-Think Male' (Schein, 1973) paradigm, meaning women are often overlooked for the managerial role because of the perceived misfit between women and the characteristics required to be a manager. We then turn our focus to the findings of a 10-year cohort study which examines gender role stereotypes and requisite managerial characteristics. We analyse changes in patterns of gender role stereotypes and requisite managerial characteristics over this 10-year period, before considering and discussing the implications of these findings from a business school, student, and organisational perspective.

Gender inequality

Gender equality is not only a fundamental human right, but also necessary for a prosperous and sustainable world (United Nations, 2020). The UN (1979) define gender discrimination as: 'Any distinction, exclusion or restriction made on the basis of sex which has the effect or purpose of impairing or nullifying the recognition, enjoyment or exercise by women, irrespective of their marital status, on the basis of equality of men and women, of human rights and fundamental freedoms in the political, economic, social, cultural, civil or any other field.' Despite the historical inequalities and discrimination that women have faced, it is now acknowledged that women and men must have the same power to shape society and their own lives in all sectors, at all levels; this is a human right and a matter of democracy and justice (Levin et al., 2020). This has led to the introduction of 'gender mainstreaming,' which was established as a major global strategy for the promotion of gender equality in the Beijing Platform for action from the Fourth United Nations World Conference on Women in Beijing in 1995. The Economic and Social Council (ECOSOC) (1997) defines gender mainstreaming as 'the process of assessing the implications for women and men of any planned action, including legislation, policies or programmes, in all areas and at all levels. It is a strategy for making women's as well as men's concerns and experiences an integral dimension of the design, implementation, monitoring and evaluation of policies and programmes in all political, economic and societal spheres so that women and men benefit equally, and inequality is not perpetuated. The goal is to achieve gender equality.' While gender mainstreaming is essential for securing human rights and social justice for women as well as men, it also recognises that incorporating gender perspectives in different areas of development ensures the effective achievement of other social and economic goals. In recent years, gender equality has become a goal that has been accepted by governments and international organisations and is enshrined in international agreements and commitments. In line with this, Kilgour (2020) advocates that the goal of gender equality is central to any concept of sustainability, business ethics, and corporate responsibility. The business case for addressing sustainability and gender equality outlines the benefits of promoting gender equality internally not only linking it to enhanced measures such as performance, such as shareholder value or profitability, but also links to reputation (Haynes and Murray, 2017).

The role of business schools in promoting gender equality

RME and the actions of a business school can play a role in reducing gender inequalities, as well as acting as a catalyst to promote gender inclusivity, not only in the workplace but within society in general. In this regard Flynn et al. (2017) point out that business schools should be role models in creating an environment, that is empowering to both men and women, to challenge social norms by providing examples of best practice to the employer community. Moreover, eradicating gender imbalance in management education and corporate leadership should be prioritised in the aims of establishing an inclusive and sustainable global economy and effective learning experiences for responsible leadership. Yet despite this, business schools themselves are characterised by significant gender gaps across all levels of the university setting, from administration and faculty through to doctoral candidates and MBA students (Flynn et al., 2015). These gender gaps from an employment perspective are because of the hierarchies that exist internally, creating differential treatment between men and women. In speaking about gender inequalities in business schools, Verbos and Kennedy (2017) caution that business schools intending to instil PRME and the Women's Empowerment Principles (WEPs) values in their students may need to clean their own houses before expecting students to embrace those principles. Interest in gender inequality in management education has heightened since the 1970s. Researchers have examined gender inequalities in business schools and management education from a range of perspectives: (1) students (e.g., numbers, relationships, MBA programs, careers); (2) faculty (e.g., promotion and tenure, working conditions and pay, research evaluation, leadership); (3) climate (e.g., harassment, environment); and (4) programs (e.g., syllabi, curricula, orientation, sex-role stereotyping) (Kilgour, 2017). Leaving these inequalities aside, it is important to acknowledge that business schools are integral to paving the way to establishing better business practices in that 'gender takes shape in, and is shaped by, teaching, learning, and leadership practices, and in relations between students, faculty, administrators, and communities' (Ropers-Huilman, 2003, p. 2). In combatting the issue of gender inequality in management education and business schools, initiatives such as PRME, WEPs, and the Athena Swan Charter have been established to ensure that business schools and universities are uniquely placed to transform business and management education through research and teaching, as well as setting best example by creating a climate of inclusion and diversity at its most senior levels, reinforcing best practice, to transform gender equality in universities, as well as influencing other sectors. However, as Verbos and Kennedy (2017) caution, simply adding women into senior level roles will not promise true inclusion or change the status quo. In this vein, business school leaders should practice ethical leadership in their efforts to enact PRME and WEPs, which in turn will help attract and retain talented female faculty, thus providing role models for aspiring female faculty and students alike.

Unequal gender representation in academia

Women's underrepresentation in management and leadership positions in the corporate sector ought to be addressed by business schools, yet business schools' record of accomplishment regarding gender equality mirrors the corporate reality (Bilimoria, 1999; Kilgour, 2013; Mavin and Bryans, 1999; Sinclair, 1995). True gender equity means allowing women to be valued equally within the culture of a business school for their unique contributions and perspectives (Verbos and Kennedy, 2017). Female representation in senior academic roles has increased globally in recent years whereby women now comprise of 34.7% of full-time faculty. This equates to 22.4% of all professorships globally, 33.9% of associate professor positions and 38.7% of all assistant professor posts (AACSB, 2020). Furthermore, 25.7% of Deanships globally are held by women, with 35.4% of associate Deanships filled be female candidates. In terms of Assistant Deans, females occupy 64.6% of posts. As female faculty begin to occupy these roles in greater numbers they become role models to other aspiring female faculty, which Bakken (2005) found to be crucially important for gendered identification with a profession. Additionally, exposing female students to such role models in the business school may inspire female students to develop similar aspirations within their chosen professions.

From a student perspective, the gender gap can be attributed to deeply engrained social roles and stereotypes set by society, and within the curriculum reinforcing gender-specific roles and skills as prescribed by society (Barry et al., 1957; Bem, 1981) (we will discuss this in greater detail in the next section). While progress has been made, thanks to the SDGs, more girls are going to school, fewer girls are forced into early marriage, more women are serving in parliament and positions of leadership, coupled with the introduction of laws to advance gender equality, many challenges remain. Discriminatory laws and social norms remain pervasive and women continue to be underrepresented at all levels of political leadership and leadership roles in general.

From an organisational perspective, we know that in our current workforce women receive higher performance evaluations but are rated as less promotable (Roth et al., 2012), women who perform as well as men have fewer promotions and less income (Joshi et al., 2015) and gender of respondent is an important variable when assessing gender bias, as male respondents rate men higher than their female counterparts during organisational decision-making processes (Koch et al., 2015). Research suggests that this discrimination occurs mainly because people believe that women lack the capacity to be leaders (Antonakis and Day, 2018), even though there is no evidence that suggests women are incompetent leaders when using either effectiveness or optimal leadership styles as measures (Hyde, 2014). Studies show that although men and women set out with the same ambitions for leadership when they complete their academic studies (Ely et al., 2014), a growing gap ensues as they enter into the workplace, in terms of what women expected and where they eventually end up. Research suggests that this discrimination occurs mainly because people believe that women lack the characteristics requisite for such roles (Schein, 1975; Schein, 2007), a belief which has created a stubborn persistence of gender stereotypes, and for many, a prototype where leaders and managers are perceived as masculine in nature (Berkery, 2017; Eagly and Karau, 2002; Schein, 1973; Schein, 1975; Schein, 2007), placing women who seek opportunities at more senior levels in the organisation at a distinct disadvantage compared to their male counterparts.

Gender role stereotypes among students

To start, gender stereotypes 'are socially shared beliefs about the characteristics or attributes of men and women in general that influence our perceptions of individual men and women' (Cleveland et al., 2000, p. 42). Through gender stereotyping, we can categorise individuals into groups based on their gender, and our perceptions will be influenced by what we know about the gender as a whole. Investigations into gender stereotypes has become an established line of enquiry, with early studies by Rosenkrantz et al. (1968), Broverman et al. (1972), Schein (1973; 1975; 1976) and continuing to the present with Booysen and Nkomo (2010), Koenig et al. (2011), Hyde (2014), Rudman and Phelan (2015), and Eagly et al. (2020). Gender stereotypes and ideologies about what is possible and or appropriate for females and males limit their societal roles, thereby affecting their participation in the labour force and their contributions to their families, in addition to influencing their choice of studies. Eagly (1987) argues that the roles assumed by individuals are based on the society to which (s)he belongs and as a result, men and women are expected to behave in ways which are consistent with their culturally defined gender roles. Furthermore, social role theory implies that individuals might question the capacity of one gender in a particular role, creating a gendered division of labour in which men and women tend to occupy different specific roles, such as different occupational and family roles (Diekman and Schneider, 2010), such as men in construction work or engineering and women as nurses and teachers. Within the classroom, our teaching faculty have the potential to positively or negatively shape and influence perceptions based on who is delivering the module and the resources used. For example, exposure to senior female academics can have a positive impact on the perception of the roles that can be held by women. On the other hand, the ongoing predominance of a male business leaders used in case studies and male role models in management textbooks signals to both male and female students that women are not suited to leadership and management positions.

Within an organisational context, a masculine orientation has developed around many roles and in particular the managerial role (Agars, 2004), which has subsequently led to the view that men are seen as more suited to the managerial role (Schein, 1973), partly because society has formed stereotypes that are incompatible with women in these roles (Arnold and Loughlin, 2019). Eagly et al. (2020) note how gender stereotypes stem from people's direct and indirect observations of women and men in their social roles. By this virtue, if men are overrepresented in managerial roles relative to their number in the general population, beliefs and stereotypes are created around the managerial role, that males are more suited to the managerial role, leading to 'a stubborn persistence of gender stereotypes' and their relationship with the managerial stereotypes (Morgenroth et al., 2020, p. 1). On the other hand, if the scales begin to balance and more women start to occupy senior level managerial roles, the perception of women's suitability to the managerial position should change, eroding traditional stereotypes. Research into gender role stereotypes and requisite managerial characteristics has grown out of the prevailing paradigm that is summarised as 'Think Manager-Think Male' (Schein, 1973; Schein, 1975). In Schein's early empirical studies respondents perceived successful middle managers as more similar to men than women. Since Schein's initial study in 1973 a series of studies have been conducted using Schein's Descriptive Index (SDI), and of particular interest to this chapter are the studies conducted pertaining to students' populations. The findings of these studies indicate the stubborn persistence of the 'Think Manager-Think Male' paradigm among male students (Berkery et al., 2014; Sauers et al., 2002; Schein, 1973; Schein, 1975; Schein and Mueller, 1992; Schein et al., 1996), while female students, particularly in more recent years, are less likely to gender type the managerial role (Berkery et al., 2014; Schein et al., 1989). While studies to date examine student populations across cultures and programmes, the results are not always directly comparable due to variance in sample sizes and the influence of national culture. To overcome this, we survey the same population of business students at 10-year intervals to assess changes in gender stereotypes within a business student population. The first cohort was surveyed in the Spring semester of the academic year 2008/09. At the time, the business school in which these students were registered was about to become a member of PRME. The second round of data collection was collected 10 years later. In the intervening years the school had become a PRME champion and had applied for a Bronze Athena Swan Award, which was subsequently awarded in May 2019. Given the changing focus on gender equality within the business school between 2008/09 and 2018/19 we expect to find a shift in student attitudes towards gender role stereotypes and expect to find a more gender egalitarian perception of the managerial role among students.

Our study

In this section we present results from a cohort study using a dataset comprised of business studies students (n = 1,282) at a business school within a large public University in the Republic of Ireland. The first round of data was collected in 2008 – the year in which the business school in which the data was collected signed up to PRME (n = 628) and the data in cohort 2 was collected during the spring semester of the 2018/19 academic year (n = 654). The surveys were administered (handed out and collected) at the end of class over a two-week period on both occasions. All survey responses were optional, and confidentiality and anonymity were assured.

Studies adapting the 'Think Manager-Think Male' paradigm use Schein's Descriptive Index (SDI) in which participants rate how characteristic 92 descriptive words and phrases are of men, women and managers in general, the results of which allow us to assess the relationship between gender role stereotypes and requisite management characteristics. Participants were presented with the original 92 descriptive items listed on SDI and were randomly assigned one of the three target conditions to rate: (1) men, (2) women, and (3) managers in general. For example, some participants were asked to report the extent to which each adjective was reflective of 'men in general.' In this instance, participants were instructed that when making their judgments, they should imagine they were about to meet the person for the first time and the only thing they know in advance is the person was a male. These instructions were modified for each of the target conditions. Participants rated the adjectives on a 5-point scale: 1-Not characteristic, 2-Somewhat uncharacteristic, 3-Neither characteristic nor uncharacteristic, 4-Somewhat characteristic, 5-Characteristic. Each participant responded to only one target condition. We had two cohorts in our sample, which were subsequently broken down by gender creating four distinct samples in this research: cohort 1 comprises of data collected during the academic year 2008/09 and data collected for cohort 2 was collected during the academic year 2018/19. The overall sample comprises 608 (47%) male respondents and 674 (53%) female respondents; this represents a gender breakdown of 45% males and 55% females in cohort 1 and 49.7% male and 50.3% in cohort 2. The overall average age of respondents in cohort 1 was 21 years old and in cohort 2 this was 20 years old.

Data was analysed using the SPSS statistical package. In line with previous studies using the 'Think Manager-Think Male' paradigm intraclass correlation coefficients (ICC, r^1) were computed using mean values of descriptive items for each group to determine the relationship between gender and requisite managerial characteristics. The ICC scores indicate an overlap or similarity of ratings, giving an estimate of the percentage of the total variance that is due to the differences among the conditions (Dodge et al., 1995). This allowed us to determine the degree of similarity between managers and men and between managers and women. A high ICC (close to 1) indicates high similarity between the target conditions. For example, an ICC score of 0.98 for the ratings of men and managers represents a high degree of similarity between the ratings of men and managers. On the other hand, a low ICC (close to zero) of 0.12 for the ratings of men and managers represents a very low degree of similarity between the ratings of men and managers. In line with research conducted by Duehr and Bono (2006), if the difference in the correlation between two sets of conditions (e.g., managers and men in general as compared to managers and women in general) exceeds 0.29, the difference is statistically significant ($p < .05$), assuming equal variance across samples. These results are outlined in Table 5.1.

Table 5.1 Analysis of variance of mean item ratings and intraclass coefficients by cohort and gender of respondent

	df	Cohort 1 = 2008 Ratings			Cohort 2 = 2018 Ratings		
		MS	F	r^1	MS	F	r^1
Males Respondents							
Managers and men							
Between items	91	.705	5.69***	.703***	.477	6.27***	.738***
Within items	92	.124			.076		
Managers and women							
Between items	91	.486	1.49*	.192*	.448	2.98**	.496***
Within items	92	.326			.150		
Females Respondents							
Managers and men							
Between items	91	.679	3.75***	.578***	.561	3.71***	.573***
Within items	92	.181			.151		
Managers and women							
Between items	91	.724	2.99***	.496***	.726	5.34***	.688***
Within items	92	.245			.136		

Notes
*** $p < 0.001$,
** $p < 0.01$,
* $p < 0.05$.
The *MS* for between items looks at the amount of variation that can be explained by accounting for differences between the descriptive items.
The *MS* for within items looks at the variation within each descriptive item across the two groups (men and managers). If men and managers are rated similarly the within item will be small compared to the between item and the *F* statistic will be significant, as is in this case.
df = Degrees of Freedom; *MS* = Mean Squared.

Implication of these findings

These tests revealed that gender stereotypes are changing within this business student population. In cohort 1, male students gender typed the managerial role in favour of men (men and managers $-r^1 = .703$, $p < .001$, women and managers $-r^1 = .192$, $p < .05$), whereas their female counterparts, did not gender type the managerial role (men and managers $-r^1 = .578$, $p < .001$, women and managers $-r^1 = .496$, $p < .001$). Among cohort 2, there was no evidence of gender role stereotypes and requisite managerial characteristics among either the male and female cohorts. These findings illustrate a significant shift in the gender role stereotypes and requisite managerial characteristics, advancing contemporary literature by illustrating a more gender egalitarian view of the management role among business students.

We now move to discuss these findings from the perspective of students, the business school, and organisations.

Implication of these findings from a student perspective

Diekman et al. (2004) propose that as women gain greater access to managerial positions, gender differences in power within organisations will begin to erode. For this to happen, women must be first perceived to be a suitable fit to the managerial role. The male students from cohort 1 have entered the workforce with the perception that women do not hold the characteristics necessary for management roles. This incongruence between the women and managerial role, coupled with deeply engrained organisational cultures, will result in women being unfairly treated and overlooked for promotions as they are seen to be lacking in managerial characteristics compared to their male counterparts. In this vein, Schein (2001) warns that participation rates of females in managerial roles will be kept low if the attitudes of male decision makers, prejudiced strongly by managerial gender types are allowed to go unchallenged. The results from cohort 2 are more encouraging as these students no longer gender type the managerial role. These results may have been influenced by the changing roles of women in Irish society, the increased numbers of women in managerial roles, and greater levels of exposure to senior female academics.

Implication of these findings from a business school perspective

Moratis and Melissen (2021) encourage business schools to critically reflect on their role in advancing an education and research curriculum that engages and supports the SDGs as a way of ameliorating their intended ethos. As business schools embrace PRME, within the student body a fundamental need to understand and develop the SDG related to gender equality (SDG 5) is both fundamentally inherent and critical. By focusing on gender equality, as many business schools do, it is hoped that there is a direct impact on the mindset of the students as they advance, developing them as advocates for gender equity. It is also important however to recognise the inter-dependencies of the SDG and their role of inciting systemic change in the world. Sachs et al. (2019) suggest that the SDGs can be operationalised by viewing them as six key transformations with interdependencies, the first of which highlights the interdependence of gender, education, and inequality. As such, this research informs this first transformation by highlighting the role of business schools in creating a more egalitarian view of management roles in relation to gender through education. The research suggests that business schools who engage in initiatives such as PRME, WEPs, and Athena Swan can influence equality and inclusion mindsets and resulting practices through their research and educational curriculums. Business schools must ensure that equity is reinforced throughout the lifecycle of the student at the university and is continually driven as part of the lifelong learning agenda of working adults to fully engage with the SDGs.

Within the classroom, we call on business schools to introduce topics such as unconsciousness bias, second-generation gender bias and the double bind phenomena across modules to create a greater awareness about un-intended biases that students may bring into the workplace with them. For example, unconscious biases are the social stereotypes we hold about certain groups of people from outside our own conscious awareness. Unconscious bias may impact on decisions in the workplace, particularly when it comes to recruitment, promotion, and performance management. When bias is prevalent, individuals will struggle to hire diverse teams, and improve workplace inclusion. Second-generation gender bias refers to practices that may appear neutral or non-sexist, in that they apply to everyone, but which discriminate against a gender because they reflect the values of the gender who created or developed the setting (Carter, 2011). Without an under-standing of second-generation bias, people are left with stereotypes to explain why for example women as a group have failed to achieve parity with men in senior management roles: If they can't reach the top, it is because they 'don't ask,' they are 'too nice,' or simply 'opt out,' inferring that women who have managed to succeed are exceptions and women who have experienced setbacks that it is their own fault for failing to be suffi-ciently aggressive or committed to the job (Ibarra et al., 2013). Finally, as for the double bind phenomena, Seikkula and Olson (2003) interpret this in the context of a family system as people being caught up in an ongoing system which produces conflicting definitions of the relationship and consequent subjective distress. Based on this definition one would expect that if women were to demonstrate more agentic characteristics and start to 'act' more like a traditional leader, they would be more accepted in the role. Unfortunately, that isn't always the case; women who demonstrate agentic leadership behaviours are penalised for acting against the traditional female gender role.

Implication of these findings from an organisation's perspective

Progress to date on achieving the SDGs has been slow and has been further compounded by the coronavirus in recent years. This lack of progress with the added complexity of interrelating systems has led to the suggestion that the implementation of the SDGs can be viewed as a wicked problem that must be addressed through the interface of public and private organisations (Eden and Wagstaff, 2021). Private business is strategically placed and, has the potential to fill the void caused by government inactivity in driving the SDGs in our societies (Kurz, 2020). However, they need to move past just the 'business as usual' strategy for implementation of normal change and look to develop systems that are transformative based on sustainable development. As Eden and Wagstaff (2021, p. 50) note, 'Gender equality is 1 of 17 "wicked problems" in the 2030 Agenda.' Immediate attention must be paid to equality, diversity, and inclusion systems within these organisations which foster and promote fairness in the promotion process. Organisations should look towards their talent management strategy to identify top performing individuals, or those with the highest potential for performance in management and technical domains in the future (Farndale et al., 2015) taking into account inherent bias. Furthermore, organisations serious about tackling gender disparity in the workplace should engage in and develop diversity and inclusion training. Such training should include and create awareness around unconsciousness bias and second-generation gender bias. A talent management strategy that is cognizant of such inherent biases would therefore need to be established to ensure that women have equal opportunities to be identified as talent (Farndale et al., 2015). Within the literature, Eagly and Carli (2003) suggest that with the increased number of women entering the field of leadership and management, theories, and practices must also change. Organisations should create a climate and culture of inclusion through the introduction of female in management initiatives/academies that champion the advancement and achievements of women within their organisation. Doing so will work towards a vision of gender equality in the workplace: common goals can be created that all members of the workforce strive towards and increase the visibility of women leaders. Finally, evidence like the research outlined in this chapter should be used to underpin the advancement of SDG 5 in businesses, as solving wicked problems must be coexistent with 'business as usual' strategies within organisations.

Conclusions

Overcoming challenges to gender equality in both business schools and the workplace has a long history, creating traditions and cultures that have become engrained and difficult to change (Flynn et al., 2016). The findings we present in this chapter illustrate a significant shift in the gender role stereotypes and requisite managerial characteristics, advancing contemporary literature, illustrating a more gender egalitarian view of the management role among undergraduate business students. In our discussion, the roles and responsibilities of business schools in creating an environment that allows learners to acquire the knowledge and skills needed to promote sustainable development, through the teaching of topical areas, such as implicit bias, second-generation bias, and the double bind phenomena, will act as a useful guide to inform business schools in their engagement with stakeholders such as learners, policy makers, and organisations in general. This, in turn, will facilitate and support dialogue and debate on critical issues related to socially responsible workplaces and sustainability.

References

AACSB. (2020). *2020 Business School Data Guide.* https://www.aacsb.edu/-/media/aacsb/publications/data-trends-booklet/2020.ashx?la=en&hash=DD37BBF79457F638BBB43C19A72F1840121796D6

Agars, M.D. (2004). 'Reconsidering the impact of gender stereotypes on the advancement of women in organisations,' *Psychology of Women Quarterly*, 28(2), pp. 103–111.

Antonakis, J. and Day, D.V. (2018). *Leadership: Past, present, and f.* Sage Publications Inc.

Arnold, K.A. and Loughlin, C. (2019). 'Continuing the conversation: Questioning the who, what, and when of leaning' in. *Academy of Management Perspectives*, 33(1), pp. 94–109.

Bakken, L.L. (2005). 'Who are physician–scientists' role models? Gender makes a difference,' *Academic Medicine*, 80(5), pp. 502–506.

Barry, H., Bacon, M.K. and Child, I.L. (1957). 'A cross cultural survey of some sex differences in socialization,' *Journal of Abnormal and Social Psychology*, 55(5), pp. 327–332.

Bem, S.L. (1981). 'Gender schema theory: A cognitive account of sex typing,' *Psychological Review*, 88(4), pp. 354–364.

Berkery, E., Tiernan, S. and Morley, M. (2014). 'Inclusive or Exclusive: An examination of sex role stereotypes and requisite managerial characteristics among irish business studies students,' *Irish Journal of Management*, 33(1).

Berkery, E.C. (2017). *Of seats, stereotypes and structures: empirical contributions on women in the workplace from a gender-organisation-systems perspective* University of Limerick].

Bilimoria, D. (1999). 'Upgrading management education's service to women,' *Journal of Management Education*, 23(2), pp. 118–122.

Booysen, L. and Nkomo, S. (2010). 'Gender role stereotypes and requisite management characteristics: The case of South Africa,' *Gender in Management: An International Journal*, 25(4), pp. 285–300.

Broverman, I.K., Vogel, S.R., Broverman, D.M., Clarkson, F.E. and Rosenkrantz, P.S. (1972). 'Sex-Role stereotypes: A current appraisal1,' *Journal of Social Issues*, 28(2), pp. 59–78.

Carter, S.B. (2011). 'The invisible barrier: Second generation gender discrimination,' *Psychology Today*. May 1.

Cleveland, J.N., Stockdale, M. and Murphy, K.R. (2000). *Women and men in organisations: Sex and gender issues at work.* Lawrence Erlbaum Associates.

Diekman, A.B., Goodfriend, W. and Goodwin, S. (2004). 'Dynamic stereotypes of power: Perceptions of change and stability in gender hierarchies,' *Sex Roles*, 50(3/4), pp. 201–215.

Diekman, A.B. and Schneider, M.C. (2010). 'A social role theory perspective on gender gaps in political attitudes,' *Psychology of Women Quarterly*, 34(4), pp. 486–497.

Dodge, K.A., Gilroy, F.D. and Fenzel, L.M. (1995). 'Requisite management characteristics revisited: Two decades later,' *Journal of Social Behavior and Personality*, 10(4), pp. 253.

Duehr, E.E. and Bono, J.E. (2006). 'Men, women, and managers: are stereotypes finally changing?' *Personnel psychology*, 59(4), pp. 815–846.

Eagly, A. (1987). *Sex differences in social behavior: A social-role interpretation.* Lawrence Erlbaum Associates.

Eagly, A.H. and Carli, L.L. (2003). 'The female leadership advantage: An evaluation of the evidence,' *The leadership quarterly*, 14(6), pp. 807–834.

Eagly, A.H. and Karau, S.J. (2002). 'Role congruity theory of prejudice toward female leaders,' *Psychological Review*, 109(3), pp. 573.

Eagly, A.H., Nater, C., Miller, D.I., Kaufmann, M. and Sczesny, S. (2020). 'Gender stereotypes have changed: A cross-temporal meta-analysis of US public opinion polls from 1946 to 2018,' *American psychologist*, 75(3), pp. 301.

ECOSOC. (1997). *Mainstreaming the gender perspective into all policies and programmes in the United Nations system.* New York: UN ECOSOC.

Eden, L. and Wagstaff, M.F. (2021). 'Evidence-based policymaking and the wicked problem of SDG 5 Gender Equality,' *Journal of International Business Policy*, 4(1), pp. 28–57.

Ely, R.J., Stone, P. and Ammerman, C. (2014). 'Rethink what you "know" about high-achieving women,' *Harvard Business Review*, 92(12), pp. 20.

Farndale, E., Biron, M., Briscoe, D.R. and Raghuram, S. (2015). A global perspective on diversity and inclusion in work organisations. *The International Journal of Human Resource Management*, 26(6), pp. 677–687.

Flynn, P., Cavanagh, K. and Bilimoria, D. (2017). 'Gender equality in business schools: the elephant in the room,' in Flynn, P.M., Haynes, K. and Kilgour, M.A. (eds.) *Integrating gender equality into business and management education: Lessons learned and challenges remaining.* Routledge.

Flynn, P., Cavanagh, K. and Bilmoria, D. (2015). 'Closing the Gender Gap: What business schools can do to increase the number of women in the corporate world,' *BizEd.*

Flynn, P.M., Haynes, K. and Kilgour, M.A. (2016). *Overcoming challenges to gender equality in the workplace: Leadership and innovation.* Greenleaf Publishing Limited.

Haynes, K. and Murray, A. (2017). 'Sustainability as a lens to explore gender equality: A missed opportunity for responsible management,' In Flynn, P., Haynes, K. and Kilgour, M. (eds.) *Integrating gender equality into business and management education.* Routledge, pp. 55–80.

Hyde, J.S. (2014). 'Gender similarities and differences,' *Annual review of psychology*, 65, 373–398.

Ibarra, H., Ely, R. and Kolb, D. (2013). 'Women rising: The unseen barriers,' *Harvard Business Review*, 91(9), pp. 60–66.

Joshi, A., Son, J. and Roh, H. (2015). 'When can women close the gap? A meta-analytic test of sex differences in performance and rewards,' *Academy of Management Journal*, 58(5), pp. 1516–1545.

Kilgour, M. (2020). 'Gender equality: taking its rightful place at the heart of sustainability education,' in Librizzi, F. and Parkes, C. (eds.) *The SAGE handbook of responsible management learning and education*. SAGE.

Kilgour, M.A. (2013). 'The global compact and gender inequality: a work in progress,' *Business & Society*, 52(1), pp. 105–134.

Kilgour, M.A. (2017). 'Gender inequality in management education: past, present and future,' In *Integrating gender equality into business and management education*. Routledge, pp. 10–25.

Koch, A.J., D'Mello, S.D. and Sackett, P.R. (2015). 'A meta-analysis of gender stereotypes and bias in experimental simulations of employment decision making,' *Journal of Applied Psychology*, 100(1), pp. 128–161.

Koenig, A.M., Eagly, A.H., Mitchell, A.A. and Ristikari, T. (2011). 'Are leader stereotypes masculine? A meta-analysis of three research paradigms,' *Psychological bulletin*, 137(4), pp. 616.

Kurz, R. (2020). 'UN SDGs: disruptive for companies and for universities?' in *The Future of the UN Sustainable Development Goals*. Springer, pp. 279–290.

Levin, L., Bridgman, J., Constantin, I., Breengaard, M.M., Costa, M. and Lynce, A.R. (2020). *Methods and tools to measure gender issues based around intersectional analysis*. https://www.tinngo.eu/wp-content/uploads/2020/11/TInnGO_D6.2_Toolbox.pdf

Mavin, S. and Bryans, P. (1999). 'New initiatives to place gender on the agenda in business schools,' *Equal Opportunities International*, 18(8), pp. 1–9.

Moratis, L. and Melissen, F. (2021). 'Bolstering responsible management education through the sustainable development goals: Three perspectives,' *Management Learning*, 53(2), 212–222.

Morgenroth, T., Ryan, M.K. and Sønderlund, A.L. (2020). 'Think Manager–Think Parent? Investigating the fatherhood advantage and the motherhood penalty using the Think Manager–Think Male paradigm,' *Journal of Applied Social Psychology*, 51(3), 237–247.

Ropers-Huilman, B. (2003). *Gendered futures in higher education: Critical perspectives for change*. State University of New York Press.

Rosenkrantz, P., Vogel, S., Bee, H., Broverman, I. and Broverman, D.M. (1968). 'Sex-role stereotypes and self-concepts in college students,' *Journal of Consulting and Clinical Psychology*, 32(3), pp. 287–295.

Roth, P.L., Purvis, K.L. and Bobko, P. (2012). 'A meta-analysis of gender group differences for measures of job performance in field studies,' *Journal of Management*, 38(2), pp. 719–739.

Rudman, L.A. and Phelan, J.E. (2015). 'The effect of priming gender roles on women's implicit gender beliefs and career aspirations,' *Social Psychology*, 41(3), pp. 192–202.

Sachs, J.D., Schmidt-Traub, G., Mazzucato, M., Messner, D., Nakicenovic, N. and Rockström, J. (2019). 'Six transformations to achieve the sustainable development goals,' *Nature Sustainability*, 2(9), pp. 805–814.

Sauers, D.A., Kennedy, J.C. and O'Sullivan, D. (2002). 'Managerial sex role stereotyping: a New Zealand perspective,' *Women in management review*, 17(7), pp. 342–347.

Schein, V.E. (1973). 'The relationship between sex role stereotypes and requisite management characteristics,' *Journal of Applied Psychology*, 57(2), pp. 95.

Schein, V.E. (1975). 'Relationships between sex role stereotypes and requisite management characteristics among female managers,' *Journal of Applied Psychology*, 60(3), pp. 340–344.

Schein, V.E. (1976). 'Think manager, think male,' *Atlanta Economic Review*, 26 (March-April), 21–24.

Schein, V.E. (2001). 'A global look at psychological barriers to women's progress in management,' *Journal of Social Issues*, 57(4), pp. 675–688.

Schein, V.E. (2007). 'Women in management: reflections and projections,' *Women in management review*, 22(1), pp. 6–18.

Schein, V.E. and Mueller, R. (1992). 'Sex role stereotyping and requisite management characteristics: A cross cultural look,' *Journal of organizational behavior*, 13(5), pp. 439–447.

Schein, V.E., Mueller, R. and Jacobson, C. (1989). 'The relationship between sex role stereotypes and requisite management characteristics among college students,' *Sex Roles*, 20(1), pp. 103–110.

Schein, V.E., Mueller, R., Lituchy, T. and Liu, J. (1996). 'Think manager—think male: A global phenomenon?' *Journal of organizational behavior*, 17(1), pp. 33–41.

Seikkula, J. and Olson, M.E. (2003). 'The open dialogue approach to acute psychosis: Its poetics and micropolitics,' *Family process*, 42(3), pp. 403–418.

Sinclair, A. (1995). 'Sex and the MBA,' *Organization*, 2(2), pp. 295–317.

United Nations (2018). Foundational Primer on the 2030 Agenda for Sustainable Development. United Nation: Geneva.

United Nations. (2020). *Goal 5: Achieve gender equality and empower all women and girls*. United Nations. Retrieved 02/11 from https://www.un.org/sustainabledevelopment/gender-equality/

United Nations Department of Economicand Social Affairs. (2010). *The World's Women 2010: Trends and Statistics*. U. Nations. https://unstats.un.org/unsd/demographic/products/worldswomen/WW_full%20report_BW.pdf

United Nations Women. (2018). 'Turning promises into action,' *Gender equality in the, 2030*. https://www.unwomen.org/en/digital-library/publications/2018/2/gender-equality-in-the-2030-agenda-for-sustainable-development-2018

Verbos, A.K. and Kennedy, D. (2017). 'Cleaning our houses: Gender equity in business schools,' in *Integrating gender equality into business and management education*. Routledge, pp. 81–95.

6 Between criticism and optimism: The derailment and rehabilitation of business schools

Guénola Abord-Hugon Nonet, Afrodita Dobreva, and Lucas Meijs

Introduction

In a video response to the latest IPCC report, UN Secretary-General António Guterres states that 'we are on a pathway to global warming of more than double the 1.5°C degree limit agreed in Paris. Some government and business leaders are saying one thing, but doing another. Simply put, they are lying. And the results will be catastrophic. This is a climate emergency. […] Leaders must lead. But all of us can do our part. We owe a debt to young people' (Guterres, 2022). Transforming our societies to become sustainable is one of the most important tasks facing institutions of higher education this century. The impact of humankind on the regenerative systems of the planet has reached a critical point. Scientists have now designated humanity's footprint on planet earth as the Anthropocene era (Wallenhorst, 2020; Wulf, 2019). Within this context of urgency, business schools are under attack, and they must transform rapidly in order to embed Agenda 2030 and contribute to achieving the 17 Sustainable Development Goals (SDGs) (Nonet et al., 2016). Proceeding from the definition of responsibility as 'response-ability,' this chapter examines which changes are needed in the education provided by business schools in order to ensure that they can become schools of prosperity for all, including our planet. This will require business schools to change not only their curriculum, but also their approach to doing business.

For more than a century now, business schools have been under scrutiny. Some have criticised the very discipline of business as insufficiently academic (Pfeffer and Fong, 2002). According to other critics, business schools are based on teaching rationality instead of managerial judgment (Spender, 2014). Moreover, they have even been criticised for being racist, given their deeply engrained white-supremacist nature (Dar et al., 2020) and they have been accused of being implicit partners in global economic and environmental crises (Phillips et al., 2016). The value of the degrees issued by business schools has been questioned (Lobo and Burke-Smalley, 2017) and the professional relevance of the management field as a whole has come under scrutiny as well (Schlegelmilch, 2020). In fact, ever since the trade school era,

DOI: 10.4324/9781003244905-9

business schools have occupied a tiresome limbo between scientific rigour and practical relevance, with no consensus on what constitutes a good management knowledge curriculum (Datar et al., 2010; Mintzberg, 2004). The deprecating voices of critical scholars resonate with what Earl Cheit observed more than 30 years ago: no professional field has been remotely as controversial as that of business (Cheit, 1985). The call to reinvent business schools is therefore loud and clear (see also Thomas and Cornuel, 2012).

While it is imperative to adopt a critical stance when evaluating the highly contested role of business schools, it is important to recall that criticism itself is not a cure. For this reason, this chapter is not intended to add to the already raging assessments of business schools. In connection to Agenda 2030, the climate commitments made in Paris and the 17 SDGs, this chapter examines the responsibility of business schools. Will they be able to shift their focus away from generating blind followers and confederates of destructive industry practices to take the lead and shape the new (and very much needed) generation of business leaders needed to achieve the current sustainability targets? In order to answer this question, we examine current educational practices and compare the current (outdated) model to a new approach to education that seeks to encourage students from the perspective of developing head, heart, hands, and soul. We argue that the multidisciplinary nature of business schools does indeed equip them to take a leading role in this shift. To do so, however, they must redefine their position in relation to the broader context. As such, this chapter is an exercise in understanding the overall scope of the challenges faced by business schools, proposing innovative solutions for business schools to become schools of responsible (or 'response-able') management. We set out to create the next best step in the history of business schools—an optimistic journey of recovery, in which the higher aims of higher education can and shall be restored.

Understanding what happened to the business school

One prominent critique of business schools, as endorsed by Spender (2014, p. 430) is 'that they promote greed in their students [and] shy away from the tough ethical and sustainability issues around doing business.' To some extent, this can be seen as the consequence of the worldwide adaptation of the promising new ideology of neoliberalism. This ideology is based on privatisation, capital deregulation and a *laissez-faire* attitude towards the market, proceeding from the seminal assumption that, if left undisturbed, it will ensure the best possible allocation of resources (Kenton, 2020). Such principles of freedom embody a highly desired opposition to the preceding collectivist regime, which existed along the same spectrum as Nazism and communism (Monbiot, 2016). The principles of neoliberalism also resulted in an organic transfer of control from the public to the private sector. This shift immediately amassed a great deal of support amongst wealthy individuals within industrialised societies, who saw it as an opportunity to ease some of their tax burden (Monbiot, 2016).

As evidence of their support for the neoliberal ideology, these wealthy individuals invested financial resources and mobilised their personal networks to promote these principles further. A well-resourced movement was set in motion. Backed by the most influential and affluent individuals, it gained momentum and began to permeate multiple layers of society in the form of policies. For example, monetary policies that were consistent with the neoliberal views were adopted by the Jimmy Carter administration in the United States and the Jim Callaghan government in Britain (Monbiot, 2016). In the 1980s, their respective successors – Ronald Reagan in the United States and Margaret Thatcher in Britain – further cemented the neoliberal doctrine by passing massive tax cuts for the rich, dismantling trade unions and promoting outsourcing and competition in public services (ibid). The replacement of collaborative social structures with individual responsibility is clearly reflected in Thatcher's illustrious statement 'There is no such thing as society. There are individual men and women, and there are families' (Thatcher, 1987). The neoliberal logic that positions individualism squarely at its very core trickled down from the political arena to all facets of society.

Even education, which has traditionally been treated as an externality (Kuttner, 1999), could not escape the merciless sieve of neoliberal ideology, which sought to attribute market value to just about any social interaction (Harvey, 2005; Brown, 2015). A clash of two competing logics occurred: the logic of the private sector, which disproportionately prioritises owners of financial capital, and the logic of the public sector, according to which everyone deserves a seat at the table. This clash continues to influence the half-hearted position of business schools with regard to the public global objectives of the SDGs.

The competitive climate of neoliberal individualism was hostile to the public sector's quest for the collective good. This generated contempt towards collective efforts and government intervention, based on the simple justification that any organisation that is not run as a business is bound to be inefficient and therefore in need of a more rigid corporate management structure (Giroux, 2014). The 'New Public Management' (see Osborne and McLaughlin, 2005) was one example.

The culture of frantic efficiency expanded to reach the field of higher education, too, which eventually succumbed to the pressure to change. In hindsight, it is evident that universities were caught in the crossfire of an ideological and economic paradigm shift and had little space to manoeuvre, let alone escape.

What is the problem?

This brief history lesson presented above contextualises the contamination of higher education with the infectious neoliberal disease that many scholars refer to as 'corporatization' (Wilshire, 1990; Damrosch, 1995, Fish, 1999; Readings, 1999; Bok, 2003; Donoghue, 2008). The phrase 'corporate university' has come to epitomise everything that is going wrong in universities. In his book *Universities in the Marketplace: The Commercialization of Higher Education,* former Harvard University President Derek Bok (2003) argues that higher education is trading its academic values for commercial ones by allowing short-term lucrative opportunities to wreak long-term damage on its fundamental mission. Bok points to the ever-increasing business interests in education, which have permeated not only teaching and research, but all other activities on campus, from restroom advertisements to professorship endowments (Clay, 2008). These developments are in line with Taylor's (2017) conclusion on the growing influence that the business community is exerting on higher education. In reality, however, the accusations related to the disconnection between business education and business practice are probably not true. The opposite appears to be the case: business schools seem to have followed business practices too closely and, as the latter began to derail, so did the former.

The industrialisation of business schools is evident at the level of both process and content. At the process level, business schools treat their students as customers (Zell, 2001; Clay, 2008). At the content level, the curriculum shamelessly and rampantly perpetuates individualism, consumerism and a particular variant of corporatism (Starkey and Tempest, 2005; Parker, 2018). For example, while society needs to move away from overconsumption, marketing theories teach students how to inflate desire. While society fights inequality, finance courses teach students how to capitalise on arbitrage opportunities and maximise and short-term gains. While society craves more human connection, human resource management teaches students how to categorise employees and treat them like yet another commodity. While the latest IPCC report (2022) indicates that we are not on track to limit global warming to 1.5°C (the average level of greenhouse gas emissions in recent decades is actually the highest in human history), and while we know that we must reverse the peak in emissions before 2025 and reduce greenhouse gas emissions by 43% by the end of this decade, business schools continue to teach economic principles of exponential economic growth, market self-regulation and unlimited natural resource use. These are the same principles that are destroying us, our biodiversity, and our biosphere.

The situation outlined above raises the question whether business schools are capable of reversing the co-dependent relationship between educating their students and responding to the interests of big business. Will they be able to shift their focus away from generating blind followers and confederates of destructive industry practices to take the lead and shape the new (and very much needed) generation of business leaders needed in order to achieve the current sustainability targets?

Finding solutions

What images come to mind upon hearing the word 'school'? Grades? Success? Intellectual work? Etymologically, the word school traces back to the Greek *scholé*, which means leisure or free time. The act of obtaining education was thus originally a leisure activity in which individuals immersed themselves in the process of pursuing the truth (Pieper and Perrin, 2014).

The Greek *scholé* transformed into the Latin *schola*, followed by the English *school*. Along the way, the concept underwent a radical shift in its implied meaning of helping students to serve the goals of the industrial revolution: to be obedient workers, to work on defined time schedules with defined breaks, to sit quietly and to avoid any form of critical thinking (Mitch, 2018). One would be hard-pressed to disagree with the observation that contemporary education has much more to do with work, pro-ductivity, and outcomes than it does with leisure. This is yet another symptom of the disease of corporatisation, which has moved universities away from their primary mission of seeking the truth (Zell, 2001).

One answer might be responsible management, but exactly what con-stitutes *responsible management* can be perceived differently, depending on context and culture. As suggested by Nonet et al. (2016, p. 728), being re-sponsible ('response-able') is 'the ability to respond in an aware and conscious manner, encompassing interaction, knowledge gathering, and decision-making which is grounded in the reality of day-to-day managerial respon-sibilities, nurtured with self-development and self-awareness, initiated from within the personal, individual level in seeking to understand other in-dividuals, guided by clear moral values, as well as the courage to stand for them, reliant on the development of soft skills (such as inspiring, caring), informed by systemic thinking, with a holistic consciousness of the con-sequences (present and future) on all stakeholders, designed to enculturate a shared vision, respectful, participative, inclusive and empowering, emerges through empowerment to build up a shared responsible vision at the in-dividual and organisational level, with a clear understanding of the issues and the development of appropriate knowledge, reinforced by a process of continuous improvement.' It is also grounded in the reality of the context, calling for the questioning of paradigms that were accepted in the past, as well as the impact that they have had on current and future well-being.

Within this context of responsible management, it is important to ex-plore ways in which business schools can become incubators for ethical, compassionate, and humble students, helping them to develop critical thinking abilities. It is also to consider how business schools could help their students to shift the context of their engagement, proceeding not from a purely intellectual and utilitarian approach, but also from a compassionate and action-oriented approach (e.g., 'head, heart, and hands'). Such a shift is needed in order to help businesses and all stakeholders achieve the objec-tives of Agenda 2030 and promote the well-being of humanity and the planet in general through the SDGs.

At this point, it would be helpful to reshape several facets of the tradi-tional business school model. In Table 6.1, we present a comparative overview of the business school of the past and (hopefully) the business school of the future.

Table 6.1 Comparison between current and proposed business school models

Category	Element	Traditional model	Proposed model
Learning Process	Teaching method	Theoretical (head)	Blend of head, heart, hands, and soul
	Learning environment	Classroom	In context, with the affected populations and within the natural environment
	Assessment	Grading on a curve	Self-feedback, group feedback, and coaching with experts
	Final assignment	Thesis	Life-relevant portfolio
Curriculum	Skills education	Low	High + consciousness
	Emphasis	Literacy and numeracy	Creativity and cultural awareness
	Duration	Fixed	Lifelong
	Progression model	Static, linear	Dynamic, circular, progression in loops
Community	Selection process	Performance-based	Values-based
	Age	Young adults	No age limit
	Goal	Employability	Growth and well-being
	Educators	Academics	Academics and non-academics
Context	Focus	Study success	An embedded view, an integrated context that acknowledges that humans cannot thrive unless Planet Earth is healthy and thriving (Kurucz et al., 2013)
		Post-colonisation principles: Eurocentric curriculum reinforcing Western, white, heterosexual male dominance and privilege	Principle of decolonisation: plurality of conceptions, spiritualities, religions, sexual orientations and cultural backgrounds, giving voice to elders, minorities, ethnic groups, and indigenous peoples
	Ranking	Yes	No
	Relationship with businesses	Unidirectional	Interactive, interweaving of multiple relationships
			Multistakeholder engagement with the private sector, the public sector, and civil society (e.g., should business schools continue to be business schools, or should they become schools of innovation and collaboration?)
	Relationship to society	Vertical	Horizontal and holistic, embracing the complexity of all stakeholders, as well as the various interests at stake

Learning process

Traditional learning has historically referred to a theoretical, top-down type of learning in which interaction is limited and the teacher is perceived as the main source of knowledge, instructing students according to such resources as textbooks, articles, and lectures. The flow of information is regulated by the instructor. Arguably, the rise of the internet ushered in the end of the vertical traditional learning experience by placing an abundance of online resources and interaction possibilities at the fingertips of most contemporary students.

New variations of traditional learning have been established in recent years, including problem-based learning, student-centred flipped classrooms (Milman, 2012) and blended learning (Benson and Kolsaker, 2015), with the latter becoming particularly prominent since the start of the COVID-19 pandemic. Each of these variations represents only a gradual improvement on what was once traditional leaning. One radical and diametrically opposed learning method is *transformative learning* developed by the American sociologist Jack Mezirow (1997). Unlike traditional learning, transformative learning is a non-linear process, which is set in motion as students experience disorienting dilemmas – events that challenge their current frames of reference (i.e., beliefs and worldviews). Disorienting dilemmas can be deliberately incorporated into educational programmes to create opportunities for students to rectify dysfunctional and outdated beliefs in a safe environment. If applied properly, transformative learning theory can promote awareness and self-expansion in terms of both knowledge and identity (Mezirow, 1997). If not applied properly, however, it could potentially cause more harm than good, leaving students confused due to a loss of trust in their own beliefs and judgment. Transformative learning is a particularly attractive concept for higher education, as it corresponds to the higher form of skills (e.g., critical thinking and critical reflection) that universities pledge to teach.

Despite its potential advantages, the possibility of implementing transformative learning in universities and business schools should not be taken lightly, as the process is not as organised, intuitive, and predictable as one might expect (Dobreva, 2021). It should not be regarded as a panacea for all of the problems associated with more traditional instructional approaches. The one-size-fits-all mentality should be replaced with flexibility to employ a blend of several methods that best matches the current developmental levels and needs of individual students.

The flexibility that is applied to the choice of teaching methods should also extend to the choice of location. In addition to debunking the false separation between knowing (*what*) and doing (*how*), the influential work of Brown et al. (1989) underscores the importance of the social and physical contexts, which were once treated as merely ancillary to learning. Their work builds on that of Miller and Gildea (1987), who investigated the difference between the learning words from dictionary definitions and from day-to-day communication, finding the latter to be much more effective than the former.

The conclusion is that words are not self-contained, but context-sensitive. Brown et al. (1989) extrapolate this notion from language to all knowledge. In the case of business education, teaching abstract business concepts in a sterile classroom setting simply cannot convey the intricacies of these concepts, nor can it ensure that students will be able to apply them properly. For example, strategic management should extend far beyond teaching Porter's Five Forces framework (see also Spender, 2014). Students should observe or, even better, participate in the strategising processes of actual managers or management consultants: taking decisions, observe their consequences, reflecting on them and adjusting them accordingly.

It is also important for students to experience the consequences of managerial decision-making. For example, when taking decisions concerning the deforestation of the rain forest or increasing working hours at low cost in harsh working conditions to help increase return on investments, students should have the opportunity to witness the effects of these decisions in the field, to discuss them with experts, peers and stakeholders (possibly through online means) and to realise the various consequences of managerial decisions. Exposure to the natural environment and the various actors affected by the decisions (especially those with little or no voice), in combination with social interaction could intensify the learning, feeling and understanding of students (Brown et al., 1989; Naidu and Bedgood, 2012). They should also have the opportunity to experience the sacredness of life, to reflect on the meaning and value of life, and to develop an educated understanding of the effects that managerial decisions can have on life. Students should have the opportunity to connect to the sacred, and management should be approached from the perspective of the soul.

Each school could find a way to ensure that their participants have opportunities for critical reflection, for feeling and for the application of theory. In other words, they should ensure that students are able to learning by feeling and by doing. Various settings are conceivable, including walks and classes in nature, field trips to hospitals or prisons, interviews with white-collar criminals, or interviews with entrepreneurs (including failed and social entrepreneurs). Other possibilities could include inviting environmental and other scientists to introduce the boundaries of the planet and the steps that are needed, or incorporating the vices of indigenous peoples and other minorities into the learning experience. It would also be beneficial to conduct projects with managers or other practitioners (e.g., as part-time lecturers), as well as with representatives from civil society. Space should be created for parents, activists, children, teachers, medical staff, farmers, and other stakeholders to help participants reflect and understand the 'wickedness' of the problems with which they are confronted, the magnitude of the challenges and the diversity of the actors affected by their potential future decisions. Business schools should support compulsory internships in all sectors: private, public, and not-for-profit (civil society). Students should be allowed the flexibility to combine part-time education and part-time work, to work with organisations continuously or to perform junior consultancy work (e.g., hackathons) and other relevant challenges involving direct interaction with all actors – not just the private sector.

Instructors should always consider taking the role of devil's advocate, in order to ensure that all perspectives are considered and encourage students to think critically and creatively. They cannot afford to teach simplistic models; it is critical to embrace the complexity (and the beauty) of life as it is.

The shift that we are proposing also calls for changes in assessment and the final assignments required of students. The outdated but, sadly, still common practice of 'grading on a curve' paradoxically makes it disadvantageous to have good peers (Calsamiglia and Loviglio, 2019). Imagine a scenario in which grades are replaced with feedback sessions in which students have the opportunity to assess their own performance in collaboration with the teacher. This would help them to develop a number of critical skills and qualities (e.g., self-evaluation, authenticity, ethics), in addition to building self-confidence and increasing an internal locus of control. It would allow a continued focus on the students' level of mastery while filtering out the harmful effects of constant, top-down comparison. Such assessment formats acknowledge and celebrate the differences between students without designating one as being better than the other. In addition to being detrimental to self-esteem and motivation, the practice of reducing a student's knowledge to a number can be conductive to cheating, stress, and anxiety (Fedesco, 2019).

The replacement of multi-interval assessment scores with narrative evaluations could enhance trust between instructors and students (Chamberlin et al., 2018). A shift away from quantitative towards more qualitative assessment of knowledge should also be manifested in the character of final assignments. Instead of producing research papers (e.g., Bachelor's or Master's theses) of questionable personal and societal relevance, students could be prompted to present an overview of the developmental processes that they have experienced throughout the course of their education. This could include changes in their personal values and purpose, of the types of meaningful connections that they have built and the ways in which their formal educational experiences have informed the further steps that they will take in their lives. Higher education should not be perceived as a discrete event, but as a part of a path of lifelong learning. This does not rule out celebrating the milestone of completing a degree. It simply calls for more integration between the periods before and after the attainment of a diploma.

In addition to promoting learning, business schools should allow their participants to 'be.' More specifically, the critical importance of 'being' should be acknowledged in the learning spaces that we create. Schools of collaboration should be spaces in which participants can develop both self- and group consciousness, nested within a larger context (e.g., the planet on which we live or the community which we are part of). Such a vision 'will support a radically progressive view of business schools as "public spheres of conscientization" (Freire, 1998): spaces where consciousness is awakened so that social action is made possible rather than psychic prisons devoted to training future servants of power!' (Kurucz et al., 2013, p. 3).

Curriculum

Transformative learning requires skills such as reflection and critical thinking. Despite the consensus concerning the crucial importance of skills across industrial sectors and organisational levels, however, such skills continue to be rare commodities in the curricula offered by most universities (Walker and Finney, 2006).

In 1999, the UK Government published a report outlining a detailed plan for actions in the short, medium, and long term that could unlock the potential of students. In that report, creative education is defined as 'forms of education that develop young people's capacities for original ideas and action,' with cultural education defined as 'forms of education that enable them [students] to engage positively with the growing complexity and diversity of social values and ways of life' (National Advisory Committee on Creative and Cultural Education, 1999, p.5). It is thus obvious that even 20 years ago it was already acknowledged that safeguarding a country's prosperity would require developing a national strategy that fosters skills amongst young people.

Today, the need for creativity and cultural understanding is probably higher than it has ever been before. We must learn to replace the dysfunctional belief that creativity is available only to a select few with the motivation to find our own creative strengths – a powerful source of personal self-esteem and achievement. We must replace the dysfunctional belief that our own culture is superior to others' with patience and respect towards diversity – a powerful source of interpersonal knowledge and relationships.

The label '21st-century skills' has become an umbrella term capturing the heterogeneous set of skills that one must possess in order to be successful in life (in the broadest sense of the word). The configuration of 21st-century skills varies, though. The skills could be grouped around *learning, literacy* and *life*, with critical thinking, creativity, collaboration and communication belonging to learning skills; information, media and technology belonging to literacy skills; and flexibility, leadership, initiative, productivity and social skills belonging to life skills (Stauffer, 2020). In a collaborative effort, the OECD developed a learning compass as a framework for arriving at the ultimate, shared destination of individual and societal well-being (Figure 6.1). As noted by the OECD Director for Education and Skills, Andreas Schleicher, 'Education today is about more than simply teaching students something. It's also about helping them develop the tools they need to navigate an increasingly complex, volatile and uncertain world' (Schleicher, 2019, p. 1). Schleicher argues that, if schools continue to teach only that which is easy to

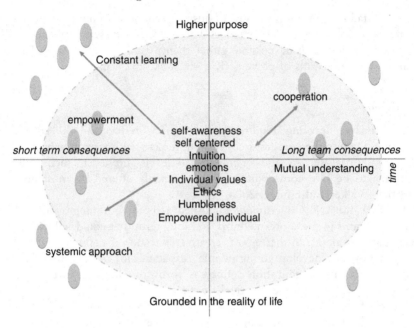

Figure 6.1 A visual representation of the set of definitions for responsible management and
factors that influence responsible management (Nonet et al., 2016, p. 729).

automate and digitise (and that will thus eventually be performed by AI), they
will in effect be producing second-class robots, instead of first-class humans.
This argument is in line with the insight that education has traditionally
lagged behind societal changes and that the majority of today's students
continue to be taught according to 20th-century didactic practices in 19th-
century educational organisations (Schleicher, 2018).

The learning compass allows students to navigate uncertain contexts
while exercising their purpose. It consists of core foundations (i.e.,
knowledge, skills, attitudes, and values), transformative competencies (i.e.,
creating new value, reconciling tension and dilemmas, and taking responsibility), student agency/co-agency and an iterative cycle of anticipation,
action and reflection (OECD, 2019; Figure 6.2). Consistent with the
SDGs, the compass ultimately points towards individual and collective
well-being.

This learning compass could be formally embedded into the concept of
planetary boundaries, as developed by Rockström et al. (2009).

Doughnut economics is a live example used by businesses, cities and
countries, in which various dimensions of well-being (e.g., education) are
embedded within the larger framework of planetary boundaries (Raworth,
2017). Business education should be designed according to an embedded
view, in which we learn to regenerate the planet on which we live. We
cannot continue to teach obsolete and false theories (e.g., the unlimited use

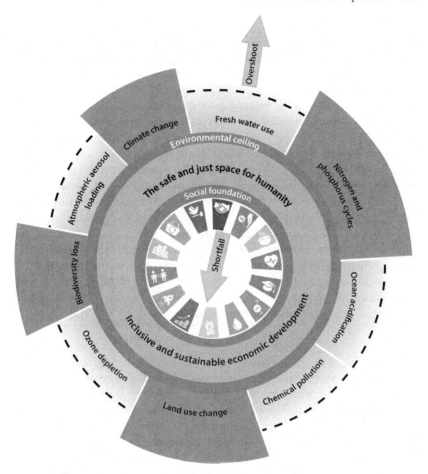

Figure 6.2 OECD Learning Compass (OECD, 2019).

of natural and human resources), as our planet is on fire and our health and economies are at stake.

The incorporation of all business school theories into the embedded-view model has therefore become critical to the survival of humanity.

One final remark should be made with regard to the duration and progression model of the business school curriculum. These elements have traditionally been standardised and fixed at the discretion of the university. Moving towards a more student-centred model of a business school will also call for changes in this regard. A dynamic, non-linear curriculum recognises that each student proceeds from a unique starting point in terms of knowledge, skills, and attitudes, while acknowledging differences in values and treating each individual's developmental path as an expression of – and not as a deviation from – the 'normal' model of learning and progression.

Community

Business schools have traditionally been rigorous in selecting young students based upon past performance. Following the argumentation presented above, the selection process should be transformed into a values-based perspective. First, a values-based perspective should be based on a selection procedure that incorporates congruence in values between students and schools (see Arieli et al., 2016). Second, it should also focus on the growth potential of students, instead of on their current level of achievement. The adoption of such a perspective of growth or added value also implies a dramatic change in the age composition of the student population. Far more than in the past, future education will be a shared enterprise. It will no longer stop at the age of 16, 18, or 21 years, as has historically been the case for the majority of people, but will be continuous and open ended. As a result, the student population might even include retired people, as the focus shifts away from the objective of employability (or maximising earnings) towards the goals of individual well-being, growth, and responsibility. Finally, the education of the future will be provided not only by schools and colleges, but by businesses and commercial organisations, the developers of new technologies, artists, scientists, other professionals, and the community at large.

Conclusion

The agenda proposed in this chapter is ambitious. Addressing the grand challenges faced by humanity will require innovation and collaboration at all levels. Given their multidisciplinary nature, business schools are uniquely equipped to play a leading role in this process, although doing so will require them to redefine their position in relation to the broader context. As is the case for relationships between businesses and the community, the first step for a business school should be to shift the focus away from the individual student and towards an embedded view of the student in our multiple contexts of well-being: individual, collective, and planetary (Kurucz et al., 2013).

To help their students become the innovators, entrepreneurs, managers, leaders, and employees that society will need in order to achieve the necessary societal and ecological transitions, business schools should promote their development as mindful, collaborative, humble, authentic, compassionate, and critical individuals. They should also help them to collaborate with others (e.g., other cultures, other stories), to engage in dialogue, to create shared value, to broker with multiple sectors and partners from all diverse groups, in order to innovate and solve the greatest challenges of the century. Finally, and most importantly, business schools should help their participants to rethink their relationship to the natural world and realise that we are the Earth (as opposed to communicating in terms of utilitarian human and environmental 'resources').

The shift that we propose calls for replacing the teaching of stand-alone knowledge with facilitating the development of abilities that will allow participants to navigate unfamiliar environments and find their own direction in a meaningful and responsible way (OECD, 2019). The relationship between business schools and the business community should become even more interactive and multidirectional. Perhaps even more importantly, the perspective should be shifted towards organisations instead of businesses and towards processes instead of structures. As a final directive, business schools should have a horizontal and holistic relationship with the broader community and society. Instead of presenting business-focused solutions, they should engage in dialogue with society about the grand challenges of the current times.

This chapter is one of many calls for action to change business schools. It is a fundamental call for transformation. We envision a change in which business schools develop into 'schools of purpose': schools that no longer focus on teaching students how to build careers, schools that no longer measure their success according to rankings, schools that no longer see themselves as isolated from the community and society, and schools that do not ignore the planet. Schools of purpose help their students – regardless of age – to find holistic ways of creating meaningful and shared value for all. Schools of purpose help create multi-stakeholder collaboration to create innovative solutions and lasting prosperity in financial terms, but primarily in terms of overall societal and environmental health.

References

Arieli, S., Sagiv, L. and Cohen-Shalem, E. (2016). 'Values in business schools: The role of self-selection and socialization,' *Academy of Management Learning & Education*, 15(3), 493–507.

Benson, V. and Kolsaker, A. (2015). 'Instructor approaches to blended learning: A tale of two business schools,' *The International Journal of Management Education*, 13(3), 316–325.

Bok, D. (2003). *Universities in the marketplace*. Princeton University Press.

Brown, J., Collins, A. and Duguid, P. (1989). 'Situated cognition and the culture of learning,' *Educational Researcher*, 18(1), 32–42.

Brown, W. (2015). *Undoing the demos: Neoliberalism's stealth revolution*. New York: Zone Books.

Calsamiglia, C. and Loviglio, A. (2019). 'Grading on a curve: When having good peers is not good,' *Economics Of Education Review*, 73, 101916.

Chamberlin, K., Yasué Maï and Chiang, I.-C. A. (2018). 'The impact of grades on student motivation,' *Active Learning in Higher Education*, (201812).

Cheit, E. (1985). 'Business schools and their critics,' *California Management Review*, 27(3), 43–62. 10.2307/41165141

Clay, R. (2008). 'The corporatization of higher education,' https://www.apa.org. Retrieved 1 August 2021, from https://www.apa.org/monitor/2008/12/higher-ed.

Damrosch, D. (1995). *We scholars: Changing the culture of the university*. Harvard University Press.

Dar, S., Liu, H., Martinez Dy, A. and Brewis, D. (2020). 'The business school is racist: Act up!,' *Organization*, 28(4), 695–706. 10.1177/1350508420928521

Datar, S.M., Garvin, D.A. and Cullen, P.G. (2010). *Rethinking the MBA: Business education at a crossroads*. Harvard Business Press.

Dobreva, A. (2021). *Perspective transformation: Raising social awareness through transformative learning*. (Master thesis). Rotterdam: Erasmus University Rotterdam/RSM. Retrieved from http://hdl.handle.net/2105/56532

Donoghue, F. (2008). *The last professors: The corporate university and the date of the humanities*. Fordham University: New York.

Fedesco, H. (2019). *Grades as a necessary evil? How they affect student motivation and what we can do about it*. Retrieved 16 August 2021, from https://cynthiabrame.org/2019/12/18/grades-as-a-necessary-evil-how-they-affect-student-motivation-and-what-we-can-do-about-it/.

Fish, S. (1999). *Professional correctness: Literary studies and political change*. Harvard University Press.

Freire, P. (1998). Pedagogy of freedom: Ethics, democracy and civic courage. Lanham: Rowman & Littlefield Publishers.

Giroux, H. (2014). *Neoliberalism's War on higher education*. Haymarket Books.

Guterres, A. (2022). 'Secretary-General warns of climate emergency, calling intergovernmental panel's report 'a fhile of shame', saying leaders are lying, fulling flames, United Nations Meetings Coverage and press releases, secretary general, statement and messages,', 4 April 2022, online, retrieved on May 14 2022: https://www.un.org/press/en/2022/sgsm21228.doc.htm

Harvey, D. (2005). *A brief history of neoliberalism*. Oxford University Press.

IPCC, 2022: *Climate change 2022: Impacts, adaptation, and vulnerability*. Contribution of Working Group II to the Sixth Assessment Report of the Intergovernmental Panel on Climate Change [Pörtner, H.-O., Roberts, D.C., Tignor, M., Poloczanska, E.S., Mintenbeck, K., Alegría, A., Craig, M., Langsdorf, S., Löschke, S., Möller, V., Okem, A., Rama, B. (eds.)]. Cambridge University Press. In Press.

Kenton, W. (2020). *Neoliberalism*. Investopedia. Retrieved 30 July 2021, from https://www.investopedia.com/terms/n/neoliberalism.asp.

Kurucz, E., Colbert, B.A., Marcus, J. (2013). 'Sustainability as a provocation to rethink management education: Building a progressive educative practice,' *Management Learning*, 0(0), 1–21. DOI: 10.1177/1350507613486421

Kuttner, R. (1999). *Everything for sale*. Chicago: University of Chicago Press.

Lobo, B. and Burke-Smalley, L. (2017). 'An empirical investigation of the financial value of a college degree,' *Education Economics*, 26(1), 78–92. 10.1080/09645292.2017.1332167

Mezirow, J. (1997). 'Transformative learning: Theory to practice,' *New Directions for Adult and Continuing Education*, 74, 5–12.

Miller, G. and Gildea, P. (1987). 'How children learn words,' *Scientific American*, 257(3), 94–99.

Milman, N.B. (2012). 'The flipped classroom strategy: What is it and how can it best be used?,' *Distance Learning*, 9(3), 85.

Mintzberg, H. (2004). *Managers, not MBAs: A hard look at the soft practice of managing and management development*. Pearson Education.

Mitch, D. (2018). 'The role of education and skill in the British industrial revolution,' in *The British Industrial Revolution*. Routledge, pp. 241–279.

Monbiot, G. (2016). *Neoliberalism – the ideology at the root of all our problems*. The Guardian. Retrieved 30 July 2021, from https://www.theguardian.com/books/2016/apr/15/neoliberalism-ideology-problem-george-monbiot

National Advisory Committee on Creative and Cultural Education. (1999). *All Our Futures: Creativity, Culture and Education*. London. Retrieved from http://sirkenrobinson.com/pdf/allourfutures.pdf

Naidu, S. and Bedgood, D. (2012). 'Learning in the social context,' Seel, M. , *Encyclopedia Of The Sciences Of Learning, 1923-1925*. New York: Springer.

Nonet, G., Kassel, K. and Meijs, L. (2016). 'Understanding responsible management: emerging themes and variations from european business school programs,' *Journal of Business Ethics* 139, 717–736

OECD. (2019). *OECD Future of Education and Skills 2030: OECD Learning Compass 2030*. Retrieved from https://www.oecd.org/education/2030-project/teaching-and-learning/learning/learning-compass-2030/OECD_Learning_Compass_2030_Concept_Note_Series.pdf

Osborne, S.P. and McLaughlin, K. (2005). 'The new public management in context,' in *New public management*. Routledge, pp. 19–26.

Parker, M. (2018). 'Why we should bulldoze the business school,' The Guardian. Retrieved 1 August 2021, from https://www.theguardian.com/news/2018/apr/27/bulldoze-the-business-school.

Pfeffer, J. and Fong, C. (2002). 'The end of business schools? Less success than meets the eye,' *Academy Of Management Learning & Education*, 1(1), 78–95. 10.5465/amle.2002.7373679

Phillips, F., Hsieh, C., Ingene, C. and Golden, L. (2016). 'Business schools in crisis,' *Journal Of Open Innovation: Technology, Market, And Complexity*, 2(1). 10.1186/s40852-016-0037-9

Pieper, B. and Perrin, C. (2014). *What is Scholé?*. Simply Convivial. Retrieved 30 July 2021, from https://www.simplyconvivial.com/2014/what-is-schole/

Raworth, K. (2017). *Doughnut economics: seven ways to think like a 21st-century economist*. Chelsea Green Publishing.

Readings, B. (1999). *The university in ruins*. Harvard University Press.

Rockström, J., Steffen, W., Noone, K., Persson, Å., Chapin III, F.S., Lambin, E., … & Foley, J. (2009). 'Planetary boundaries: exploring the safe operating space for humanity,' *Ecology and society*, 14(2).

Schlegelmilch, B. (2020). 'Why business schools need radical innovations: Drivers and development trajectories,' *Journal Of Marketing Education*, 42(2), 93–107.

Schleicher, A. (2018). 'Educating learners for their future, not our past,' *ECNU Review of Education*, 1(1), 58–75.

Schleicher, A. (2019). 'A new tool for navigating through a complex world - OECD Education and Skills Today,' Retrieved 17 August 2021, from https://oecdedutoday.com/education-skills-learning-compass-2030/

Spender, J.C. (2014). 'The business school model: a flawed organizational design?,' *Journal of Management Development*, 33(5), pp. 429–442. 10.1108/JMD-02-2014-0019

Starkey, K. and Tempest, S. (2005). 'The future of the business school: Knowledge challenges and opportunities,' *Human Relations*, 58(1), 61–82.

Stauffer, B. (2020). *What Are 21st Century Skills?*. Aeseducation.com. Retrieved 13 August 2021, from https://www.aeseducation.com/blog/what-are-21st-century-skills.

Taylor, A. (2017). 'Perspectives on the University as a Business: The corporate management structure, neoliberalism and higher education,' *Journal For Critical Education Policy Studies*, 15(1), 108–135.

Thatcher, M. (1987). 'Interview for *Woman's Own* on September,', 23. Retrieved from http://briandeer.com/social/thatcher-society.htm

Thomas, H. and Cornuel, E. (2012). 'Business schools in transition? Issues of impact, legitimacy, capabilities and re-invention,' *Journal of Management Development*, 31(4), pp. 329–335. 10.1108/02621711211219095

Walker, P. and Finney, N. (2006). 'Skill development and critical thinking in higher education,' *Teaching in Higher Education*, 4(4), 531–547.

Wallenhorst, N. (2006). What type of citizenship in the Anthropocene?, *Le Telemaque*, 2, 45–58.

Wallenhorst, N. (2020). La vérité sur l'Anthropocène. Pommier: Paris.

Wilshire, B. (1990). *The moral collapse of the university*. State University of New York Press.

Wulf, C. (2019). 'La formation à l'ère de l'anthropocène. Mimésis, rituels, gestes (Education in the Anthropocene: Mimesis, Rituals, Gestures),' *Mimésis, rituels, gestes (Education in the Anthropocene: Mimesis, Rituals, Gestures)*.

Zell, D. (2001). 'The Market-Driven business school: Has the pendulum swung too far?,' *Journal Of Management Inquiry*, 10(4), 324–338. 10.1177/1056492601104006

7 Reflections of an engaged marketing scholar: An SDG-guided journey towards being a 'called professional'

Ranjit Voola

Introduction

In this chapter, I critically reflect on my journey to align my personal values with my professional goals, as an Associate Professor of Marketing. In 2015, inspired by my experience at the 2014 United Nations Global Compact Leaders' Summit in New York, I proactively and strategically pivoted my scholarly journey by framing my scholarly worldview through the lens of the Sustainable Development Goals (SDGs). Various lived experiences relating to vulnerability, sacrifice, being the recipient of extreme kindness (i.e., recipient of a kidney from a live donor), and the desire to be authentic in all aspects of my life, including professional life, motivated me to re-imagine my role as a scholar. To critically reflect on these experiences, I adopted the 'called professional' framework (Bloom et al., 2021), which provides insights into the characteristics of those professionals who are 'called.'

Callings 'capture the most positive and generative manifestation of the connection between people and their work that scholars have studied' (Wrzesniewski, 2012, p. 45). I utilise this framework for two reasons. First, it is aligned with my lived experiences, and it provides an evidence-based insight into how one can become a called professional. Second, Moratis and Melissen (2022) find that most RME initiatives do not consider that the SDGs require a holistic transformational change, at various levels (e.g., personal, organisation). Furthermore, this 'superficial' approach to RME may result in 'bluewashing,' where firms attempt to gain legitimacy by superficially engaging with the SDGs. Therefore, at the personal level, to contribute to a systematic and transformational change relating to RME and the SDGs, I strongly believe that scholars should consider reflecting on their 'calling.'

In this chapter, I first provide an overview of the current dominant pessimistic view of management and marketing (e.g., relevance to society, cause of the problems facing humanity), to situate my reflection. However, I take a more positive view and suggest that these critiques have made the management and marketing academies reflect on their role and as evidenced by the number of calls for papers on the SDGs, as well as the desire

DOI: 10.4324/9781003244905-10

for business schools to be part of the PRME network, the SDGs are slowly becoming mainstream. Then, I reflect on my journey to become an SDG-marketing scholar by applying the 'called professional framework.' I conclude by providing some key learnings that may be useful for other scholars who are interested in incorporating the SDGs.

Hopelessness and hopefulness of business education

There have been and continue to be wide-ranging critiques of the contemporary business school. These range from the business school scholarship ignoring key challenges facing humanity (Harley and Fleming, 2021), being racist (Dar et al., 2021), and contributing to hubris (Sadler-Smith and Cojuharenco, 2021). Importantly, business schools are seen as key players in creating detrimental human suffering relating to inequality and climate change (McLaren, 2020). In fact, the critiques are so relentless that there is a sense of hopelessness around the purpose and value of business and business schools (Spicer et al., 2021).

In the context of marketing, researchers argue that marketing scholarship does not engage with important issues relating to marketers, policymakers, and broader society (Kohli and Haenlein, 2021; Van Heerde et al., 2021), partly due to the narrow and implicit boundaries of what consumer research should investigate (MacInnis et al., 2020). Furthermore, Chandy et al. (2021, p.1) state that 'we still know too little about marketing's role in improving – or harming – our world' and call out marketing scholars for becoming detached from urgent world challenges. However, I agree with Spicer et al. (2020), who sense hopelessness, but also hope that the business school can re-imagine itself to address these critiques. I also believe that management education provides a mechanism for reflecting on the importance of business engagement with society and nature, to address the challenges arising from inequalities and climate change (Moratis and Melissen, 2020).

Marketing is crucial to addressing the wicked challenges facing humankind. As the famous naturalist David Attenborough noted, saving our planet is now a communication challenge (BBC, 2020), suggesting that, although the rationale (based on logic and science) for engaging with societal challenges is clear, convincing and persuading the various stakeholders that the problems exist and that actions need to be taken to address it, is a difficult proposition. There have been various calls for marketing scholars to engage with the SDGs (e.g., Scott et al., 2022; Voola et al., 2022a). For example, Voola et al., (2022a, p. 13). argue that 'by not extending this rich body of literature on sustainability specifically to the SDGs, marketing scholars are at risk of missing a valuable opportunity to participate in the meta-narrative of the world, which is important to various stakeholders (e.g., governments and firms), and increasingly to marketing practitioners and students.'

I situate this reflection of my journey as an SDG-marketing scholar, within the intense critiques of the business school, and the call for RME to effect transformational change. I take a hopeful stance, as opposed to a hopeless stance, and reflect on the ability of individual scholars to engage in transformational RME. To this end, I critically reflect on my journey to be a 'called professional' as an SDG-marketing scholar. I specifically reflect on my lived experiences and the various stages of the 'Narrative Model of Authoring an Identity as a Called Professional' (Bloom et al., 2021), which is visually represented in Figure 7.1.

Called Professional framework

Experiencing work as a calling has been espoused as an 'ideal of a truly positive experience of work' (Bloom et al., 2021), 'where they [callings] capture the most positive and generative manifestation of the connection between people and their work that scholars have studied' (Wrzesniewski, 2012, p. 45). Although, Figure 7.1 provides the framework in its entirety, I believe that I have only completed part of the journey towards being a called professional. Bloom et al. (2021) highlight two broad plot lines that people follow to transform themselves by re-imagining work as a calling: 1) discernment and 2) exploration. Whilst the discernment narrative revolves around finding one's destiny, the exploration narrative revolves around realising that something critical is missing in one's work and being very motivated to fill the gap. Although these are two different narratives, once they have discovered their calling, professionals need to reflect on how to align their personal values and their calling with the profession they are in. As they started to live their calling, two motives guided their actions: the need for professional legitimacy and personal authenticity. They experience authenticity and legitimacy, by receiving membership, where they are accepted by the wider professional community where their authenticity is acknowledged. This results in the person to author an 'integrated identity as called profession' (Bloom et al., 2021, p. 308).

My discernment journey towards a destiny

I believe that three major lived experiences have defined a plot line that led me towards a destination, where I wanted to align my personal goals with my scholarly goals or attempt to find my calling or my eventual destination. As I have stated previously, I don't believe I have gone through the whole process, but, at present, I can articulate destination to mean being a management/marketing scholar who challenges existing notions about business including its purpose and construct a compelling case for why businesses should adopt the SDGs, as a framework for strategy, to have impact at the wider societal level, and to reach its traditional economic goals.

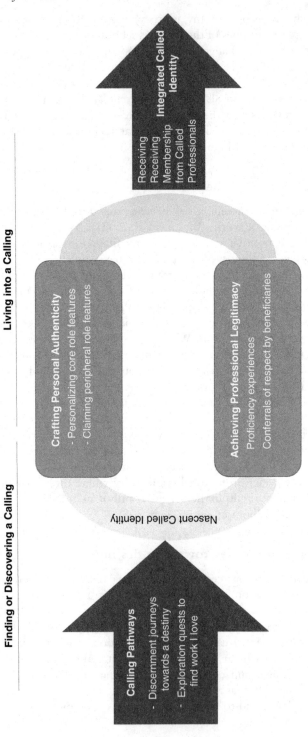

Figure 7.1 A narrative model of authoring an identity as a called professional (source: Bloom et al., 2021).

My parents

I believe my path followed the discernment as opposed to the exploration plotline,. where the goal was always to find my destiny. In other words, as Bloom et al. (2021, p. 308) state, 'discernment, portrayed finding as a calling as an organic evolving process wherein knowledge and insights about oneself and one's future world emerged over time.' It started when I was a child. When I was about seven years old, I remember asking my mother why she always slept in a saree (Indian traditional outfit), as opposed to a nightdress. She told me that because she is a gynaecologist in a non-profit Christian hospital, she may be called anytime to assist poor women in giving birth; therefore, she had to be always ready. This experience, as well as various other sacrifices that my parents made on a daily basis because they worked in a non-profit setting, had an indelible influence on what I wanted to become, although, at time, it was not clear to me what exactly that would be. As I grew older and learned how much a gynaecologist and a surgeon could earn if they worked in private practice, made me realise that following your passion or what you believe in requires significant sacrifice. However, one critical realisation that had a profound effect on finding my calling was that the greater good trumps individual gain. In my parents' case, helping poor patients trumps having less money and little free time. For example, I was sent to a boarding school when I was eight because they did not have time to take care of me. *I wanted to be like my parents.*

My daughters

Growing up in India, I witnessed both explicit and implicit gender in-equalities, including challenges that girls face in obtaining an education and pursuing their passions (although, I live in Australia now, similar yet more implicit inequalities are evident). Much later, as an adult professional, when I was conducting research in India relating to poverty, I had asked a recipient of a microfinance program, who in this case was considered ultra-poor (i.e., earning less than 1 USD a day), if she was happy being a successful entrepreneur. Rather than discuss the money she was making, she described success as the opportunity to own a business, the opportunity to be recognised as an individual entity (rather than a wife/mother/daughter of male kin), and to be visible in her own village. For her, it was equally important to have connections with others (which she did not have previously, as a homebound mother). As a male and relatively richer person, I took opportunities, connections, and visibility for granted. This further highlighted to me the basic challenges girls and women face in their daily lives. Now that I have two young daughters of my own, I am conscious of a world where gender inequalities are the norm for adults. However, I am very aware of the challenges of tackling these inequalities, as I benefit from this patriarchy in some situations, without realising it! I am cognizant of the fact that I alone cannot address patriarchy, or that those gender inequalities will not stop by the time my daughters are adults. However, I am confident that I, as a management/marketing scholar by challenging future business leaders to question this inequality, as well as disseminating research on tackling these inequalities, can play a small role in reducing inequalities, specifically gender-based inequalities. *I wanted to make a difference for my daughters.*

My kidney donor

In 2018, I had kidney failure, which resulted in being on peritoneal dialysis for about 15 months. This involved being connected to a machine, for about 10 hours, every night. After hearing about my kidney failure, the pastor of my church offered his kidney and after five months of rigorous tests, the kidney transplant occurred in 2019. This act of unfathomable kindness made me reflect on whether I got my means and ends confused, and inculcated kindness in my personal as well as professional life. It made me question the purpose of my scholarly career. Earlier, the end was primarily about getting promotions, accolades/awards, and top-tier publications. However, upon observing how my donor practiced what he preached, I realised that these ends were important, but were not the most important. I realised that the 'end' for me was to align what I believe in with all that I do in my life, including being an academic. In other words, although the ends previously were to get promoted and get scholarly accolades, I re-imagined them as means to a greater end, which was to seek transformational change in the world. Practically, this meant engaging business and marketing students with the SDGs, disseminating research on SDGs, and championing the counterintuitive argument that for-profit businesses can and should engage with the SDGs whilst making profits. *I wanted to operationalize kindness like my donor.*

Introspection

Based on my childhood experiences with my parents, my two daughters, and my journey through kidney failure and transplant, I realised that there were several things that were important to me. It was clear from my childhood that I wanted to be like my parents, who had forgone money to serve people, and I wanted to do what I can in my capacity to reduce gender inequality. My kidney donor further impressed upon me to demonstrate kindness and generosity. These experiences lay the foundation for reflection. Below I reflect on several important moments in my journey towards being an SDG-marketing scholar.

A professor at the University of Newcastle, where I was undertaking a Master of Marketing, suggested that I write well and encouraged me to undertake a Ph.D. This resulted in me becoming a marketing scholar, with my first (and so far, only) job as a full-time scholar at the University of Sydney. I started teaching in the areas of marketing strategy and international marketing. At this stage, although I enjoyed teaching and researching in the marketing discipline, I felt an underlying and nagging cognitive dissonance between my role as a marketing scholar and my latent calling. This was partly because at the early stage of my academic career, I believed that marketing was at the front line of exploitative capitalism practices and that it encouraged the pursuit of endless profits, without much regard for societal consequences. My lived experience at that time made me realise that there were limited choices for marketing and management students to engage in studies that allowed them to reflect and question traditional assumptions (e.g., the primacy of shareholders and that firms can engage in alleviating societal issues as well make profits). Motivated by my discernment journey, as well as my realisation that in my specific context existing structures were not conducive to pursuing my destiny, I recognised that I had to create my own destiny. Specifically, to be like my parents, who sacrificed wealth for the greater good, to engage in alleviating gender inequalities, and to be kind like my donor, I needed to question assumptions and challenge existing structures to align my personal values with my professional values. Two different frameworks allowed me to realise these goals.

As a marketing scholar, I was aware of the market-driven versus market-driving distinction (Sheth and Parvatiyar, 2021), where the former is responsive to markets, whilst the latter requires shaping the market. Being responsive to markets is easy, but shaping markets is difficult, as it requires engaging with latent needs (as opposed to expressed needs). The chances of failure are high, but the reward is also high. By reshaping my scholarly context, I could drive engagement specifically with the SDGs, through teaching, research, and broader community engagement. Shaping an environment that was conducive to engaging with the SDGs required talking to the relevant academic managers to make the case for teaching and researching in the SDG area.

At the beginning of my shaping journey, several people discouraged my ideas relating to the SDGs as it was difficult to link SDG relevance in the business and marketing context. This was a new idea in the discipline with relatively few scholarly publications in marketing to reference. There was also a potential downside for my career in attempting to shape the 'market.' As my Ph.D. was related to marketing strategy, the obvious way for promotion was to delve deeper into this area and get published in top-tier journals. However, the 'shaping the market' approach required me to pivot towards a new theoretical space revolving around the SDGs, which could potentially hinder my publications. Secondly, in the context of teaching, it is easier to teach the same subject, repeatedly, as it requires less effort and there is time for other academic functions such as research and stakeholder engagement. On the other hand, developing novel subjects, such as conceptualising the SDGs as a framework for marketing strategy, requires creativity, diligence, hard work, overcoming failure, including negative student feedback, and facing colleagues who question the legitimacy of my status as a marketing scholar.

Although, the 'shaping the market' approach gave me a theoretical foundation for my 'calling,' the Japanese concept of *Ikigai* – translated as 'to live (iki) and reason (gai)' – allowed me to think deeper about my calling (Figure 7.2). I made a concerted effort to implement its essence in my scholarly career. I engaged my students in finding their Ikigai, as I believe that it provides one viable foundation from which one can engage with the SDGs, not only as a scholar but also as a practitioner. The following is an excerpt from one of the subjects (Marketing and Sustainable Development) that I created for the Bachelor of Commerce program. It is a personal example of my Ikigai to encourage my students to engage with their Ikigai.

In the first week, I briefly talked about the importance of finding your Ikigai. I think this is important because if as marketers we want to engage with the SDGs, our drivers must be inside-out (our values, what is important to us) more than outside-in (what the world thinks we should do). This is because engaging with the SDGs requires a passion for social issues, as well as an attitude of not giving up. The SDGs (e.g., poverty, gender equality, climate change, hunger, education) are emotional issues, difficult to fake your engagement with them. Secondly, the attitude of not giving up is important because this is still a counterintuitive proposition (engaging with the SDGs at a profit) and it is difficult to implement in companies. Therefore, if it is not based on values or what is important to you, then at the first sign of resistance you will give up on implementing the SDGs.

What I love? I love to make a significant difference to the lives of vulnerable people and to tackle inequalities.

> *Why reason 1. I spent all my childhood watching my parents, doctors who were spending insane hours treating poor patients in India (for very little money). This motivated me to engage with alleviating poverty. As I did a Ph.D. in Marketing, I decided to engage with poverty alleviation through my profession of teaching and research.*

> *Why reason 2. I have two daughters, aged 13 and 6. I really don't want to see the incredible gender inequalities that exist today and I think businesses and marketers can do something about this inequality.*

> *Why reason 3. A friend of mine donated his kidney to me (as I had kidney failure), without asking. This kindness I wanted to reciprocate. I believe the SDGs provide a viable framework to be kind and, in the context of business, make money.*

What does the world need? The world needs businesses and marketing people who can engage profitably with the SDGs. Therefore, I teach and research in this area. Specifically, I have developed this unit as well as another unit at the master's level titled 'Poverty Alleviation and Profitability.'

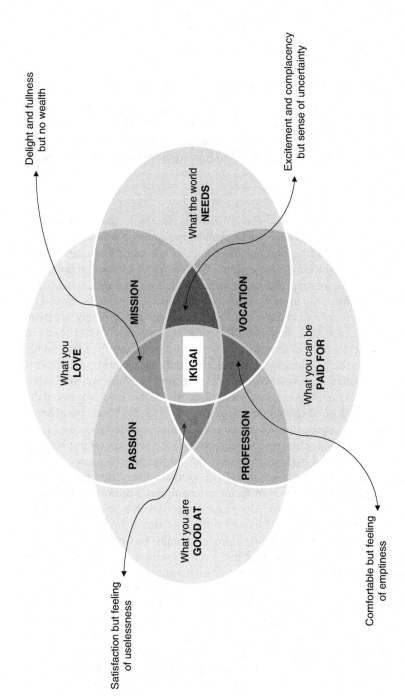

Figure 7.2 Ikigai (source: Toronto Star, diagram by Mark Winn).

What I am good at? I would like to think teaching and research and catalyzing students to be marketing activists (market driving) that hopefully, one day will make a change in how companies engage with the SDGs.

What can I get paid for? I get paid to teach and research. (However, I proactively developed these units and proactively researched in these areas.)

Living into a calling with legitimacy and authenticity

Bloom et al. (2021, p. 318) find that operationalising one's calling required 'authoring called identity that integrated their true selves and roles' or to be a 'living manifestation of the calling.' To achieve this, the person has to author an identity that embodies both professional legitimacy and personal authenticity.

Crafting personal authenticity

When I started the SDG journey in 2015, it was clear to me that the journey to be an SDG-marketing scholar will be challenging and sometimes very difficult in mainstream marketing/business disciplines or educational settings – particularly due to traditional assumptions about what a business school or a marketing scholar is supposed to be like and do. For example, when I first started this journey, my ideas were met with scepticism, especially around the purpose of business is to engage in societal challenges and difficulty in solving societal challenges. The key critique was that businesses should focus on making money, whilst fulfilling a customer's need. Additionally, I was advised against taking the SDG route by a senior scholar, as it would be difficult to publish and therefore have implications for promotion. More recently, whilst presenting at an international conference about the SDGs, it was suggested that it is nice and feels good to want to change the world for the better, but where is the money? My arguments about marketing being ambidextrous (i.e., make the world better *and* achieve economic goals) failed to make an impact.

These experiences highlighted to me the importance of proactively developing personal authenticity, to be true to my 'calling.' Because I realised that if I don't, it will be very difficult to champion a minority perspective and I would probably follow the majority perspective to obtain rewards such as promotions. I would like to note here that I do not believe that obtaining rewards such as promotions is morally incorrect or a negative thing to aim for. As a result of my lived experiences and reflecting on aligning my personal values with my professional values, I re-imagined promotion to be a means to a greater end and not the end itself. Furthermore, as a Bob Marley (1973) fan, the lyrics 'you can fool some people sometimes, but you cannot fool all the people all the time' resonated with me and encouraged me to be authentic in my quest to be an SDG-marketing scholar. This led me on a journey to discover the essence of the SDGs and their meaning in the contemporary world and business. With support from the business school, I went to both the UN headquarters in

New York and Geneva to engage in talks on the SDGs. I also started reading about the SDGs, to make myself familiar with how other disciplines and scholars were engaging with the SDGs. I started discussing it with my colleagues and the school leadership.

Another strategy I adopted was to engage with the wider audience to persuade them that the SDGs are relevant and valid. This helped me to address the imposter syndrome that I am acting as an expert in SDGs when I felt that I was not. To this end, I proactively took part in several outward-facing events such as a radio interview with a national broadcaster, the Australian Broadcasting Corporation (Voola, 2015), an interview with the University of Sydney Alumni Magazine (Voola, 2017), and broader community-focused events such as the Raise the Bar Sydney event, where I engaged with the wider public (Voola, 2018; Azmat and Voola, 2020).

I also started to focus on developing a compelling narrative that emphasises why I do what I do, as opposed to what I do. I wanted my audience (i.e., students, colleagues, co-authors, wider community) to know that I am genuine about my desire to engage with the SDGs. For example, I changed my bio on my website to emphasise the why. The first paragraph of the bio reads as follows:

Associate Professor Ranjit Voola spent all his childhood watching his parents (gynecologist and surgeon) providing subsidized and/or free treatment to the poorest of the poor in a non-profit hospital in India. This experience provided unique insights into the lived realities of the poor and created a desire to address some of the vulnerabilities the poor confront daily. Furthermore, as a kidney transplant recipient from a live donor, the relentless nature of the disease as well as the kindness of the donor, has provided Ranjit with a lived experience of vulnerability and kindness. These experiences have shaped the type of academic he wants to be, an academic whose research, teaching, and engagement attempt to make lives better, by reimagining the purpose of for-profit firms. With its tagline of 'leaving no one behind', the 17 UN Sustainable Development Goals (e.g., End poverty, No hunger, Gender equality) provide an ideal context to realize these academic goals.

In the specific context of teaching, I found that personal examples of struggles and triumphs engaged students more with the topic of the SDGs, because of the personal authenticity it portrays. Furthermore, by extrapolating my personal life circumstances to the SDGs in my classes I tried to highlight authenticity. For example, one key characteristic of students attempting to engage with the SDGs is their ability to re-imagine a problem into an opportunity. This attitude is essential because I believe that based on traditional business education, the first instinct is to view the SDGs as a problem that businesses must confront, rather than as an opportunity that the SDGs provide businesses. In my classes, I relate my experiences of dialysis to how I attempted to re-imagine a problem into an opportunity and then relate it to the SDGs, explaining how they can be re-imagined as opportunities from a business perspective.

I was on peritoneal dialysis for about 10 hours every night, where I was linked to a pipe with about a two-meter radius. Due to infection concerns, it was not advisable to disconnect and connect multiple times to the dialysis machine. In fact, in the 14 months I was on dialysis, I only disconnected twice. I explained to the students that it is entirely possible that I could have seen this as a major problem in life (e.g., dialysis affecting my health, inability to travel without extensive planning) as well as being bored. However, my discernment path and related introspection provided the foundation for me to re-imagine the 'problem' into an opportunity. I proactively reflected on what the opportunity of being stuck to a machine for 10 hours every day, was. I realised that the opportunity was that it gave me a lot of time! Then I started to proactively engage in scholarship including reading and writing, for the first few hours of dialysis. This approach led me to increase my citations and number of quality publications (e.g., since kidney dialysis in 2018, I was able to publish eight A and four A* publications based on the ABDC rankings, and my citations in the year 2017 doubled to around 300 in 2021. Then, I demonstrated to the students, through evidence of my citations and the number of publications how one can re-imagine a problem into an opportunity and the possibility of having positive outcomes (Figure 7.3). I also felt that students saw me as being authentic and hopefully understood that I had genuine motivations for engaging in teaching SDGs. Although, my achievements are

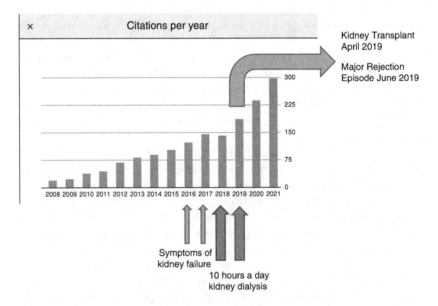

Figure 7.3 Re-imagining a problem to an opportunity: Google Scholar citation (until December 2021) and kidney failure journey.

not extraordinary in terms of publications or citations, the demonstration of *how* I was able to re-imagine problems into opportunities and relate them to the SDGs, allowed me to role model how business and marketing students can approach the SDGs.

Achieving professional legitimacy

According to Bloom et al. (2021, p. 320) one mechanism to achieve professional legitimacy is by demonstrating mastery in enacting the profession. In my case, I adopted a triangulation perspective (in teaching, research, and engagement) in attempting to achieve professional legitimacy. As explained previously, I engaged in market shaping in teaching, by developing new curricula relating to the SDGs. Below I explain the three subjects.

Poverty Alleviation and Profitability (Master of Management, CEMS)

Based on the Roundtable that I organised around the theme of Poverty Alleviation and Profitability in 2014, as well as advocating for sustainability and the SDGs within the business school, a senior scholar encouraged me to develop a curriculum and teach in the CEMS Master of Management program. This program focused on pre-experience management students. Although this unit was initiated in 2014, prior to the SDGs, as I engaged with UN Geneva and UN New York, I incorporated the SDGs (specifically SDG 1). The subject outline states the following:

> *There is an increasing recognition that businesses are more than profit-making entities. This notion goes beyond being socially responsible and environmentally aware. Poverty alleviation and profits are co-equal in their importance and occur simultaneously. This perceived contradiction raises a myriad of ethical and moral challenges. This unit is designed to critically evaluate the role of business, specifically poverty alleviation and its links with profitability. Basic theories and frameworks relating to the motivations of businesses are critiqued. Poverty is defined as not only income deprivation but capability and freedom deprivation. Contemporary ideas relating to the purpose of business, such as Shared Value, are evaluated. The Base of the Pyramid thesis is critically evaluated, including co-creation of value with the poor, marketing to the poor, transformative consumer research and cross-sector collaborations.*

In between this unit and the next, I had a few years of health issues. Therefore, I focused more on publications as opposed to developing a new curriculum. However, since mid-2020, I have been able to concentrate more on new curriculum development in marketing and in business education. In the context of marketing, I made the case with the Head of Discipline of Marketing to include a subject on the SDGs in the Bachelor of

Commerce (Marketing major) program, which the Head encouraged. This resulted in developing a unique subject relating to the interplay between marketing and the SDGs. However, during this process, I was afraid that although there is sufficient material about sustainability, there was not much about the SDGs. Based on my personal experiences on my values, motivations, experiences at the UN, and publishing scholarly work, I was able to overcome the initial mental struggle and develop a novel curriculum. The subject outline states the following:

Marketing and Sustainable Development (Bachelor of Commerce)

Marketing plays a critical boundary spanning role between the for-profit firm and its various stakeholders. Marketing is also a critical consideration in developing business strategy. As debates continue on the purpose of for-profit business, specifically the shift from a focus solely on shareholders to various stakeholders (e.g., suppliers, customers, employees and broader society), including calls for responsible business and marketing leaders that tackle grand challenges facing the world (e.g., poverty, gender inequality and climate change), it is important that marketers are proactive in shaping these debates and facilitating changes in marketing practice. This unit is designed to critically evaluate the role of marketing theory and practice in engaging with grand challenges as highlighted by the 17 United Nations Sustainable Development Goals (e.g., ending poverty, tackling climate change and addressing gender inequality), at a profit. This unit adopts a holistic perspective of marketing and theories from both consumer behaviour and marketing strategy are used to understand how marketers can engage in facilitating the implementation of the 17 United Nations Sustainable Development Goals within marketing strategy.

During this time, I was also involved in planning for a foundation unit for the Master of Commerce unit, titled Responsible Business Mindset. This subject has over 1,000 students each semester and it highlights the importance of a responsible business mindset. I specifically developed a curriculum for week 13 (the semester has 13 weeks) relating to strategy and the SDGs and I have started teaching this subject in 2022. The subject outline states the following:

Responsible Business Mindset (Master of Commerce)

The grand challenges of sustainability, climate change, social inequality, health and wellbeing, and corporate misconduct have revealed a critical need to transform business beyond the singular mindset of shareholder primacy. Coupled with this, a business must be proactive in establishing and maintaining its social license to operate as increasing risk and uncertainty has exposed a loss of trust in business. In response, this unit centers on co-creating a responsible business mindset with students based on an understanding that a business is deeply connected with the society and environment in which it operates. It is oriented towards examining the practices of business where organizational and personal considerations for ethical, sustainable, environmental and community objectives are embedded within, and not in conflict with, the desire to be profitable. An understanding of how a responsible business mindset can be shaped by the Sustainable Development Goals, ethical, Indigenous and other relevant frameworks is interwoven with consideration of the evolving legal and institutional structures for corporate governance and the role of business culture in the context of a broader set of stakeholders. Multidisciplinary insights from the legal, workplace, marketing, accounting and finance perspectives provide context and texture, as students orient themselves with developing responses to practical market realities, drawing on theoretical understandings of a responsible business mindset. This unit integrates a responsible business mindset in all aspects of organizational planning, processes, reporting and decision-making, with the aim to develop future leaders who are not only mindful of the outcomes of responsible business actions, but can also bring critical reflection to such theories and practices.

Research

I realised that, although there was knowledge on the SDGs, it was primarily emanating from social sciences, and not much from business/marketing. Therefore, I attempted to become an activist for the SDGs, in mainstream marketing scholarly publications. For example, I attempted to encourage marketing scholars to engage with the SDGs by leading a special issue on Marketing and the SDGs titled 'Re-imagining Marketing Scholarship in the era of the UN Sustainable Development Goals' in the Australasian Marketing Journal (Voola et al., 2022b), and a forthcoming special issue in 2023 in the Journal of Marketing Education, titled 'Marketing Education and the UN Sustainable Development Goals: Are Marketing Students and Faculty Prepared to be Agents of Change for Sustainability?' I was also involved in laying a foundation for marketing scholarly work on the SDGs by presenting future search opportunities at the interface of B2B marketing and the SDGs (Voola et al., 2022a) and consumer behaviour and the SDGs (Voola et al., 2022c). I continue to look for opportunities to engage in shaping the debates and knowledge on the SDGs and marketing and management, via ongoing scholarly work relating to the SDGs including working with practitioners. Gaining credibility in research allows for gaining knowledge so that I can teach well. I have also tried to shape the business school's approach to SDGs by becoming a member of the steering committee for the Principles for Responsible Management Education (PRME) and leading research in this area nationally by becoming a steering committee member for research at the PRME Australia and New Zealand chapter.

Key learnings and conclusions

I don't believe I have gone through the whole process of being a called professional as espoused by Bloom et al. (2021). The result of this process is to develop an 'integrated called identity (which) is a relatively explicit and permanent assertion that they are faithfully embodying their calling' (p. 323). I believe that my journey is about halfway, and I have a few more years to achieve an integrated called identity. Below I highlight several learning from my discernment journey. Although this is a very personal journey, I believe some of these learnings may be applicable to others following an SDG route.

Learning 1: Why am I a scholar?

I don't believe I would have engaged with the SDGs, as I did if I did not answer this reflective question. It was important for me to understand my roots, which lay the foundation to pursue an SDG journey – why am I a scholar? To understand my roots, I needed to know what motivated me. In my case, it was my parents, my daughters, and my kidney donor. Being clear about my roots insulated me from the temptation to give up on the SDGs and instead pursue academic rewards such as promotion. More importantly, it provided a passion to fulfil my calling to be an SDG-marketing scholar. This may be extrapolated to other scholars starting this journey in that understanding their motivations and their 'why,' is likely to provide a strong foundation to succeed in their journey to be an SDG-marketing scholar.

Learning 2: Why should I sacrifice?

As Moratis and Melissen (2022) highlight, passion, in its original Latin and Greek meaning, also includes suffering. In the context of my journey, the 'suffering' relates to my mental struggle relating to the possibility of a lack of scholarly publications, potentially affecting when I got promoted. Additionally, I spent a lot of time developing a new curriculum when I could have saved time by teaching traditional marketing units and focusing on research. I learned that sacrifice is necessary to follow your passion, especially if it is not a mainstream idea. This insight may assist others in expecting to make sacrifices (perhaps to embrace suffering) and have the discernment to make the appropriate sacrifices to follow their passions.

Learning 3: Why should I talk about my life experiences with my students?

Initially, I was very hesitant to talk about my motivations and my vulnerabilities including my kidney transplant story, primarily because it may not seem 'professional.' However, I realised that engaging students (and other scholars) with my life stories allowed me the opportunity to be authentic and therefore more persuasive in my arguments about the SDGs. For example, my story of using dialysis time as research time (re-imagining it from a problem to an opportunity), talking about this to the students, and then extrapolating it to the context of SDGs, I believe, allowed me to be more authentic and more persuasive. This insight highlights that relating your motivations and life experiences to SDGs may enhance one's authenticity and therefore the persuasiveness of their SDG arguments.

Learning 4: Why are so many people resisting my ideas?

When I first started my journey in 2015 and even now in 2022, there is still a lot of scepticism about SDGs and the role of business in implementing SDGs. From my experiences, this suggests the nascence of the idea. As I get pushback to my ideas from various stakeholders, I hone my response to their objections of the SDGs and marketing. However, I am very aware that it is extremely difficult to quickly change the dominant argument about the purpose of business, especially among business students, where the dominant education paradigm revolves around business and profits. Therefore, when I do engage with people who resist these ideas, I acknowledge that the dominant discourse relating to the purpose of business is making money. However, I throw a challenge to this traditional *modus operandi* by proposing opportunities for businesses to engage with the SDGs whilst realising their traditional goals. The learning for others may be to expect resistance, but don't be surprised and embrace this resistance by proactively developing answers for these objections to the SDGs and business.

Learning 5: Why are some people helping me on my journey to be a called SDG-marketing Scholar?

Apart from my passion to be a called SDG-marketing professional, the other major learning was that some people went out of their way to support an idea that was counterintuitive. Although, initially, I did not understand the importance of these people, I recognised that identifying and taking their counsel was key to moving forward in my journey to be a called SDG-Marketing scholar. Additionally, I also learned that many people will not support you. Therefore, focusing on identifying allies in your journey to be a called professional, is critical.

In conclusion, various lived experiences relating to vulnerabilities, sacrifices, and kindness have encouraged me on the journey to becoming a called SDG-marketing professional. In the contemporary scholarly academic world, where the dominant approach is to focus on publishing in top-tier journals, getting high student evaluations, grants, and promotions, the journey of following my calling, as conceptualised by Bloom et al. (2021), has been refreshing and fulfilling. Furthermore, reflecting on my calling allowed me to proactively consider how, as an SDG-marketing professional, I can be part of a transformational approach to RME, where I am passionate to engage in transformational change in students. I believe that scholars who are engaging in the RME movement that is systematic and transformational will benefit from reflecting on their calling.

Although there is sacrifice involved, personally, I am happy to forgo promotion or other accolades to follow my calling. However, I don't believe that in the long run, following one's calling is mutually exclusive to obtaining scholarly 'rewards,' such as promotion. In my personal context, re-imagining rewards such as promotions as means to a greater end has been life-changing, as it allowed me to start a journey of aligning personal values with my professional values. It has also given me the privilege of being on an ongoing extraordinary journey to find and operationalise my calling.

References

Azmat, F. and Voola, R. (2020). 'Sustainable development goals more urgent than ever in a post-COVID world,' *Sydney Business Insights*. https://sbi.sydney.edu.au/sustainable-development-goals-more-urgent-than-ever-in-a-post-covid-world0

BBC (2020). 'Sir David Attenborough joins Instagram to warn 'the world is in trouble',' *British Broadcasting Corporation*. https://www.bbc.com/news/entertainment-arts-54281171

Bloom, M., Colbert, A.E. and Nielsen, J.D. (2021). 'Stories of calling: How called professionals construct narrative identities,' *Administrative Science Quarterly*, 66(2), pp. 298–338.

Chandy, R., Johar, G., Moorman, C. and Roberts, J. (2021). 'Better marketing for a better world,' *Journal of Marketing*, 85(3), pp. 1–9.

Dar, S., Liu, H., Martinez Dy, A. and Brewis, D.N. (2021). 'The business school is racist: Act up!' *Organization*, 28(4), pp. 695–706.

Harley, B. and Fleming, P. (2021). 'Not even trying to change the world: why do elite management journals ignore the major problems facing humanity?,' *The Journal of Applied Behavioral Science*, 57(2), pp. 133–152.

Kohli, A.K. and Haenlein, M. (2021). 'Factors affecting the study of important marketing issues: Additional thoughts and clarifications,' *International Journal of Research in Marketing*, 38(1), pp. 29–31.

MacInnis, D.J., Morwitz, V.G., Botti, S., Hoffman, D.L., Kozinets, R.V., Lehmann, D.R., Lynch Jr, J.G. and Pechmann, C. (2020). 'Creating boundary-breaking, marketing-relevant consumer research,' *Journal of Marketing*, 84(2), pp. 1–23.

McLaren, P.G. (2020). 'Strengthening capitalism through philanthropy: The Ford Foundation, managerialism and American business schools,' *Management Learning*, 51(2), pp. 187–206.

Moratis, L. and Melissen, F. (2020). Reflections on 'true' business sustainability: Challenging definitions, recognizing couplings and developing intelligence'. Complementary academic paper with the report 'Challenging business as usual: Conceiving and creating sustainability value through hybrid business models'. Antwerp: Antwerp Management School.

Moratis, L. and Melissen, F. (2022). 'Bolstering responsible management education through the sustainable development goals: Three perspectives,' *Management Learning*, 53(2), pp. 212–222.

Parker, M. (2018). *Shut down the business school: What's wrong with management education*. London: Pluto Press.

Sadler-Smith, E. and Cojuharenco, I. (2021). 'Business schools and hubris: Cause or cure?,' *Academy of Management Learning & Education*, 20(2), pp. 270–289.

Scott, M.L., Hassler, C.M. and Martin, K.D. (2022). 'Here comes the sun: Present and future impact in marketing and public policy research,' *Journal of Public Policy & Marketing*, 41(1), pp.1–9.

Sheth, J.N. and Parvatiyar, A. (2021). 'Sustainable marketing: Market-driving, not market-driven,' *Journal of Macromarketing*, 41(1), pp. 150–165.

Spicer, A., Jaser, Z. and Wiertz, C. (2020). 'The future of the business school: Finding hope in alternative pasts,' Academy of Management Learning & Education, 20(3), pp. 459–466.

Spicer, A., Jaser, Z. and Wiertz, C. (2021). 'The future of the business school: Finding hope in alternative pasts,' *Academy of Management Learning & Education*, 20(3), pp. 456–466.

Van Heerde, H., Moorman, C., Moreau, C., Palmatier, R. (2021). 'Reality check: Infusing ecological value into academic marketing research,' *Journal of Marketing*, 85(2), pp. 1–13.

Voola, R. (2015). 'The business helping the poor for a profit,' ABC Radio Sunday Extra (October 4th) https://www.abc.net.au/radionational/programs/sundayextra/social-good/6806120

Voola, R. (2017). 'On My Mind, Sydney Alumni Magazine,' The University of Sydney, http://sydney.edu.au/news-opinion/news/2017/04/06/on-my-mind.html

Voola, R. (2018) 'Profits with Purpose,' Raise the Bar, Sydney, (October 17th), http://www.rtbevent.com/ranjit-voola/

Voola, R., Bandyopadhyay, C., Voola, A., Ray, S. and Carlson, J. (2022a). 'B2B marketing scholarship and the UN sustainable development goals (SDGs): A systematic literature review,' *Industrial Marketing Management*, 101, pp. 12–32.

Voola, R., Carlson, J., Azmat, F., Viet Ngo, L., Porter, K. and Sinha, A. (2022b). 'Reimagining Marketing Scholarship in the era of the UN Sustainable Development Goals,' *Australasian Marketing Journal*, 30(2), pp. 97–106.

Voola, R., Bandyopadhyay, C., Azmat, F., Ray, S. and Nayak, L. (2022c). 'How are consumer behavior and marketing strategy researchers incorporating the SDGs? A review and opportunities for future research,' *Australasian Marketing Journal*, 30(2), pp. 119–130.

Wrzesniewski, A. (2012). 'Callings,' in *The Oxford handbook of positive organizational scholarship*. New York: Oxford, pp. 45–55.

Part III

Creative pedagogies and assessments

8 The use of news articles as a pedagogical tool for responsible management education

Ruth Areli García-León

Introduction

The 2030 Agenda for Sustainable Development is an ambitious action plan with 17 Sustainable Development Goals (SDGs) which seeks a better and more sustainable future for all (United Nations, 2021). It includes ensuring sustained and inclusive economic growth, social inclusion, and environmental protection in order to eliminate extreme poverty, reduce inequality, and protect the planet (UNSSC, 2021). To overcome this challenge, it is necessary to change our lifestyles, thinking, and behaviour to develop more sustainable societies (UNESCO, 2017).

Education systems are part of this challenge. Business and management schools aim to provide future leaders with skills to balance economic and sustainability goals (PRME, 2021). Since its inception in 2007, via mandate from the UN Secretary-General, the Principles for Responsible Management Education (PRME) were launched to develop responsible leaders for the future through management education with the skills and the mindset to achieve the SDGs (Morsing, 2022a). Empowering management students to contribute actively to sustainable development requires a transformation of how they think and act, and of their knowledge, skills, values, and attitudes (UNESCO, 2017).

For management education, this challenge involves integrating these topics into the curriculum. In order to develop future sustainable leaders with the required new skills, values, and attitudes to impact the direction of the world by making influential decisions, it is critical to develop programs, courses, and learning content that addresses these topics. Nevertheless, the question is no longer why sustainability should be integrated across management education curriculum, but instead how to do it (Morsing, 2022b). This poses a challenge as there is no consensus on how to teach these subjects, and there are constraints on effective integration of topics such as corporate social responsibility, sustainability, and sustainable development (Doh and Tashman, 2014). As such, it has become necessary to integrate new pedagogies into the management curricula to develop students' competences to address the world's complex problems (Morsing, 2022a) in

DOI: 10.4324/9781003244905-12

order to convey sustainable development issues via dynamic and holistic ways of teaching (Molderez and Fonseca, 2018).

The aim of this chapter is therefore to contribute to new pedagogies of Responsible Management Education (RME) by showing how news articles can be used as an actual pedagogical tool to include sustainable development issues in the content of a management course in order to develop more conscientious students interested in contributing to the SDGs. The use of news articles as a pedagogical tool is based on the educational social constructivist theory of learning (Vygotsky, 1978), collaborative learning, and on my experience of more than eight years in adding sustainable development topics with the use of news items to different management courses for graduate and undergraduate students of different nationalities in the faculties of Business Administration, Law, and Automotive Engineering at Ostfalia University of Applied Sciences in Germany.

For this purpose, the chapter is structured as follows. I begin by explaining how news articles can be used to address sustainable development issues in management education. Then, I present the social constructivist theory, the collaborative learning approach, and my experience using news articles to address sustainable development issues in management courses as the foundations of this proposal. I then address the points involved in designing an activity with the use of news articles. Further, I explain the steps to follow when implementing an activity including news articles and present two examples that I have used with my master's students during the winter semester of 2021/2022. As a conclusion, I recommend some variations to obtain different final outcomes and offer insights about the importance of the instructor in designing activities, as well as the advantages of the use of news items in the classroom.

The use of news articles in the classroom

The first time I had the idea of using news articles for RME, I was looking for some Harvard-type cases (Andersen and Schiano, 2014) in order to address sustainable development topics in the classroom. I wanted to bring my students closer to a real situation in which they could see themselves involved, and through which they could reflect on their own behaviour. At that time, almost nine years ago, it was very difficult for me to find cases addressing problems related to sustainability.

Today, although these cases offer a hypothetical or real scenario about companies' situations from which students formulate solutions to a problem, they do not present a vivid or confrontational situation in which the students can consider their own behaviour seriously, as sustainability issues are hardly presented in a holistic way considering the different actors involved in a sustainable development situation (Montiel et al., 2018). Cases of this type present a few themes, sectors, perspectives, and countries (Jack, 2018). Female leaders are poorly represented, and when they do appear, they are often portrayed as less risk-taking and less visionary than men (Jack, 2018; Sharen and McGowan, 2019). Normally, they place an importance on the outcomes of a single company, presenting the voices of managers rather than employees, and without capturing the complexity of social and environmental issues (MacAskill and Tilley, 2021; Starkey and Tempest, 2009). Sustainable development topics should be addressed considering the sustainability dimensions (i.e., economic, social, and environmental) and the complexity of integrating them harmonically (Lennerfors et al., 2020). Besides, a systemic understanding of all sustainability challenges (Figueiró and Raufflet, 2015) and actors involved in sustainable development should be considered.

In my experience, working with cases has become more difficult because students do not see the purpose of dealing with a problem that was already solved by the company months or years ago. For them, these situations seem 'outdated' in a world dominated by new technologies, where almost all the information about these cases, could be found online. Besides, issues about sustainable development, climate change, or corporate responsibility are constantly emerging and new strategies, laws, policies, and regulations regarding these issues are evolving and changing with the times. Therefore, it is difficult to find cases about these topics containing all the necessary information to use in the classroom.

Furthermore, working with cases of companies in management education is becoming difficult with new generations of students. In the past, students were more suited to work with larger cases involving firms' real situations with a lot of information and suggested readings because they did not use smartphones and mobile devices with internet access as extensively as they do today. In just a few minutes, students are able to find on the internet the solutions that other students have already uploaded, clues to solve the case, or the steps that the company followed to solve it.

On the contrary, news articles are real situations occurring in the present and can easily be found using mobile devices, and there are no 'solutions' to find online. Moreover, news items are not always company-focused: they include a wide range of topics, including entertainment, arts, weather, culture, foreign affairs, international, politics, and crime. They can be hard, soft, or general. Hard news has a high level of newsworthiness, demands immediate publication, and usually refers to events regarding politics, economics, or social matters, while soft news refers to offbeat events, gossip, or human-interest stories with a low level of substantive information value (Lehman-Wilzig and Seletzky, 2010; Tuchman, 1972). General news contains important utilitarian information that citizens can use and refers to recent economic or demographic information, reports, or new data influencing only certain groups which must be published, but not necessarily immediately (Lehman-Wilzig and Seletzky, 2010).

Regarding their journalistic genre, they can be informative (e.g., interview or report), opinionative (e.g., editorial or column), interpretive (e.g., analysis or survey), diversional (e.g., human interest history or colour history), or utilitarian (e.g., indicator or service) (Marques de Melo and Assis, 2016). These broad characteristics have helped to effectively use news articles in the classroom for teaching purposes. For example, research has demonstrated that newspaper articles as a pedagogical tool increase students' interest and attention, and their use in the classroom could be useful to promote critical thinking, science literacy, information literacy, and critical analysis, among others (Jarman and McClune, 2007; Majetic and Pellegrino, 2014; Park, 2011; Singh, 2011).

News articles can be used as a pedagogical tool for current and real situations that students can read the same day in the classroom on their smartphones or computers when the instructor shares the link with them. Another advantage is that news stories are short, and students do not require a lot of time to read them, therefore they can be read before collaborative work and can also be accessed via the internet in the classroom depending on the time available. Additionally, online newspapers or news sources include pictures, videos, and hyperlinks with more details about the story. Students can access the hyperlinks and look for more information or past news items about the same topic. In addition, the videos can be used by the instructor to provide a visual element in the classroom or to introduce the students to the topic in the plenary session.

The idea is that by designing an activity using news items as the focal point, students can work collaboratively, raise awareness about their own role in sustainable development, and learn more during this process.

Learning collaboratively with news articles

The design of an activity using news items is centred on the chosen news, the contents of the course, the SDGs to study, and the questions or activities that will trigger analysis and critical thinking. Therefore, learning will emerge as a result of collaborative work and will help lead students to raise awareness of their own behaviour regarding sustainable development.

The psychological theory of learning known as constructivism is derived from the cognitive theories of Piaget, Vygotsky, and others (Fosnot and Perry, 2005). Social constructivism emphasises the role of social interactions in learning and assumes that knowledge, understanding, significance, and meaning are developed jointly with other human beings. Therefore, cognitive growth occurs on a social and cultural level where individuals learn by interacting with other people, through the context surrounding the individuals, and by mediation of different objects before this construction of knowledge occurs within the individual (Vygotsky, 1978). Therefore, as a developmental process, learning is led and influenced by social interactions (Cobb, 1994), since during these interactive processes, individuals mutually process, understand, experience, agree or establish, and this external activity with others is reconstructed internally and occurs then internally (Vygotsky, 1978). As such, this social process is fundamental for the learning development of the individual (Cole and Scribner, 1978). Instructional models based on social constructivism involve learning with others and stress the necessity of collaboration among learners; therefore, social constructivist educational approaches could include reciprocal teaching or working collaboratively with others (Lave and Wenger, 1991).

Collaborative learning is an educational approach where students work collaboratively with others in groups and discuss to find understanding, solutions, meaning, or to create a final product (Smith and MacGregor, 1992). Collaborative learning gives students a social context of learning with peers where they learn about the same topics (Bruffee, 1981). When solving a problem or completing a task or activity designed by the instructor, students help each other by searching for ideas, collecting data, and discussing interchanging ideas to finally construct the knowledge (Brufee, 1984). Collaborating with peers, presenting their ideas, conveying information to others, explaining how to complete the task, and justifying their ideas are among the communication processes that may trigger internal cognitive processes associated with learning (Webb, 2013). Webb (2013) explains that speakers and listeners involved in these processes can learn, for example, by activating and strengthening their understanding of what they have learned, filling gaps in their understanding, or repairing fragmented mental models. Therefore, by designing an activity with news articles, in which students collaborate to fulfil an activity, instructors can activate the communications that will trigger the internal processes associated with learning.

In a collaborative classroom, the transmission of knowledge by the instructor shifts to the generation of knowledge by the students since they assume active roles, taking responsibility for their own and others' learning, and the instructor's influence becomes more indirect (Sheridan et al., 1989). The educator's main task is to develop a suitable activity for the production of knowledge, and in the classroom, to encourage students to talk to each other, search for ideas, and discuss in order to finish the activity that will influence the construction of knowledge derived from this interchanging of ideas (Brufee, 1984). Thus, instructors act as expert designers of intellectual experiences for students to facilitate the learning process (Smith and MacGregor, 1992).

The educator, as a facilitator of learning, must constantly be willing to monitor current news articles in order to find those related to sustainable development issues involving the learning outcomes described in the syllabus. As such, the educator needs to have the disposition to work creatively on the design of an activity that will awaken students' interest in order to determine the learning objectives and outcomes to be fulfilled through the activity, and to allot necessary time within the classroom or online teaching setting to work on it. Furthermore, the instructor should generate an appropriate environment in which the teams can work collaboratively to analytically answer the questions asked and/or the desired result. Educators act as tutors during discussions and learning processes. When students search for information and determine the best way to answer the questions to develop the desired outcome established by the instructor, they could develop further collaboration and critical thinking.

In the following sections, I will explain in detail how to design a collaborative activity with news articles, including sustainable development topics in a management course. This proposal is built on my experience of more than eight years working with news articles to focus on sustainable development issues with the topics of management courses, and it has drawn on my past research about the same topic (see García-León, 2019). I have used news articles to address the SDGs within the management courses for students of the Bachelor's in Business Administration and the Bachelor's in Engineering (i.e., industrial engineering), as well as for the students of the Master's in Automotive Service Technology and Processes and the Master's in International Law and Business. In particular, I have used news articles in the courses Consumer Behaviour, Distribution and Communication Policy, International Strategic Management, International Business, International Management/Marketing, and Case Studies International Marketing.

With the objective to help instructors use news articles to include sustainable development issues in their management courses, the following section addresses several preliminary considerations and important elements necessary for the design of an activity. These considerations relate to identifying suitable news items, developing the discussion questions or final result, determining the suggested and supportive literature, determining the time necessary to complete the activity, and delivering the materials for the activity.

Activity design

Suitable news item identification

The chosen news item must include information regarding desired sustainable or undesired unsustainable behaviours and their consequences. This is the first step to persuade individuals to engage in sustainable actions (McKenzie-Mohr, 2000).

Therefore, the management educator should constantly read newspapers or other sources of news items in order to find one that is suitable for the purposes of the class. I recommend choosing a news item no older than one week as novelty is a useful component to surprise students and to raise their interest. As such, they will find the same information in other media and no solutions by the time they use the news item in the classroom.

The chosen news item should be related to one of the SDGs and to one of the course's learning subjects, and can be a national or international issue. It is better if the news is related to the students in some way to make it more tangible and relevant (e.g., the situation occurring in the city or country where they live is related to persons of their age). Working on an activity related to a situation that occurred in their own country, region, or neighbourhood may intensify the desire to take environmental actions (Scannell and Gifford, 2013).

Development of discussion questions or final result

Aside from determining the learning objectives of the activity, it is necessary to develop discussion questions to lead the students' analysis. These questions should target specific sustainable development issues, as well as the chosen learning content of the course. It is recommended to include around five questions, as a longer list of questions can make the collaborative work tedious and boring.

The last questions should be related to the students' own role in helping to achieve the SDGs. It is important to include one or two questions with which the students have the opportunity to think about their own behaviour regarding the issue reported in the news article and related to the SDGs (e.g., food waste, carbon footprint, gender inequality). These last questions should be asked to encourage students to actively generate ideas on how their behaviour could help to produce a change towards more sustainable societies (e.g., How does this situation affect you? How are you contributing to this situation? What immediate changes can you make to contribute to SDG 7 (or any other)? Can you imagine a better future regarding this issue? How can you help to reach the goal?). They can take a step further by implementing specific actions to engage in sustainable development. Psychologists suggest that specifying where, when, and how exactly they are going to perform an action may be helpful in moving towards sustainable development (Kurz et al., 2014). Moreover, the process of envisioning their preferred future provides students direction and energy, generates impetus for action, motivates students to choose to act in the present, and helps them realise how their actions will contribute to this vision of the future, taking ownership and responsibility for working towards it (Tilbury and Wortman, 2004). Besides knowledge generation, the goal of the questions is to trigger the generation of ideas and to help students think analytically about the situation presented.

Additionally, the instructions on how they need to submit their answers or final results (e.g., PowerPoint presentation, short video, *viva voce*) should be included. Aside from the questions, other activities can be used to grow student awareness of their contribution to sustainable development (e.g., creating a video or advertising about how to contribute to water conservation).

Suggested and supportive literature

Besides the chosen news item, students need information about the topic in question, the content of the course, as well as the chosen SDGs. Relevant information should be available in the form of books, magazines, or journals. Besides physical information, students should be able to access valuable information available on the internet with the help of their electronic devices. Therefore, the instructor should give a list of literature or links available on the internet that may be useful to answer the questions for analysis.

The educator should be prepared to receive questions involving ethical or moral issues. Interdisciplinary education principles including ethics may be used to address, or at least shed light on, some sustainability issues. We should not forget that SDGs issues involve tensions, paradoxes, and ethical dilemmas in decision-making (Moratis and Melissen, 2022).

Time determination

It is relevant to determine how much time students will need to work on the activity. Instructors can establish a timeframe by trying to solve the activity themselves, or with another person's help. Although this step may seem unimportant, insufficient time to accomplish an activity correctly may lead to failure of the initial objective of increasing student awareness of their own behaviour in terms of sustainable development.

Delivery of materials

It is important to think in advance about the best way to present the news item and the instructions to the students. In exceptional cases, questions and instructions could be handed out in printed version by giving one copy to each team. The teacher can hand out the news articles, the questions, and the instructions for the final outcome during the class or before. These elements could be available on a virtual learning platform, such as Moodle or Blackboard. Depending on how the instructor organises the time to work on the activity, she/he can ask the students to read the news article before class, or to read the news item and the suggested and supportive literature (e.g., internet links) in advance. Another possibility is to reveal the questions and instructions for the final activity's outcome only on the designated day for collaborative work.

It may be interesting to bring a newspaper to the classroom to highlight the place that the news item occupies in the newspaper, as well as to identify or analyse other news related to the selected topic and the pages and sections in which they appear. Another possibility is to analyse what the other news articles (e.g., the editorial or column) say about the same topic.

Steps during classroom teaching

Students read the news item individually

As previously mentioned, students may read the news article in advance. In the classroom, depending on the length of the article and the availability of electronic devices with internet access, the students could read the news item by themselves, or the news item could be projected on the board with the help of a beamer. If the university has a newspaper subscription available for students, and the educator wants to use this source, it is recommended to verify that students are registered and have access to them before working in the classroom. The best option could be to use an open access newspaper or media in order to have speedy access to the news, but as open access newspapers are changing gradually to subscriptions, it is important to be sure that the university allows students to access online newspapers.

Team composition

The instructor forms teams based on the number of students or based on the available devices with internet access. Depending on the number of participating students, each team can consist of three to six students. The instructor can help to compose the teams with the intention that the students know each other better to avoid constant chatting among groups of old friends, or to integrate foreign students into the different teams of local students. When the majority of the students are international, the instructor could form balanced teams of international students without having the majority of one country in particular, or build teams based on countries or regions to see differences regarding cultural background or worldview with respect to the issues addressed in class.

Instructions

In teams, students read the questions and in general, the expected result to complete the activity. In my experience, although at this point the students had already read the news item individually, during teamwork they spend more time clarifying the information contained in the news article and in the instructions. I recommend allowing students to do this. Normally, they clarify the information by asking each other or by asking the instructor. Therefore, the teacher should take the time to answer questions during this time and during the time in which the students are working to fulfil the activity in general.

Teamwork

Students work in teams to answer the questions and produce the final result within the given timeframe by using the supporting or suggested literature and resources provided by the instructor. An advantage of using mobile devices with internet access is that students can find more information related to the topic, which will make them feel free to look for helpful information. Social networks, the internet, laptops, and smartphones are resources *for* learning. Therefore, the educator verifies that students can use these resources intelligently, which in turn motivates them to use the resources in the service of their own knowledge. The instructor tutors, monitors, guides, and amends if there is any part of the activity that has not been correctly understood. During this time, the educator verifies that the students understand the questions, resolves doubts, and ensures that the electronic devices are used for the intended purposes.

Regarding questions related to their own contribution to sustainable development, it is important to say that students may answer questions very fast that are not related to them directly. In my experience, frequently, they are quick to judge others concerning their role regarding sustainable development, but when confronting their own behaviour and commitment, their answers are often not speedy, conclusive, or precise. Therefore, it is essential to give students time to consider their own role in the matter and help them, without forcing them, to offer ideas on how they can contribute to creating a more sustainable world.

Students present their answers and results

Depending on the teacher's strategy, classroom resources, and time available, this can be done through a formal presentation with slides, a creative video, or a simple discussion where the instructor acts as moderator. Regarding the questions related to their own behaviour, it is important to have specific answers from the students. Therefore, the educator should not accept phrases like 'I don't know' or 'it is difficult to say' as answers. Here is the step where students need to give specific examples to explain how they can contribute to sustainable development. During the students' presentations, the instructor can dive deeper into the answers by questioning or commenting about something interesting or relevant, or by providing more information regarding some topic or issue important to the students' knowledge.

In the following section, there are two practical examples of the use of news articles that I used with my Master's of International Law and Business students within the course International Management/Marketing during the winter semester of 2021/2022 at Ostfalia University of Applied Sciences in Germany.

Examples of the use of news for RME

Food waste example

Course: Master's Degree Course International Management/Marketing
Course content: Introduction
SDG: 12. Ensure sustainable consumption and production patterns.
Learning outcome: Students will learn basic concepts related to sustainability and will have a first approach to the food waste issue.
News item: 'How food waste is huge contributor to climate change' from The Guardian.
Time (Duration): 50 to 60 minutes
Participants: Teams of 3 to 5 students.
Tools: Electronic devices with internet access.

The Guardian

How food waste is huge contributor to climate change

Food production, transportation, and rotting waste all cause release of greenhouse gases
Weather watch
Food waste
Jeremy Plester
Sat 4 Sep 2021 06.00 BST

Cutting food waste can help the climate. Every day in the UK we waste 20m slices of bread, 280 tonnes of poultry, 4.4 m potatoes and much more.

Households squander about 70% of the UK's 9.5 m tonnes of waste food every year. About a third of all the world's food goes to waste, and producing, transporting and letting that food rot releases 8–10% of global greenhouse gases. If food waste were a country, it would have the third-biggest carbon footprint after the US and China, according to the UN's Food and Agriculture Organisation.

Food waste fell sharply last year during lockdown as people stuck at home began to use leftovers, plan meals and freeze food rather than throw it away. Once lockdown ended, however, food waste rose again. Growing, processing, packaging, and transporting food all contribute to climate change. For example, about a third of fruit and veg is rejected for being the wrong size or shape before it even reaches the

---

shops. And when food is thrown away, it rots and releases yet more greenhouse gases into the atmosphere.

Source: Plester (2021). https://www.theguardian.com/news/2021/sep/04/how-food-waste-is-huge-contributor-to-climate-change

Questions:

1 What is climate change?
2 What are greenhouse gases?
3 What is a carbon footprint?
4 How much food waste is produced every year in Germany?
5 Do you contribute to the food waste in Germany?
6 How can you avoid/reduce food waste?
7 What advice would you give to companies to help prevent food waste?

Instructions

1 Read the news individually (2 minutes).
2 In teams, use any electronic devices with Internet access to look for information in order to answer the questions (remember that Wikipedia is not a recommendable source). Prepare a PowerPoint presentation with your answers and do not forget to include sources (30 minutes).
3 In the end, one or two persons from your team should present your answers.

In order to involve students in implementing their intentions to reach sustainable behaviour, I used the first news item as an introduction to the topic of sustainability and to the contents of the course. As a first step for subsequent activities related to sustainability within the class, I wanted to be sure that the students really comprehended the meaning of the concepts of 'climate change,' 'greenhouse gases,' and 'carbon footprint,' and did not simply recognise them by name because they had heard about them before.

The first news item shows undesirable information about food waste and its consequences as a first step to persuade individuals to engage in sustainable actions (cf. McKenzie-Mohr, 2000). Students were required to look for information about how much food waste was produced every year in Germany in order to bring this issue to their own country and reality. In addition, the students were asked if they were contributing to the food waste produced every year in Germany in order to make this issue more tangible and relevant to them (cf. Scannell and Gifford, 2013). Moreover, they were asked to provide ideas for reducing food waste in order to bring them to action, intensifying the desire to use pro-environmental methods. The last question was related to the course in general by asking them how companies can help to prevent or avoid this problem altogether.

The students responded to the first 3 questions by explaining the concepts detailed. They admitted to contributing to food waste in Germany by buying too much food and then throwing it away due to poor weekly meal-planning, by cooking too much and not storing food properly, or by opening new food before consuming old food, among others. Regarding the solutions that they could employ to avoid/reduce food waste, students mentioned meal-planning by using leftovers in new meals and freezing or storing them correctly, by sharing big meal portions with family or friends, and by using apps or joining communities to share excessive food like foodsharing.de, toogoodtogo.de, or foodwatch.org.

Regarding the advice they could give companies to help prevent food waste, students pointed out that companies could help by donating food, offering smaller packages, giving smaller portions in the workers' cafeteria, and educating consumers regarding food waste by using short messages on their packages.

After class, students had the opportunity to provide feedback about the activity. It was interesting to learn that students knew the main concepts and understood them completely. Most of them did not know how much food waste was produced in Germany every year, and they accepted that they were contributing to the food waste in their country. Most of them said that this activity helped them understand more about their own contribution to climate change, and that it encouraged them to change their own behaviour to avoid or reduce food waste.

Use of animal fur example

Course: Master's Degree Course International Management/Marketing
Course content: Characteristics and Basic Orientations of International Companies and International Strategy
SDG: 12. Ensure sustainable consumption and production patterns.
Learning outcome: Students will analyse the international strategy followed by the Kering Group, and will formulate a strategy for LVMH regarding the use of animal fur. In addition, students will remember the 17 SDGs and will recognise their importance for the development of international strategies.
News item: 'Luxury group Kering to ditch fur completely' from Reuters.
Time (Duration): 45 to 70 Minutes
Participants: Teams of 3 to 5 students
Tools: Electronic devices with internet access.

Reuters

September 24, 2021
Retail & Consumer
5:46 PM CEST
Luxury group Kering to ditch fur completely
Last updated 11 days ago
2 minute read

Reuters

PARIS, Sept 24 (Reuters) – France's Kering (PRTP.PA) will stop using animal furs in all its collections, joining a growing list of luxury fashion houses to respond to customer demands for ethical and sustainable clothing and accessories.

The decision comes four years after its star label Gucci announced it would forego fur. A number of fashion houses followed suit, including Italy's Prada (1913.HK), Burberry (BRBY.L) and outerwear specialist Canada Goose (GOOS.TO), which had come under fire for its use of coyote fur.

With an eye to building future generations of luxury customers, fashion labels have doubled-up efforts to burnish their sustainability credentials with younger, environmentally conscious shoppers.

Starting from the fall 2022 collections, none of the group's houses will use fur, the statement said.

'The time has now come to take a further step forward by ending the use of fur in all our collections. The world has changed, along with our clients, and luxury naturally needs to adapt to that,' François-Henri Pinault, Chairman and CEO of Kering, said.

While the group's houses, which include Balenciaga, Bottega Veneta, Alexander McQueen, Brioni and Saint Laurent, have phased out fur in recent years, Friday's company-wide ban closes the door to its use in the future, even in the event of a change in creative direction.

Larger rival LVMH (LVMH.PA) leaves the decision on fur use to its creative directors.

Although coats made entirely from fur have fallen out of fashion in recent years it has continued to be used as a trim, or in luxury handbags.

Images of mass cullings of coronavirus-infected mink in Denmark at the height of the coronavirus pandemic prompted public outcry and heightened demands to ban the use of animal products in the fashion industry.

'The announcement is a significant blow to the declining fur trade and puts pressure on the few remaining fashion brands that continue to sell fur to follow suit,' said the Humane Society.

Reporting by Dominique Vidalon, Mimosa Spencer; Editing by Sudip Kar-Gupta, Kirsten Donovan and Louise Heavens

Source: Vidalon and Spencer (2021). https://www.reuters.com/business/retail-consumer/french-fashion-company-kering-says-it-will-be-going-entirely-fur-free-2021-09-24/

Questions:

1 Kering group will stop using animal furs in all its collections starting from autumn 2022. What is behind this decision?
2 Do you consider that the strategy adopted by Kering as one of the four international strategies described by Bartlett and Ghoshal (1990), or one of the four orientations from Heenan and Perlmutter (1979)?
3 LVMH decided to leave the decision on fur use to its creative directors. If you were CEO of LVMH, would you make the same decision? What strategy would you adopt and why?
4 What SDG, if any, is Kering pursuing with this decision?
5 Should companies consider the SDGs when choosing an international strategy and why?

Instructions

1 Read the news individually (3 minutes).
2 In teams, use any electronic device with internet access to read the information suggested, to watch the videos, and to look for information in order to answer the questions (remember that Wikipedia is not a recommendable source). Prepare a PowerPoint presentation and do not forget to include sources (40 minutes)
3 In the end, one or two persons from your team should present your answers.

Suggested Literature/Links:

DW News, 2020. https://www.dw.com/en/danish-pm-admits-to-mistakes-over-mink-cull/av-55742859

DW News, 2020. https://www.dw.com/en/mink-fur-boom-in-china-raises-virus-fears/av-55820479

Jackson, 2021. https://www.businessinsider.com/canada-goose-jackets-fur-free-by-the-end-of-2022-2021-6
https://www.reuters.com/business/retail-consumer/french-fashion-company-kering-says-it-will-be-going-entirely-fur-free-2021-09-24/

United Nations, 2021. https://sdgs.un.org/goals

Vidalon and Spencer, 2021. https://www.reuters.com/business/retail-consumer/french-fashion-company-kering-says-it-will-be-going-entirely-fur-free-2021-09-24/

Kering Group's decisions affect the international markets where its products are sold. Therefore, I chose this second news item for consideration as one of the contents of the class Characteristics and basic orientations of international companies. The cited content of the course includes reviewing the four international strategies of Bartlett and Ghoshal (1990) and the EPRG Model from Heenan and Perlmutter (1979). As such, the second question is centred on these two topics in particular.

Once the students read the news item in the classroom, I showed them the three videos contained in the suggested literature. In these videos, they could see minks living on farms, as well as testimonials and opinions from farmers and other persons involved in the fur trade. This provided students with more information and details regarding the animals' living conditions.

The students submitted the expected answers regarding the first two questions, meaning they considered the details provided by the news articles for the first question, and the information about the two theories contained in the course literature. During collaborative work, it was interesting to hear that students were not sure if the Kering Group was making the decision to ban fur as a greenwashing action, or as a real commitment to the world.

To answer the third question, students sought additional information to that which was contained in the suggested literature. Students looked for details about the SDGs and about how minks are sacrificed for their fur. Using this and other information, the teams discussed in detail which decision was better under these circumstances. The answers to this question were divided. Some teams decided to follow the same strategy as LVMH, others decided to ban fur for all brands, and there were students that decided to adopt a more conservative strategy considering local preferences regarding the use of animal fur per country or region, which was a result of the international strategies learned in the course.

To answer the fourth question, all teams chose SDG #12: Responsible Consumption and Production, followed by SDG #13: Climate Action.

All teams agreed that companies should consider the SDGs when choosing an international strategy, but the reason for this answer was divided. Some students believed that firms should make decisions according to the desires and necessities of the customers. Other students thought that companies should consider the SDGs in order to contribute, with their decisions, to educating consumers about what is happening regarding climate change and sustainability, and how they should act. They considered that corporations like the Kering Group and LVMH dictate fashion and trends for generations of consumers, and that they could encourage pro-environmental trends and serve in this manner as educators for their customers as well. Students discussed other essential topics such as circular economy and how companies could take advantage of them.

As a result of this activity, it was observed that students were able to make decisions based on information (i.e., suggested and personally searched additional information). To this end, the use of mobile devices with internet access was fundamental. Moreover, students made informed decisions when deciding which strategy would be best for LVMH, and they discussed ways to make better decisions considering the SDGs and not just the company's profits.

Conclusions

I am convinced that news articles are an excellent tool to attract students' attention on sustainable development issues. As such, the aim of this chapter was to describe the use and the advantages of using news items as a pedagogical tool to include sustainable development issues in management courses in order to create future leaders who contribute actively to achieving the SDGs.

The examples described in this chapter were centred on the use of questions as part of an activity. Nevertheless, depending on the time available, it is possible to include other activities in order to obtain diverse final results. For example, students can produce videos to educate others about sustainability issues in their community or household (e.g., food waste or food consumption). Research indicates that constructing media artefacts (e.g., videos or blog entries) could help enhance students' environmental awareness and activism (Karahan and Roehrig, 2015). They could choose a company for which to develop printed advertising or new packaging with messages inviting consumers to consume wisely to avoid food waste. Role-playing activities can also be used regarding decision-making on boards of directors, or to convince others about positive sustainable behaviours. The use of role-play could be interesting because, as an experiential pedagogy, it is comparable with the real world, which is characterised by teamwork, decision-making under pressure, and imperfect information (Truscheit and Otte, 2004). Role-play identifies feelings and develops communication, problem-solving, listening, and conflict resolution skills when students assume a particular role in a real-world scenario

(Alkin and Christie, 2002; Rao, 2011). Furthermore, studies have demonstrated its effectiveness in addressing sustainable development topics, because it helps them embrace the complexity of these issues (Buchs and Blanchard, 2011; Gordon and Thomas, 2018; Kim, 2014).

As demonstrated, instructors have a very important role in designing course activities. The process of reading newspapers constantly to find a suitable news item, which could be linked with the content of the course and the SDGs, as well as designing an activity to attract students to think about their own role regarding sustainable development can be time-consuming. It can take several days to develop the final activity. The information contained in the news articles could vary from country to country, be tendentious, incomplete, or in favour of companies, governments, or countries. Some newspapers are more analytic and address the readers with logic and rational information and are ruled by professional ethics, while others lack ethics and are more sensationalist, or play with readers' emotions through images (Lehman-Wilzig and Seletzky, 2010). The instructor should keep this in mind when choosing news items. Additionally, when applying the activity in the classroom, the management educator may be confronted with ethical and moral issues that were not considered when designing the activity. Altogether, and while this can prove to be a tough job, the experience of using news items as a pedagogical tool for RME has been very gratifying for me, because, when confronted with new and actual situations and realities, students show interest and enthusiasm to solve the problems, working collaboratively with other students to enhance their own knowledge.

News articles do not have all the information, answers, or defined strategies that may help students make decisions, which is important. Students should learn that sustainability is evolving, and results are produced from ongoing negotiations (Wals and Jickling, 2002). Novel sustainability problems lacking solutions show students that these issues are taking form, that new laws and policies are being developed, that companies are designing modern strategies, and that new actors, leaders, and companies are making decisions and introducing new ideas and solutions. Therefore, students should understand that when investigating, discussing, finding solutions, and working together on an issue or sustainability problem lacking clear strategies, policies, or laws, and thinking in innovative ways to participate in favour of sustainable development, they are active participants of transformation. This shows them that it is in this changing world where they can participate in different ways as leaders, today and in the future, balancing economic, and sustainability goals.

Acknowledgements

I would like to thank Lars Moratis and Frans Melissen for their constructive feedback on an earlier draft of this chapter.

References

Alkin, M.C. and Christie, C.A. (2002). 'The use of role-play in teaching evaluation,' *American Journal of Evaluation*, 23(2), pp. 209–218.

Andersen, E. and Schiano, B. (2014). *Teaching with cases: A practical guide*. Boston: Harvard Business School Publishing.

Bartlett, C.A. and Ghoshal, S. (1990). *Internationale unternehmensführung. innovation, globale effizienz, differenziertes marketing*. Frankfurt am Main: Campus Verlag.

Bruffee, K. (1981). 'Collaborative learning,' *College English*, 43(7), pp. 745–747.

Brufee, K. (1984). 'Collaborative learning and the "Conversation of Mankind",' *College English*, 46(7), pp. 635–652.

Buchs, A. and Blanchard, O. (2011). 'Exploring the concept of sustainable development through role-playing,' *The Journal of Economic Education*, 42(4), pp. 388–394.

Cobb, P. (1994). 'Where is the mind? Constructivists and sociocultural perspectives on mathematical development,' *Educational Researcher*, 23(7), pp. 13–20.

Cole, M. and Scribner, S. (1978). 'Introduction,' in Cole, M., John-Steiner, V., Scribner, S. and Souberman, E. (eds.) *Mind in society: The development of higher psychological processes*. Reading: Harvard University Press, pp. 1–16.

Doh, J.P. and Tashman, P. (2014). 'Half a world away: The integration and assimilation of corporate social responsibility, sustainability, and sustainable development in business school curricula,' *Corporate Social Responsibility and Environmental Management*, 21, 131–142.

DW News. (2020, November' '26). *Danish PM admits to mistakes over mink cull*. Available at: https://www.dw.com/en/danish-pm-admits-to-mistakes-over-mink-cull/av-55742859

DW News. (2020, December 4). *Mink fur boom in China raises virus fears*. Available at: https://www.dw.com/en/mink-fur-boom-in-china-raises-virus-fears/av-55820479

Figueiró, P.S. and Raufflet, E. (2015). 'Sustainability in higher education: A systematic review with focus on management education,' *Journal of Cleaner Production*, 106, 22–33.

Fosnot, C.T. and Perry, R.S. (2005). 'Constructivism: A psychological theory of learning,' in Fosnot, C.T., (ed.) *Constructivism: Theory, perspectives, and practice*. Teachers College Press, 2nd ed., pp. 8–33.

García-León, R.A. (2019). 'Noticias como recurso didáctico en la Educación para el Desarrollo Sostenible,' *Conference Proceedings of the 4th Virtual International Conference on Education, Innovation and ICT, EDUNOVATIC 2019*, 444–448. (ISBN 978-84-09-19568-8).

Gordon, S. and Thomas, I. (2018). '"The learning sticks': Reflections on a case study of role-playing for sustainability,' *Environmental Education Research*, 24(2), pp. 172–190.

Heenan, D.A. and Perlmutter, H.V. (1979). *Multinational organization development: A systems approach*. Addison-Wesley Pub. Co.

Jack, A. (2018, October 29). 'Why Harvard's case studies are under fire,' *Financial Times*. https://www.ft.com/content/0b1aeb22-d765-11e8-a854-33d6f82e62f8

Jackson, S. (2021, June 24). 'Luxury parka maker Canada Goose will stop using fur in all products by the end of 2022 following years of activist pressure,' *Business Insider*. https://www.businessinsider.com/canada-goose-jackets-fur-free-by-the-end-of-2022-2021-6

Jarman, R. and McClune, B. (2007). *Developing scientific literacy: Using news media in the classroom*. Maidenhead: McGrawHill.

Karahan, E. and Roehrig, G. (2015). 'Constructing media artifacts in a social constructivist environment to enhance students' environmental awareness and activism,' *Journal of Science Education and Technology*, 24, pp. 103–118.

Kim, D.-Y. (2014). 'Understanding integrated environmental assessment in a multi-stakeholder negotiation via role-play,' *Simulation & Gaming*, 45(1), pp. 125–145.

Kurz, T., Gardner, B., Verplanken, B. and Abraham, C. (2014). 'Habitual behaviors or patterns of practice? Explaining and changing repetitive climate-relevant actions,' *WIREs Climate Change*, 6(1), pp. 113–128.

Lave, J. and Wenger, E. (1991). *Situated learning: Legitimate peripheral participation.* Cambridge: Cambridge University Press.

Lehman-Wilzig, S.N. and Seletzky, M. (2010). 'Hard news, soft news, 'general' news: The necessity and utility of an intermediate classification,' *Journalism*, 11(1), pp. 37–56.

Lennerfors, T.T., Fors, P. and Woodward, J.R. (2020). 'Case hacks: Four hacks for promoting critical thinking in case-based management education for sustainable development,' *Högre utbildning*, 10(2), pp. 1–15.

MacAskill, K. and Tilley, C. (2021). 'Case studies in professional-oriented education: engaging with sustainability and complexity,' *EESD2021: Proceedings of the 10th Engineering Education for Sustainable Development Conference, 'Building Flourishing Communities.* University College Cork, Ireland, 14–16 June.

Majetic, C. and Pellegrino, C. (2014). 'When science and information literacy meet: An approach to exploring the sources of science news with non-science majors,' *College Teaching*, 62(3), pp. 107–112.

Marques de Melo, J. and Assis, F. (2016). 'Journalistic genres and formats: A classification model,' *Intercom*, 39(1), pp. 39–54.

McKenzie-Mohr, D. (2000). 'New ways to promote proenvironmental behavior: Promoting sustainable behavior: An introduction to community-based social marketing,' *Journal of Social Issues*, 56(3), pp. 543–554.

Molderez, I. and Fonseca, E. (2018). 'The efficacy of real-world experiences and service learning for fostering competences for sustainable development in higher education,' *Journal of Cleaner Production*, 172, 4397–4410.

Montiel, I., Antolin-Lopez, R. and Gallo, P.J. (2018). 'Emotions and sustainability: A literary genre-based framework for environmental sustainability management education,' *Academy of Management Learning & Education*, 17(2), pp. 155–183.

Moratis, L. and Melissen, F. (2022). 'Bolstering responsible management education through the sustainable development goals: Three perspectives,' *Management Learning*, 53(2), pp. 212–222.

Morsing, M. (2022a). 'PRME–Principles for Responsible Management Education: Towards transforming leadership education,' in Morsign, M. (ed.) *Responsible Management Education: The PRME Global Movement.* Routledge, pp. 3–12.

Morsing, M. (2022b). 'Part I. PRME Into the Decade of Action,' in Morsign, M. (ed.) *Responsible Management Education: The PRME Global Movement.* London: Routledge, pp. 1–2.

Park, Y. (2011). 'Using news articles to build a critical literacy classroom in an EFL setting,' *Tesol Journal*, 2(1), pp. 24–51.

Plester, J. (2021, September 4). 'How food waste is huge contributor to climate change,' *The Guardian*. https://www.theguardian.com/news/2021/sep/04/how-food-waste-is-huge-contributor-to-climate-change

PRME. (2021). *About: What is PRME?* https://www.unprme.org/about

Rao, D. (2011). 'Skills development using role-play in a first-year pharmacy practice course,' *American Journal of Pharmaceutical Education*, 75(5), pp. 1–10.

Scannell, L. and Gifford, R. (2013). 'Personally relevant climate change: The role of place attachment and local versus global message framing in engagement,' *Environment and Behavior*, 45(1), pp. 60–85.

Sharen, C.M. and McGowan, R.A. (2019). 'Invisible or Clichéd: How are women represented in business cases?' *Journal of Management Education*, 43(2), pp. 129–173.

Sheridan, J., Byrne, A.C. and Quina, K. (1989). 'Collaborative learning: Notes from the Field,' *College Teaching*, 37(2), pp. 49–53.

Singh, V. (2011). 'Using NASA science news articles to enhance learning in the classroom,' *The Physics Teacher*, 49(8), pp. 482–483.

Smith, B.L. and MacGregor. J.T. (1992). 'What is collaborative learning?' in Goodsell, A., Maher, M., Tinto, V., Smith, B.L. and MacGregor, J.T. (eds.) *Collaborative learning: A sourcebook for higher education*. Pennsylvania State University: National Center on Postsecondary Teaching, Learning, and Assessment (NCTLA), pp. 9–22.

Starkey, K. and Tempest, S. (2009). 'The winter of our discontent: The design challenge for business schools,' *Academy of Management Learning & Education*, 8(4), pp. 576–586.

Tilbury, D. and Wortman, D. (2004). *Engaging People in Sustainability*. Commission on Education and Communication. IUCN, Gland, Switzerland and Cambridge, UK. http://education21.ch/sites/default/files/uploads/pdf-en/2004_IUCN_Engaging-People-in-Sustainability.pdf

Truscheit, A. and Otte, C. (2004). 'Sustainable games people play: Teaching sustainability skills with the aid of the role-play 'NordWestPower.'' *Greener Management International*, 48, 51–56.

Tuchman, G. (1972). 'Objectivity as strategic ritual: An examination of newsmen's notions of objectivity,' *American Journal of Sociology*, 77(4), pp. 660–679.

UNESCO. (2017). *Education for sustainable development goals: Learning objectives*. UNESCO. Available at: https://www.unesco.de/sites/default/files/2018-08/unesco_education_for_sustainable_development_goals.pdf

United Nations. (2021). *Take action for the sustainable development goals*. Available at: https://www.un.org/sustainabledevelopment/sustainable-development-goals/

United Nations. (2021). *The 17 Goals*. Available at: https://sdgs.un.org/goals

UNSSC. (2021). *The 2030 Agenda for sustainable development*. Available at: https://www.un.org/development/desa/jpo/wp-content/uploads/sites/55/2017/02/2030-Agenda-for-Sustainable-Development-KCSD-Primer-new.pdf

Vidalon, D. and Spencer, M. (2021). 'Luxury group Kering to ditch fur completely,' *Reuters*. Available at: https://www.reuters.com/business/retail-consumer/french-fashion-company-kering-says-it-will-be-going-entirely-fur-free-2021-09-24/

Vygotsky, L. (1978). *Mind in Society*. Boston: Harvard University Press.

Wals, A.E.J. and Jickling, B. (2002). 'Sustainability in higher education: from doublethink and newspeak to critical thinking and meaningful learning,' *Higher Education Policy*, 15, 121–131.

Webb, N.M. (2013). 'Information Processing Approaches to Collaborative Learning,' in Hmelo-Silver, C.E., Chinn, C.A., Chan, C.K.K. and O'Donnell, A. (eds.) *The international handbook of collaborative learning*. Routledge, pp. 19–40.

Woods, K.H. (2018). 'Today's student, tomorrow's leader: Using case studies to prepare college students to make real-world ethical decisions,' in Stachowicz-Stanusch, A. and Amann, W. (eds.) *Fostering sustainability by management education*. Information Age Publishing, Inc, pp. 283–304.

9 Supporting transformation towards sustainable development: The use of Appreciative Inquiry in responsible management education

Mirjam Minderman

Introduction

Sustainable development requires transformation. The Sustainable Development Goals (SDGs) can only be realised if we radically change the way we produce and consume globally (Setó-Pamies and Papaoikonomou, 2020; World Business Council for Sustainable Development [WBCSD], 2021).

Transformation means changing systems and mindsets. This requires questioning why something is done in the way it is done – not with the intention to make existing processes more efficient, but with the goal of designing new processes. Herein lies the crucial difference with incremental change, which concerns adjustments within current systems and processes. Optimising current processes can be useful to some extent, yet this may get us locked in unsustainable structures and systems only even further. Moreover, incremental change often addresses symptoms rather than root causes.

Responsible Management Education (RME) provides current and future leaders with the knowledge, skills, and attitude to develop pathways towards a sustainable future. An essential part of this education is creating the awareness that incremental change and a focus on eco-efficiency are not enough, and that transformation is imperative for dealing with the world's challenges as summarised in the SDGs (Moratis and Melissen, 2021; Setó-Pamies and Papaoikonomou, 2020).

Yet management education has traditionally been shaped with concepts at odds with transformation, such as risk management, control, and problem analysis. The focus has been on preserving and optimising the financial capital, the organisation, and its operations (Ghoshal, 2005; Giacalone and Wargo, 2009). Generally speaking, a focus on incremental change is the default setting of management education providers.[1] Even though many of these schools have changed or are changing their curricula to include corporate social responsibility and sustainable development-related contents and competences, the traditional view on business is still underlying many

DOI: 10.4324/9781003244905-13

courses (Saravanamuthu, 2015; Snelson-Powell et al., 2020). In order for RME to be successful, management education providers need to strengthen their curricula with transformative methods and pedagogies to equip their students with a mindset that is more open to transformation (Aboytes and Barth, 2020; Boström et al., 2018; Saravanamuthu, 2015).

This chapter addresses this educational challenge by suggesting Appreciative Inquiry (AI) as one suitable method in this regard. While acknowledging that there are many, and often interrelated, ways for management education providers to include transformation for sustainable development in their curricula, research, and organisation, this chapter focuses on curricula and the use of one specific method, namely AI. First, AI is explained. Then its application in RME is discussed and illustrated with the example of AIM2Flourish in the fulltime MBA program of TIAS School for Business and Society (the Netherlands). This combination of theory and practice leads to several considerations about how AI can strengthen RME.

AI – a transformative approach

AI is a method for instigating positive change in people, organisations, and systems. It emerged in the mid-80s from the Ph.D. research of David Cooperrider at Case Western Reserve University: when inquiring into the organisational processes of one of the best hospitals in the US, he discovered that it made a massive difference in tone, direction, and outcome when he focused his surveys and interviews on what did not work within the organisation versus what made it an excellent hospital. Simply put, deficit-related questions surfaced a long list of problems and issues, while inquiring into the strengths resulted in creative and innovative examples of organisation and governance and in addition provided positive energy and inspiration to all involved. Together with his mentor Suresh Srivastva and colleague Ronald Fry, Cooperrider continued to work out what became AI and evolved from a research approach into a process for organisational development and change. Over the years, the scope of its use has widened and ranges from persons to systems and everything in between (Bushe, 2012; Grieten et al., 2018).

'Appreciative' refers to acknowledging strengths and successes; discovering what is of value and what gives life to the current situation. 'Inquiry' links to exploration and discovery; to being open to gathering information and hence to new options, indicating the future-oriented direction of AI (Stavros et al., 2015).

It is important to note that the focus on the positive (life-giving forces and strengths) does not imply ignoring the negative. Negative experiences and issues should be acknowledged, but instead of doing a detailed problem analysis, at some point the issue should be flipped and framed as an 'affirmative topic,' meaning the outcome of the positive opposite. The underlying reasoning is that it gives more energy and is more engaging to explore what you want and how to get there, instead of discussing what you do not want (Stavros and Torres, 2021). The use of SOAR instead of a SWOT analysis for strategy development is a good example of this: analysing the current weaknesses (W) and threats (T) to design a future strategy can be energy-draining and demotivating for all involved, outweighing the strengths (S) and opportunities (O) that are identified as well. Flipping these weaknesses and threats into opportunities and drafting joint aspirations (A) creates an energising and inspiring setting that unlocks creativity and new possibilities. Formulating results (R) that indicate how to meet and measure the aspirations ensures that the brainstorming and envisioning part of the process is balanced with concrete plans and outcomes (Stavros and Hinrichs, 2019).

AI is based on five principles that Stavros and Torres (2021, pp. 111, 156–157) formulate as follows:

1 Constructionist Principle: Understanding, interpersonal dynamics, meaning, and ultimately our social reality are created through language and in conversation. *Words create worlds.*
2 Simultaneity Principle: Change begins at the moment a question is asked or a statement is made. *Inquiry is intervention.*
3 Poetic Principle: Every person, organisation, or situation can be seen and understood from many perspectives. *You have a choice in how you see things.*
4 Anticipatory Principle: We move in the direction of our thoughts and the images that we hold. What we focus on expands. Anticipating what you want instead of fearing what you do not want. *We see what we expect to see; what we look for, we find.*
5 Positive Principle: The more positive and generative the question, the more positive and long-lasting the outcomes. *Positive images and positive actions produce positive results.*

In the development of AI, several other principles have been included and removed, but the above are the five fundamental principles that are commonly used. Still, in the context of sustainable development, it is relevant also to mention the 'Principle of Wholeness,' indicating that 'the whole system can have a voice in the future' (Cooperrider et al., 2005, p. 267).

AI is an engaging participatory process and should involve all stakeholders of an issue. These stakeholders jointly construct a pathway to the desired outcome that they have formulated and agreed upon at the start of the process. The entire process consists of five steps or phases, captured in the so-called 5-D Cycle (Cooperrider et al., 2005; Grandy and Holton, 2010; Stavros and Torres, 2021):

• *Define*: This is a preparatory phase in which the 'Affirmative topic or task' that is central to the entire process is formulated. Positive framing of this topic is key. Also, generative questions to use in the Discover phase are carefully crafted. The topics' and questions' focus and formulation are crucial for making the inquiry an engaging and effective process. Sometimes this phase is not included as an initial step, in which case the following 4 phases form the 4-D Cycle.

• *Discover*: Examples and stories of what works well and what gives life to the current system are actively explored in one-on-one interviews and small group discussions. This phase is about appreciating the best of 'what is' and identifying strengths that can elicit possibilities for the future.

• *Dream*: inspired by the Discover phase, the participants shift their attention from now to the future. They challenge the status quo by wondering how the ideal situation would look like. They envision what could be and draft images of the future.

• *Design*: The Dream phase's compelling images are then 'translated' into more concrete plans and pathways. What is needed to get there? Co-constructing and prototyping are key to this part of the process.

• *Deploy / Deliver* (also: *Destiny*): The prototypes are tried and tested in this final phase. This phase is about empowering, learning, improvising, and sustaining on the co-created pathway. The destiny phase is ongoing and will result in new Define and Discover phases when further questions and topics arise along the way.

This cycle is perfectly suited for use in a whole system setting, also referred to as an 'Appreciative Inquiry Summit.' Here, large groups (up to 1,000 persons) that represent an entire system gather during several (often 3–5) days and in both plenary and subgroup sessions design whole system strength-based change. These settings inspire both collaboration and innovation, with design thinking as an integral component (Laszlo and Cooperrider, 2010). Literature on AI stresses widespread engagement as a critical contributing factor to successful AI-driven change processes (Bushe, 2012). Tapping into the collective intelligence of a large and broad group of stakeholders (regardless of whether this concerns one organisation or an entire sector or system) that collectively design where they want to go and how to get there, creates a level of ownership and commitment that is difficult to equal. This process is more effective than a small group that develops a change plan that consequently needs to be 'sold' to the rest of the organisation or system. Such a small group approach is likely to result in less commitment and alignment and more miscommunication and resistance (Laszlo and Cooperrider, 2010).

AI in RME – in theory

The use of AI in higher education, including management education, has been labelled Appreciative Education and Appreciative Pedagogy. Appreciative Pedagogy is the application of AI to the method of providing education (Yballe and O'Connor, 2000; Grandy and Holton, 2010). In the same realm, Appreciative Education 'involves intentionally designing educational approaches that are based on principles of positive psychology and appreciative inquiry' (Mather and Smith, 2021, p. 1). Both concepts are closely related.

In general, designing and delivering higher education following the principles of AI has implications for students' individual and interpersonal development. By inquiring into strengths in themselves and their peers, and by being more appreciative of those strengths, their (self-)reflection and self-confidence increase and relationships with other students improve. This development may also result in a safer and more engaging learning environment (Cockell and McArthur-Blair, 2020; Neville, 2008; Dematteo and Reeves, 2011; Mather and Smith, 2021). Such a learning environment encourages exploration of assumptions and worldviews that underlie perspectives and paradigms. On the one hand, this creates a better understanding of, and respect for, different views and opinions. On the other hand, this creates awareness of what has formed paradigms and how to construct new ones. Equipping students with an 'appreciative eye' in addition to the traditional 'analytical eye,' stimulates their creativity and curiosity, enabling a more holistic view. By jointly inquiring into 'what might be,' students can experience how collaboration can lead to innovation (Neville, 2008; Roberts, 2010).[2]

Grandy and Holton (2010) explored AI as a pedagogical tool in a business school context. They found that 'the experiential nature of the AI process was a success in promoting inquiry and dialogue, encouraging collaboration and team building, and empowering individuals toward a collective vision' (p. 178).[3] Neville (2008) describes Appreciative Pedagogy as a successful method to have students in an undergraduate business course explore their underlying assumptions about business in society. This exploration results in a much higher level of critical thinking, especially concerning the paradigms underlying business education, and increased awareness about the interrelatedness between business, society and indeed themselves. Cooperrider and Fry stress the role universities and business schools can play in enabling (future) leaders to create sustainable value, driving business, and management innovation based on environmental and social impact concerns. To do so, they stress the importance of creating 'strong learning environments in which students can develop an appreciative eye through experiential exercises and AI theory and application' (Grieten et al., 2018, p. 109). Cooperrider states that currently, the discipline of organisational development is focused on intervention rather than innovation and expects this to change (Grieten et al., 2018).

Remarkably, an essential connection between AI and RME concerning the so-called competencies for sustainable development seems to be missing. There is a vast body of literature on these competencies in relation to higher and management education. The recurrent competences that are mentioned as key to sustainable development are systems thinking, long-term perspective, collaboration, and ethics (Lambrechts et al., 2013; Wiek et al.; Ploum et al., 2018; Rieckmann, 2011). These competencies and AI have essential similarities. Given its focus on the future, whole systems, stakeholder engagement and collaboration, AI is supportive in acquiring precisely these competencies. Also, the ability to question assumptions and worldviews (critical thinking), respect different perspectives, and design thinking are important competences in both RME and AI. The same similarities exist between AI and what Isabel Rimanoczy (2020) has defined as a 'Sustainability Mindset.' The underlying idea is that in order to be capable of translating sustainability-related knowledge into action, people need to complement this knowledge with 'a way of thinking and being that results from a broad understanding of the ecosystem's manifestations, from social sensitivity, as well as an introspective focus on one's personal values and higher self' (Rimanoczy, 2020, p. 10). Key elements of the Sustainability Mindset are in line with the aforementioned competencies and include long-term perspective, collaboration, interconnectedness, right-brain perspective (holistic, intuitive), creativity, reflection, and self-awareness (Hermes and Rimanoczy, 2018). Besides of these similarities, AI is complementary in that it adds a more explicit transformative element/perspective to these competencies and mindset.

In the context of management education providers, it is relevant to stress the benefits of training students in AI to provide them with an additional method in organisational development, change management or innovation courses, or a combination thereof. In addition to the usual deficit and problem analysis-based change management theories and models that management education providers offer in their courses, AI provides students with a more complete 'toolbox.' This toolbox strengthens them in addressing wicked/complex problems in general and supports them in contributing to transitions related to sustainable development in particular.

The international platform AIM2Flourish provides a low-threshold way for introducing AI in combination with the SDGs into management education. TIAS School for Business and Society has included AIM2Flourish in the curriculum of its full-time MBA program.

AI in RME – in practice

TIAS School for Business and Society

TIAS is the business school of Tilburg University and Eindhoven University of Technology and is located in Tilburg and Utrecht, in the Netherlands. It offers a broad portfolio of executive (part-time) Masters, MBAs, Master Classes, and in-company programs targeted at the for-profit, non-profit, and public sectors. TIAS is much aware of its role and responsibility concerning the challenges that the world is facing, which led to a change of name to *School for Business and Society* in 2014, and to the following purpose statement: *We develop leaders to serve society by transforming business*. To translate this purpose into its curricula, TIAS has adopted an integral competency-based approach to 'Business & Society.' It has developed the TIAS Business & Society Competency Framework that consists of four competency areas: Responsible Leadership, Collaboration, Business Modelling, and Sustainable Innovation. These competency areas and the underlying 12 competencies are integrated throughout all programs and courses.

One of TIAS's programs is the full-time International Master of Business Administration, an AMBA-accredited MBA program. Each cohort consists of 30–35 participants from Asia, Africa, Latin America and Europe with diverse backgrounds, including finance, technical engineering, IT, and social sciences. Part of this program is the course 'SDGs in Business Practice' (2 ECTS). As the SDGs can seem quite broad and abstract, this course has been designed to make these Global Goals more 'tangible' and locally relevant to the students. The course has been built around participation in AIM2Flourish. At the time of writing, four cohorts have participated in AIM2Flourish and the fifth cohort is about to start.

AIM2Flourish

AIM2Flourish is an international, United Nations-supported platform for sharing stories about business innovations in support of the SDGs, with the mission to change the narrative about business from best *in* the world, to best *for* the world. It is a program of the Fowler Center for Business as an Agent of World Benefit at the Weatherhead School of Management – Case Western Reserve University, the home or 'founding' university of AI. Both David Cooperrider and Ronald Fry are still working here and supporting AIM2Flourish. Through its website and team, AIM2Flourish provides educators of other schools with various materials to enable them to run AIM2Flourish with their students. This works as follows: students get basic training in both AI and the SDGs. Following this training they select a business or business innovation that contributes to one or more of the SDGs and is financially profitable as well. They conduct an AI-driven interview with the business leader concerned and write their AIM2Flourish story following a specific format, featuring their interviewee's inspiration, the business innovation, and its social, environmental, and business impact. With the approval of their professor and the interviewee, the students can upload their story to the AIM2Flourish platform. One of the AIM2Flourish editors (volunteering professors) consequently edits and publishes the story. Each year, AIM2Flourish honours the most inspiring stories with 17 Flourish Prizes – one for each SDG. Since its launch in 2015, AIM2Flourish has grown to currently featuring some 3,500 stories, written by students from over 500 schools worldwide. So far, 44 TIAS-related stories have been published on AIM2Flourish, and four stories have won Flourish Prizes.

AIM2Flourish at TIAS

Even though TIAS aims to integrate business and society-related contents and competences as much as possible within existing courses, the course 'SDGs in Business Practice' is added to give explicit and more in-depth attention to three elements:

First of all, the course allows for a more in-depth discussion about the contribution of business to the SDGs. SDGs are also addressed in other courses, but on a more general level and with less space for stimulating critical reflection and debate on the lines between so-called 'rainbow-washing' (greenwashing through flaunting the SDGs), incremental change, and transformation. In addition, the course also allows for illustrating the use and meaning of the TIAS Business & Society competencies in practice: the four competency areas are usually essential elements in the AIM2Flourish stories. Last but not least, the AIM2Flourish assignment provides a perfect opportunity to introduce AI and discuss its relevance concerning transformation in general and sustainable development in particular. This last part happens during a one-day workshop that addresses the AI principles, the 5-D Cycle, SOAR, and the application in the context of the SDGs. The students do various exercises to experience the power of strength-based and generative conversations and practice formulating affirmative topics. The AIM2Flourish assignment usually works in teams of two and follows the procedure as outlined in the previous paragraph about AIM2Flourish.

Overall, the course is well received and evaluated by the students. Usually, some students initially are sceptical about the positive and generative aspect of AI and feel a bit lost concerning the AIM2Flourish assignment, which is different from the problem-based, analytical, and academic assignments they are used to. However, after the submission of their assignment, nearly all students indicate that the course has been insightful and inspirational. They particularly value the personal contact with the business leader they interviewed. Some of them have even indicated that the course has inspired them to pursue a career related to sustainable development. The following quotes from students illustrate this:

'The AIM2Flourish assignment was quite a new and motivational assignment for us. Most of the assignments at a business school are related to strategy and business growth, but this assignment touches the overall impact a business can have on the company, society and all other stakeholders. We really felt quite engaged and got a new perspective to understand business and companies. In our terms, we can say that this assignment has added a new dimension to our sustainable leadership thoughts.' (two students from the 2019-20 cohort)

'The impact the AIM2Flourish experience has on us personally can be summarized as one that has taught us how rewarding it can be to address an

SDG. The leadership style our interviewee has introduced us to, is one that cannot only be admired but also one that sets an example and is an aspiration for both of us. Besides an inspirational insight into this leadership style, the AIM2Flourish experience has opened our eyes in terms of future job opportunities in ventures that are driven by social responsibility.' (two students from the 2020-21 cohort)

In summary, during the course, the MBA students experience how the four competency areas of Responsible Leadership, Collaboration, Business Modelling, and Sustainable Innovation contribute to business transformation, how such transformation contributes to the SDGs, and how AI can support these transformative processes. This brief example indicates that combining AI and the SDGs in management education can indeed contribute to shaping sustainability leadership.

Considerations

Looking at AI in theory and in the practice of AIM2Flourish at TIAS leads to the following considerations concerning its use in RME.

Positive/negative duality

An important critique on AI is that it does not provide space for including the wrongs in an organisation and the negative emotions of stakeholders, thus leading to frustration and disengagement (Barge and Oliver, 2003; Bushe, 2012; Grieten et al., 2018). In response to this positive/negative duality, Cooperrider and Fry stress the importance of the generative character of AI. They indicate that it may be more helpful to use the label 'generative' instead of 'positive' as the latter can be misleading. For example, a conflict does not evoke the connotation of 'positive,' yet it can be very constructive and 'life-giving' (Grieten et al., 2018).

Based on the experience at TIAS, it is helpful to discuss this critique in the classroom and explore to what extent it is possible to acknowledge negativity and still create a generative process where all stakeholders feel involved and motivated to design the desired future situation. In line with this, flipping a negative issue and framing the opposite outcome as an affirmative topic for an AI process requires careful facilitation and practice; if applied too easily or quickly, the result will be a superficial discussion that does not address the real issue at stake.

Educational disconnect

AIM2Flourish is an effective way to indicate how AI can be supportive of sustainable transformation. However, if AI is only addressed in one course, it is likely that students cannot relate its use to a broader context and that the learning outcome will be very limited. This so-called educational disconnect has also been described concerning corporate social responsibility courses and RME (Barber et al., 2014; Carrithers and Peterson, 2006; Remington-Doucette et al., 2013; Stubbs and Cocklin, 2008).

Consequently, in order to have transformational impact, AI and its underlying elements need to be included in a broader variety of programs, both as an appreciative pedagogy underlying the courses and as a method for complementing the 'toolbox' of students. Think, for example, of including AI in organisational change courses, introducing SOAR in addition to the standard SWOT analysis, and if design thinking is part of a program, it could be linked to AI (and vice versa). In the TIAS MBA, there is a link between elements of positive psychology in personal development training and AI in the course 'SDGs in Business Practice.'

Language and metaphors

The educational disconnect may be reinforced by the use of language concerning management and business vis-à-vis AI. One of the main sources for models, analogies, and metaphors in strategic management education has been the domain of warfare, as reflected in words and phrases such as *target, attack, capture, declare victory, defend, lead the charge* and *strike* (Audebrand, 2010). This vocabulary stresses, if not promotes, competition and adversarial relationships. Moreover, as indicated in the introduction of this chapter, traditional management courses are usually focussed on concepts concerning control, risks, and problems. Contrary to this war- and risk-related vocabulary, AI is about collaboration and using positive, strengths-based language. In this regard, the constructionist principle underlying AI needs to be stressed, which comes down to 'words create worlds.' Both Cooperrider and Fry call 'to develop a new language/theory of non-deficit-based, life-centric or strength-based change' (Grieten et al., 2018, p. 111). Hence the use of different metaphors and language will be very supportive to, if not imperative for, the successful integration of AI and indeed the implementation of RME.

Words create worlds

The fact that AI is such a highly linguistic concept and process is something to consider when designing a related educational program. The formulation of affirmative topics, generative questions, and associated conversations are all about language – again, words create worlds. This dynamic may resonate less with people who have a more quantitative aptitude. In the MBA program at TIAS, students with a background in accounting and finance seem to struggle more with the AI-related part of the course compared to peers with a background in social sciences. It is helpful to address this potential tension upfront and through ensuring sufficient experiential learning, to avoid that students miss the point entirely and in frustration wonder why they need 'to write an article for The Sun tabloid instead of an academic journal' as once happened in the early stages of the AIM2Flourish assignment at TIAS.

Dealing with anxiety and transformation

A last consideration is that AI becomes even more critical in relation to sustainable development and RME considering some basic neuroscience.

Neuroscientific research has demonstrated that negative emotions trigger the fight-or-flight (or freeze) response in the human brain: more stress hormones such as cortisol, norepinephrine, and testosterone are released, and more oxygen is sent to the part of the brain that is responsible for primary instincts such as survival and reproduction (i.e., our 'reptile brain'). This reaction results in a narrow focus, blocking the ability to be creative, connect, and collaborate (Stavros and Torres, 2021). This state of mind is also known as 'below the line,'[4] 'fixed mindset,' or 'defensive mode' (Webb, 2016). However, the opposite works as well: positive emotions stimulate the release of 'happy hormones' such as oxytocin, endorphins, serotonin, and dopamine. As a result, the parts of the brain responsible for emotional intelligence (empathy, connection, and collaboration), creativity, and critical thinking are stimulated (Stavros and Torres, 2021). This state of mind is also called 'above the line,' 'growth mindset,' or 'discovery mode' (Webb, 2016).

Change, in general, is usually contested and met with resistance. Yet, the transformation that the SDGs require is so vast, complex, and uncertain, that it is likely to trigger feelings of anxiety or powerlessness, or both. This has been described as climate change anxiety and depression, a phenomenon that also affects (management) students (Moratis and Melissen, 2021; Sims et al., 2020).

If students are aware of the above, they can consciously use the strengths-based and generative character of AI to better deal with this anxiety and, moreover, can intentionally foster a mindset in themselves and others that is more open to transformation.

Conclusion

AI is a method to foster positive change at an individual, organisational, and system level.

An important contribution of AI to management education is that it complements the traditional 'analytical eye' with an 'appreciative eye,' stimulating creativity and curiosity, enabling a more holistic view and supporting students to be more open to, and appreciative of, other perspectives. This resonates very well with the competences and elements of a sustainability mindset that are addressed in RME, such as systems thinking, long-term perspective, collaboration, creativity, reflection, and self-awareness.

As a change method in itself, AI provides a relevant addition to the 'toolbox' of management students, enabling them to drive transformation for sustainable development in their professional lives.

The experience with AIM2Flourish at TIAS has shown that AIM2Flourish is a low-threshold and successful way of introducing business students to AI. Moreover, its connection of AI with sustainable development and the SDGs enables students to experience how business can be a force for good. Indeed, several students have indicated that the assignment changed how they see their future careers and that the assignment inspired them to become sustainable leaders themselves.

Working with AIM2Flourish has resulted in insights about what is needed for successful use of AI in support of RME. A basic requirement is explaining and discussing how and why AI is based on different language and metaphors than most students are used to. In the experience at TIAS it became very clear that especially the more 'quantitative' oriented students struggle with the fact that AI is a highly linguistic concept and process. Lecturers need to bear this in mind and ensure experiential learning in order to still provide a meaningful learning process for these students as well.

Also the positive/negative duality needs to be addressed in order to avoid the impression that AI is just a superficial feel-good process that ignores the wrongs and problems at stake. Careful facilitation is required to explain the concept of generativity and when to address affirmative topics.

The most important lesson learned is that broader integration of AI throughout the curriculum is required to avoid the so-called 'educational disconnect.' Or, in other words, how to make it really 'stick' with all students. To have optimal effect, AI is preferably included simultaneously in two manners: one way is to explicitly include AI in a change management course, where it is presented to students as a 'tool' for driving inclusive and long-term transformational processes. The other way is to use AI as appreciative pedagogy underlying all courses of a program, including the abovementioned language and metaphors.

Provided these lessons have been taken into account, AI is a worthwhile method to use in support of RME and the SDGs. Its strengths-based, generative, and transformative nature can significantly strengthen both the process and contents of RME and contribute to shaping sustainability leadership.

Notes

1 The term 'management education providers' is used in this chapter to cover the wide variety of institutions that offer management and business education, from undergraduate to executive and from public to private.
2 Neville (2008) provides an extensive overview of the pedagogic implications of each of the five Appreciative Inquiry principles.
3 Grandy and Holton (2010) also stress the relevance of Appreciative Inquiry for organisational learning and change in the business school itself, supporting the business school to become a learning organisation. This is a relevant application of

Appreciative Inquiry that also relates to management education providers and RME, yet this is beyond the scope of this chapter.
4 The Conscious Leadership Group provides an illustrative explanation of this concept in its video 'Locating yourself – A key to conscious leadership.'

References

Aboytes, J.G.R. and Barth, M. (2020). 'Transformative learning in the field of sustainability: a systematic literature review (1999–2019),' *International Journal of Sustainability in Higher Education*, 21(5), pp. 993–1013. doi 10.1108/IJSHE-05-2019-0168

Audebrand, L.K., 2010. 'Sustainability in strategic management education: The quest for new root metaphors,' *Academy of Management Learning & Education*, 9(3), pp. 413–428.

Barber, N.A., Wilson, F., Venkatachalam, V., Cleaves, S. and Garnham, J. (2014). 'Integrating sustainability into business curricula: University of New Hampshire case study,' *International Journal of Sustainability in Higher Education*, 15(4), pp. 473–493.

Barge, J.K. & Oliver, C. (2003). 'Working with appreciation in managerial practice,' *Academy of Management Review*, 28(1), pp. 124–142.

Boström, M., Andersson, E., Berg, M., Gustafsson, K., Gustavsson, E., Hysing, E., ... Öhman, J. (2018). 'Conditions for transformative learning for sustainable development: A theoretical review and approach,' *Sustainability*, 10(12), pp. 4479. doi:10.33 90/su10124479

Bushe, G. (2012). 'Foundations of appreciative inquiry: History, criticism and potential,' *AI Practitioner*, 14(1), pp. 8–20.

Carrithers, D.F. and Peterson, D. (2006). 'Conflicting views of markets and economic justice: Implications for student learning,' *Journal of Business Ethics*, 69(4), pp. 373–387.

Cockell, J. and McArthur-Blair, J., (2020). *Appreciative inquiry in higher education. A transformative force* (2nd ed.). Victoria, Canada: FriesenPress.

Cooperrider, D.L., Whitney, D.K. and Stavros, J.M. (2005). *Appreciative Inquiry Handbook: The first in a series of AI workbooks for leaders of change*. Brunswick, OH: Crown Custom.

Dematteo, D. and Reeves, S. (2011). 'A critical examination of the role of appreciative inquiry within an interprofessional education initiative,' *Journal of interprofessional care*, 25(3), pp. 203–208. doi:10.3109/13561820.2010.504312

Ghoshal, S. (2005). 'Bad management theories are destroying good management practices,' *Academy of Management Learning & Education*, 4(1), pp. 75–91.

Giacalone, R.A. and Wargo, D.T. (2009). 'The roots of the global financial crisis are in our business schools,' *Journal of Business Ethics Education*, 6, 147–168.

Grandy, G. and Holton, J. (2010). 'Mobilizing change in a business school using appreciative inquiry,' *The Learning Organization*, 17(2), pp. 178–194. doi:10.1108/09696471011019880

Grieten, S., Lambrechts, F., Bouwen, R., Huybrechts, J., Fry, R. and Cooperrider, D. (2018). 'Inquiring into appreciative inquiry: a conversation with David Cooperrider and Ronald Fry,' *Journal of Management Inquiry*, 27(1), pp. 101–114. 10.1177/10564 92616688087

Hermes, J. and Rimanoczy, I. (2018). 'Deep learning for a sustainability mindset,' *The International Journal of Management Education*, 16(3), pp. 460–467.

Laszlo, C. and Cooperrider, D.L. (2010). 'Creating sustainable value: A strength-based whole system approach,' in Thatchenkery, T., Cooperrider, D.L. and Avital, M. (eds.) *Positive design and appreciative construction: From sustainable development to sustainable value.* Bingley, U.K.: Emerald, pp. 17–33.

Lambrechts, W., Mulà, I., Ceulemans, K., Molderez, I. and Gaeremynck, V. (2013). 'The integration of competences for sustainable development in higher education: An analysis of bachelor programs in management,' *Journal of Cleaner Production*, 48, 65–73. doi: 10.1016/j.jclepro.2011.12.034.

Mather, P.C. and Smith, T.M. (2021). 'Implementing appreciative education in a first-year seminar,' *Journal of Appreciative Education*, 7(1), pp. 1–14.

Moratis, L. and Melissen, F. (2021). 'Bolstering responsible management education through the sustainable development goals: Three perspectives,' *Management Learning*, 2021, 1–11.

Neville, M.G. (2008). 'Using appreciative inquiry and dialogical learning to explore dominant paradigms,' *Journal of Management Education*, 32(1), pp. 100–117.

Ploum, L., Blok, V., Lans, T. and Omta, O. (2018). 'Toward a validated competence framework for sustainable entrepreneurship,' *Organization & environment*, 31(2), pp. 113–132. doi: 10.1177/1086026617697039

Remington-Doucette, S.M., Hiller Connell, K.Y., Armstrong, C.M. and Musgrove, S.L. (2013). 'Assessing sustainability education in a transdisciplinary undergraduate course focused on real-world problem solving: A case for disciplinary grounding,' *International Journal of Sustainability in Higher Education*, 14(4), pp. 404–433.

Rieckmann, M. (2011). 'Future-oriented higher education: Which key competencies should be fostered through university teaching and learning?' *Futures*, 44(2), pp. 127–135.

Rimanoczy, I. (2020). *The sustainability mindset principles: A guide to develop a mindset for a better world.* Routledge.

Roberts, G.W. (2010). 'Advancing new approaches to learning and teaching – introducing appreciative inquiry to a problem-based learning curriculum,' *Journal of Applied Research in Higher Education*, 2(1), pp. 16–24. 10.1108/17581184201000002

Saravanamuthu, K. (2015). 'Instilling a sustainability ethos in accounting education through the Transformative Learning pedagogy: A case-study,' *Critical Perspectives on Accounting*, 32, 1–36.

Setó-Pamies, D. and Papaoikonomou, E. (2020). 'Sustainable Development Goals: A powerful framework for embedding ethics, CSR, and sustainability in management education,' *Sustainability*, 12(5), pp. 1762. 10.3390/su12051762

Sims, L., Rocque, R. and Desmarais, M. É. (2020). 'Enabling students to face the environmental crisis and climate change with resilience: Inclusive environmental and sustainability education approaches and strategies for coping with eco-anxiety,' *International Journal of Higher Education and Sustainability*, 3(2), pp. 112–131.

Snelson-Powell, A.C., Grosvold, J. and Millington, A.I. (2020). 'Organizational hypocrisy in business schools with sustainability commitments: The drivers of talk-action inconsistency,' *Journal of Business Research*, 114, 408–420. 10.1016/j.jbusres.2019.08.021

Stavros, J.M., Godwin, L.N. and Cooperrider, D.L. (2015). 'Appreciative inquiry: Organization development and the strengths revolution,' in Rothwell, W.J., Stavros, J.M. and Sullivan, R.L. (eds.) *Practicing organization development: Leading transformation and change* (4th ed.). Hoboken, NJ: Wiley, pp. 96–116.

Stavros, J.M. and Hinrichs, G. (2019). *The thin book of SOAR. Creating strategy that inspires innovation and engagement* (2nd ed.). Bend, OR: Thin Book.

Stavros, J.M. and Torres, C. (2021). *Conversations worth having: Using appreciative inquiry to fuel productive and meaningful engagement* (2nd ed.). Oakland, CA: Berrett-Koehler.

Stubbs, W. and Cocklin, C. (2008). 'Teaching sustainability to business students: Shifting mindsets,' *International Journal of Sustainability in Higher Education* 9(3), pp. 206–221.

Webb, C. (2016). 'How small shifts in leadership can transform your team dynamic,' *McKinsey Quarterly*, 2, 74–81.

Wiek, A., Withycombe, L. and Redman, C.L. (2011). 'Key competencies in sustainability: a reference framework for academic program development,' *Sustainability Science*, 6(2), pp. 203–218.

World Business Council for Sustainable Development (2021). *Vision 2050: Time to transform*. Retrieved from https://timetotransform.biz/wp-content/uploads/2021/03/WBCSD_Vision_2050_Time-To-Transform.pdf

Yballe, L. and O'Connor, D. (2000). 'Appreciative pedagogy: Constructing positive models for learning,' *Journal of Management Education*, 24(4), pp. 474–483.

10 Applying authentic assessment to teaching the Sustainable Development Goals

Sarah Williams and David F. Murphy

Introduction

Prior to April 2020, the MBA module 'Local–Global Challenges in Ethics, Responsibility and Sustainability (ERS)' was delivered as a compulsory on-campus residential within an otherwise online degree programme. The module then, and now, draws students from across the eight specialist MBAs that the University of Cumbria delivers in partnership with Robert Kennedy College (Switzerland). Due to the Covid-19 pandemic, the module was moved online while still achieving both the university's academic requirements and student needs for the residential module. This meant the module was redesigned to emphasise authentic assessment in order to more fully engage students and increase university confidence in original work. This chapter demonstrates how current ideas regarding authentic assessment have been applied to the module within the context of responsible management education (RME) for leading the SDGs.

The online module starts by framing the teaching of ethics, responsibility, and sustainability in terms of personal individual values and sense-making, with climate change being the focus of the month-long pre-course work. The approach helps to set a relevant context of complex global sustainability problems that are experienced both locally and personally. The teaching for SDG 13 (Climate Action) in the third week, for example, emphasises the local-global challenge of the climate emergency and encourages students to think about how climate change is likely to increasingly affect their communities and, as a result, how community engagement for climate action could help to build local resilience and enable communities to adapt to the changes that are already underway and intensifying. This approach is consistent with PRME Principle 6 (Dialogue) as it facilitates cross-sector interaction on a critical issue related to global social responsibility and sustainability (PRME, 2007).

The module emphasises an authentic assessment approach as this methodology is recognised as engaging students in tasks that match real-life management challenges and can help bridge the gap between knowledge and practice (Custer et al., 2000; Gulikers et al., 2004). In a review of literature,

DOI: 10.4324/9781003244905-14

Sokhanvar et al. (2021) conclude that authentic assessment can improve the learning experience of higher education students through enhancing their engagement in learning as well as helping to equip students with essential management skills such as critical thinking and problem-solving skills, self-awareness, and self-confidence. Following Villarroel et al. (2018, 2020), the module's design for authenticity also helps to improve the confidence in student work by tightly contextualising the assessment in real-life.

This chapter explores some of the techniques utilised to support authentic assessment within an RME context and how the summative assessment has been used as a tool for increasing student engagement while reducing the risk of contract cheating. The extent of contract cheating by students – using a third party as a ghost writer to prepare a new piece of work that will by-pass anti-plagiarism software, such as Turnitin (Walker and Townley, 2012) – appears to be in the minority with our MBA students. Nonetheless, as with all subjects, it is still a significant risk and a major academic offence at master's level that threatens confidence in the students' work and employer confidence in the qualification.

This chapter is organised as follows. We will start with a discussion on authentic assessment, including why this is important, some of the techniques that can be used, and how the SDGs have provided a useful framework for management education in a genuinely authentic online context. Second, we discuss how the module evolved through three iterations over two years and the resulting learning that enabled and strengthened the pedagogical development of the teaching. This includes the use of the SDGs as a framework for the second and third (current) versions. Third, we discuss the use of the SDGs as a teaching framework in more detail before our final comments on the use of the SDGs as part of an authentic assessment approach.

Using authentic assessment for RME

In developing work on authentic assessment for the ethics, responsibility and sustainability module, the ideas of Villarroel et al. (2018, 2020) have been used, along with those of Williams et al. (2018). The Villarroel et al. research reviews a two-part project, identifying three elements of authentic assessment, namely the need for the work to be: (1) realistic, (2) contextualised and (3) problematised. To be realistic, the assessment needs to link knowledge and learning from the teaching with everyday life; to be contextualised, the knowledge from student learning needs to be applied in a relevant analytical, thoughtful way that is relevant to the students' own real-life experiences; and to be problematised the work should enable students to demonstrate how their learning can be applied to solve a real-life problem or to meet a genuine organisational need. Thereby, authentic assessment aims to integrate what happens in the classroom with employment, replicating the tasks and performance standards typically faced by professionals in the world of work. It is worth emphasising here that the students on this module are a mix of professionals working at a senior level within their professional sphere along with aspiring leaders who are currently working at a more junior level. This means that students can anchor their learning within their actual work context. However, students are also given the opportunity to use a community role as the context for their report. This enables a similar level of realism, contextualisation, and problematisation within a similarly specific setting but one that may be more suitable for local community activists or those working for non-governmental organisations (NGOs). However, this also means that students are usually managing several significant external demands and the additional learning commitment needs to support their work in a genuine way to be engaging.

The approach has emphasised:

- the importance of tightly contextualising the assessment
- redesigning the module to support authentic assessment throughout the study
- maintaining and utilising current and other relevant academic and practitioner resources
- engaging students proactively to avoid their anonymity and tendency to hide in the background
- using subject specialist teachers with the professional credibility to support professionals from business
- supporting learning throughout with skills development
- providing clear ongoing guidance and feedback throughout the module
- rewarding effort as well as academic skills
- and continual tutor engagement to develop a personalised relationship and double loop learning.

The use of the SDGs as the framework for teaching ethics, responsibility, and sustainability is well suited to authentic assessment as the concepts and applications are relevant to all sizes and forms of organisation. In exploring how UK-based multinational organisations are engaging with corporate social responsibility (CSR), Williams (2021) found that larger organisations are utilising the SDGs as a framework for engaging with sustainability, considering sustainability broader than CSR and the SDGs as being more explicit and relevant. In this sense, larger organisations have the potential to use the SDGs as both a strategic framework – choosing where to focus their sustainability efforts – as well as an operational tool for supporting projects, engaging stakeholders, and reporting their contribution towards the wider global effort. As part of this research, interviewees argued that small and medium-sized enterprises (SMEs) would also find the SDGs a useful framework for engaging with sustainability, making use of the opportunity to engage in a blended quantitative and qualitative approach that focused on the local contribution of smaller organisations (Williams, 2021). The applicability of the SDGs as a framework for all sizes and types of organisations has been supported by the experience of teaching the module under discussion in this chapter.

Authentic assessment is used to engage students by keeping the teaching relevant to their work contexts while also helping to prevent and design out contract cheating. It is the authors' experience, that from about 2015 onwards there has been a general increase in this form of cheating in both undergraduate and postgraduate work. Our observation supports the longitudinal study of Newton (2018) who found an increase in this practice over time. Walker and Townley (2012) recognised a lack of research on this form of cheating implies a reliance by academics on anecdotal or speculative evidence to explain the reasons behind this phenomenon. We clearly recognise increasing pressures on students studying within UK higher education institutions who also work full-time and to minimise the needs for loans while seeking promotions, salary increases, and greater responsibilities. This contrasts with the experiences of other students who take on more casual jobs to support learning grants while studying.

In addition to pressure on university students to succeed alongside increased external pressures, a further increase in contract cheating is likely to be due to the ease with which students can access this via web-based services. Indeed, Amigud (2020) found that students are proactively approached by contractors using automation tools to generate leads with students segmented by subject area. McCarthy (2021) confirms that there has been a further increase in contract cheating due to the rise in social media approaches to students, the growth of online student file sharing sites and heightened student perceptions of a decline in tutor support with moves to online teaching. As part of their marketing to students, ghost writers may even mislead students by suggesting that they are part of their university's student support service. This includes using aspects of the university's online branding to make it more difficult for students to recognise who is approaching them. Added to this is the tendency of ghost writers to demonstrate familiarity with the students' course materials; to have the ability to 'link in' to student networks offering coaching and support; and to communicate a message that students can legitimately turn to them (Rowland et al., 2018). The overall result is that it is clearly not difficult for students to access this form of cheating.

In fighting against the rise of contract cheating and ghost writing in higher education, Ali and Alhassan (2021) identify several approaches that can be used including being explicit to students that ghost writing is a form of cheating and one that is taken seriously. As the module used in this current paper focuses on the personal ethics and personal responsibility of students as leaders, it is important to emphasise how inappropriate cheating is and how unfair gaining advantage against other students who are working honestly is perceived by the tutors and the university. In addition to highlighting this explicitly in the assessment brief and module guide, students make a written statement to confirm that the work is their own and they should therefore understand the penalties for acting otherwise. This is supported within the teaching in two ways. First, during pre-course study leading to an interim/formative submission, students explore their values and sensemaking and how their values link with their personal behaviour and responsibility. Second, in the first full week of teaching on SDG 16 (Peace, Justice and Strong Institutions), including leadership and governance dimensions, the students are introduced to personal responsibility and ethical decision-making frameworks. During the first live session, the ethical decision-making frameworks are used as an explicit exercise to explore differences between private behaviours and actions and those in public view, as well as the 'Golden Rule' (How would you feel if others were cheating you?) and Kant's categorical imperative (If I do this once, would it be alright for me to do it like this always? If I do it this way, is it alright for everyone else to take this approach too?) In addition, as part of the teaching on SDG 16, we explicitly discuss corruption within the supply chain and within different regional contexts. This helps students to gain a broader worldview and explore the pressures they might be under at work to accept bribes, for example, or to make a personal statement of authorship that was untrue. As Villarroel et al. (2020) conclude, being proactive in looking to tackle contract cheating is essential. Learning from how students tackle the assessment and questioning why they would approach the work in such a way, is an important source of continuing academic learning.

Evolving versions of adopting the SDGs as a teaching framework

In moving the module online, we have we evolved the approach as we have learned from the students. This has included learning from the need for ever greater focus and explicitness to better ensure authentic work. There have been three iterations of online delivery from April 2020 to date:

April to August 2020

The first version ran from April 2020 until August 2020. The teaching closely reflected what the students had covered during the original week-long on-campus residential (Hurford and Chapman, 2019; Hurford, 2019) including individual and group reflective exercises. This first version looked to maintain the intensity of the one week on-campus residential and, in doing so, was very different from the other online modules in their MBA studies. While their other modules were delivered over 12 weeks, this iteration included just three weeks of teaching for 20 credits. Like the on-campus residential, we maintained a pre-course unit of study with a formative assessment. The pre-course work drew on the work of Schaefer et al. (2020) and Sagiv et al. (2017) to help frame the module in terms of personal values and how values help us to make sense of complex sustainability issues. The tool developed by Williams and Preston (2018), based on the Schwartz Values System, is used to enable personal reflection on individual level values. Students follow a reflective process whereby they identify their most significant values, the experiences that have shaped these and how those values influence how they view and act on issues related to ethics, responsibility, and sustainability.

The pre-course unit used climate change as an example of a complex sustainability issue where an understanding of values can help us to understand why we disagree about climate change and what could be done about it. The original one-week residential was then delivered online over three weeks – with each separate week looking at part of what had been one final summative assessment. The first week looked at issues relevant to ethics, responsibility, and sustainability. The second week explored the role of leadership and partnership in addressing those issues. The third week reflected on students' experiential learning and how they could apply specific learning from the module within their own organisation or community. There was no specific reference to the SDGs within this iteration except in the session on partnerships (SDG 17). To build tutor relationships with students as well as to develop a sense of the class working together, and to support students with formative feedback throughout the module, assessments were submitted in three parts at the end of each week of teaching. This meant the three-part assessment that had previously been submitted as one piece of work was now assessed on a week-by-week basis. This put a lot of pressure on staff to be able to give supportive, timely, and detailed feedback to students as support for their subsequent pieces of work, but the upside was that the quality of student work rapidly improved. To further support students, we offered online tutorials for three days each week, for each of the three weeks: to our surprise and delight it was found daily attendance was regularly over 80% and a genuine sense of a class working developed using break out rooms, group work, and plenary discussions. The interactive group work carried over into the online forum. Over the course of the module with the high level of student engagement and the high level of tutor support it became obvious when work was not authentic because such submissions were easily recognisable as being overly general and did not reflect engagement with the module's specific teaching materials.

September 2020 to January 2021

However, by the summer of 2021, it became clear that we needed an approach that would be more sustainable for both students and staff over a longer period, as the ongoing pandemic made it clear that it would be some time before most students would be able to travel to the UK for a week-long on-campus delivery. We therefore redesigned the module in a way that would allow us to maintain the intensity and authenticity of the work – both over a slightly longer period but crucially by using the SDGs as an explicit teaching framework for management education. We did this by designing a new version of the module whereby the pre-course work was delivered over a four-week period, with students still submitting a formative assessment based on values and climate change but crucially with the pre-course work introducing the SDGs as a framework for leaders to engage with, and develop, more ethical, responsible, and sustainable businesses and other community-based organisations.

The original three-week delivery model was expanded to six weeks with an additional seventh week to enable students to complete their summative assessments. The teaching utilised the SDGs as a framework with each week looking at different goals, grouped around governance and partnerships (SDGs 16 and 17), planet (SDGs 6, 14, and 15) with climate action (SDG 13) considered separately, prosperity (focussing on SDG 12 and 7) and people (SDGs 1, 2, 3, 4, and 5). At the beginning of each week's study, students were provided with a tailored Teaching Resource Pack (TRP) to cover the week's learning materials. The TRP contains a link to a tutor-presented teaching video, the teaching slides but, again crucially, with hyperlinks to all the additional resources that the students required for their independent study each week. The individual TRPs include links to up to 50 resources (videos, academic readings, practitioner tools, news releases, and other relevant information) to support weekly study of that unit. Each week, students were asked to use one of the targets linked with one of that week's SDGs, to write a critical analysis of an issue that was relevant to them, based on five or six readings from the TRP. Students were encouraged to work with resources in depth and draw on ideas that were relevant to them related to their chosen SDG target. To engage leaders with action on the SDGs, students were asked to summarise what their organisation was already doing regarding the target chosen and to then highlight explicit recommendations that they could make to their organisation to deliver the target based on their learning that week.

February 2021 to April 2022

While using the SDG targets as a focus for student assessment work resulted in largely authentic work, some students were either increasingly reliant on the UN SDG resources or confused by which targets would be relevant to them. Either of these approaches resulted in less specific submissions which weakened student engagement and success. This led to the third evolution of the module. With each of the weekly TRPs, the students were given an 'set assessment exercise' to work on for that week. The set assessment exercise builds week by week into a portfolio which is their final summative assessment. To make the assessment work more specific, each class has an original set of assessment questions each based on ideas from the relevant SDG targets and linked to the teaching. With classes starting every four weeks, and up to four classes running concurrently, this means that any written work being sourced externally may be a good answer to the wrong question and lacking both depth and an explicit response to the specific question asked. The inclusion of a specific question has also helped some students to focus and improve their written work, and has improved their ability to critically analyse specific ideas.

To support students with their academic skills, while reducing any perceived need for external ghost writing and empower students to have the skills required for MBA study, significant tutor support is provided. This includes detailed formative feedback on the pre-course work, but in addition students are invited to send the tutor an example of one of their draft set assessment exercises within the first three weeks of teaching. This enables the tutor to make sure their work is on the right track as well as providing students with support to strengthen the final submission. Often, the support that students require is to make better use of the readings linked from the TRP as some students still draw predominantly on more general external resources that are not related to the assessment. The tutor needs to consider each piece of work individually and make time for guidance, but the tutor must also question the approach the student has taken, and why they would have taken that approach. For example, it is very clearly stated in the overall assessment brief, in all the tutorial slides and in each weekly set assessment exercise that students should focus on resources linked from the weekly TRP to answer the question. If the work does draw instead on dated or generic resources, the tutor must question why the student would take such an approach. In such as case, this suggests that the submission may have been written by a third-party author or that the student has not en-gaged with the teaching. The student would subsequently be invited to a one-to-one video meeting to discuss the approach they are taking to their module studies. Having this conversation enables the student and tutor to discuss any potential misunderstandings, and to let the student know that the tutor is available if any further clarifications are needed. This also enables the tutor to remind the student they are expected to use appropriate resources and to explain that making effective use of them helps to demonstrate their depth of learning and critical thinking. Another possible explanation is that the student may not be preparing the work themselves and is instead buying a generic literature review. A discussion with students about their choice of resources can help to identify this type of malpractice. When considering the authenticity of a student's submission, there are cases where the student ap-pears to have purchased a literature review but may have written the ac-companying reflection, methodology, or findings themselves. In such instances, the tutor would be able to identify discrepancies in the standard and style of writing between different parts of the submitted work.

In addition to providing formative feedback within the module, aca-demic clarity is provided so that students feel supported, particularly those who might otherwise turn to cheating either because they do not understand the assignment brief or that they have doubts about the availability of the tutor to discuss such matters (Ali et al., 2021). Weekly online tutorials further support each part of the summative assessment and help the tutor build a relationship with individual students – and for students to develop a personal commitment to the tutor and the class. The unfairness of cheating is addressed explicitly in week 1, as part of the SDG teaching on leadership and good governance. In addition, effort is acknowledged in the assessment process by encouraging students to include their online forum posts in the appendixes of their final report. The forum discussion is guided each week through reflective in-teaching activities (prompts) within the TRPs that ask students to reflect on their own experience and to share this on the forum. While the posts are optional, inclusion in the report can support their demonstration of experiential learning and, again, further develop the sense of the class being empowered and enabled to work and learn together.

SDG teaching framework

The SDGs form a useful framework for engaging students from around the world, and from different sectors and sizes of organisations, to explore issues of ethics, responsibility, and sustainability. From the first tutorial, students quickly start to think in terms of their own ethical decision making in relation to corporate social responsibility (CSR). Students are encouraged to explore responsibility from a personal perspective as an individual who operates at different levels within society from discerning consumers and engaged citizens to active agents within supply chains or as leaders and managers working in larger corporate entities. Within this frame, students are encouraged to examine CSR through a critical lens and to actively explore who is responsible and what they are responsible for, seeing responsibility as a broader concept which can start with the individual and extend to a whole community or a distant global corporation, while exploring who has the power, urgency and legitimacy to act (Parent and Deephouse, 2007).

Below are several example of student feedback:

> '*I understand that as an individual I cannot change the world on my own, but I can take responsibility for my actions. I now question every new business proposal and ask 'Is this ethical?, Would I take responsibility?, Is this sustainable?*''

> '*I have come to realise that every decision is always partnered with the effects and consequences of its actions. As a leader, the responsibility is not limited to profitability, but I must be ethically accountable for my actions. Knowledge and awareness of oneself and others are essential to sustain survival.*'

'The world belongs to us all and it is the responsibility of every living person, myself included, to preserve and protect our environment for us and generations to come.'

The module also invites students to investigate the global-local nature of sustainability challenges, and the SDGs offer a suitable framework in this regard. Previous work by Williams (2021) has shown how the SDGs can be applied from large to small organisations, and how organisations can anchor the SDGs into the values of the organisation. The pre-course work introduces the SDGs as a global agenda with business at the heart of delivery (after Scheyvens et al., 2016). This is supported by exploring how our individual values help us to filter information, frame our worldviews and motivate our action; in other words, our sensemaking (after Weick, 1995). In the pre-course unit, we use climate change as an example of why we disagree about complex sustainability issues and students are encouraged to carry out a simplified, qualitative-based Schwartz Value System survey (Williams and Preston 2018) to reflect on. Students explore their 11 value priorities and which three values are most important to them, what the experiences and influences are that shape those values and how those values are linked to how they think and act on the issues inherent in the SDGs.

Examples of student feedback include:

'Open-mindedness and a willingness to learn from and understand the beliefs and values of others help me to see issues from different perspectives, and to arrive at solutions that might be framed to appeal to people with different interests and values.'

'I have realised how curiosity motivates me and how, in my opinion, it is very important for us to be inquisitive and find new and innovative ways to do things. We may not have a solution today, but if we are mindful of our environment and our society, this value would help us evolve with critical thinking abilities.'

The module does not look at all the SDGs in detail. To start, students explore SDG 16 and the role of leadership and governance in addressing issues of ethics, responsibility, and sustainability. The teaching then moves on to explore three of the planet-oriented SDGs (SDG 6 (Clean Water and Sanitation), SDG 14 (Life Below Water), and SDG 15 (Life on Land)) and focuses on the recent and rapid decline of biodiversity as a theme related to each of these three goals. Students are encouraged to look at recent and developing work on why biodiversity is important to human society, as well as organisational approaches to reduce the impact of human activities on biodiversity loss, to identify where harm is created, how to cause less harm, and, ultimately, to the creation of positive net benefit.

There is then an explicit return to climate issues, while acknowledging that climate change is related to the megatrends driving sustainability, including biodiversity loss. In focusing on SDG 13 (Climate Action), the teaching uses climate change as an example of a global issue that can be experienced and made sense of at a local level. Students are encouraged to build on the work from the TRP by bringing in research that shows how climate change is likely to impact their own region and any research that might suggest how the region could respond, acknowledging that the focus of climate action is on building resilience and adapting to the changes that are already underway or on the horizon. Students are invited to add a photograph that represents their personal experience of climate change to a global map (in Padlet) and add a brief narrative. Students also interact with other exercises that reflect on what the generations above them are saying about climate change, the landscapes they see changing and the issues they see their organisations and communities may face. They also explore how they could take a leadership role in supporting their communities with the help they need to adapt to these changes through acknowledging the information and help they would need to achieve this. This is a week where authentic work also becomes more obvious in that external copywriters tend to focus either on defining what climate change is, discussing whether climate change exists or mainly talking discussing mitigation ideas. Those students who have engaged with the teaching are much more likely to at least try to look at how climate change is likely to affect their own region and what can be done to support communities in adapting to the changes that are increasingly evident.

With regards to SDG 12 (Responsible Consumption and Production) and SDG 7 (Affordable and Clean Energy), the teaching comes from the perspective of resource efficiency and how models developed from the waste hierarchy (EU Waste Framework Directive) have evolved into the circular economy (Esposito et al., 2018) and where ideas may be drawn from the 'Blue Economy' (Pauli, 2010) to emphasise local solutions that create abundance. For example, implementing marine biodiversity protection areas as part of facilitating the restoration of delta and costal ecosystems can help promote sustainable practices, livelihoods, and cultures (Bax, 2021). Climate change is also addressed in this unit, by linking resource efficiency and the circular economy to ideas to mitigate future climate change by decoupling resource use and carbon consumption from production.

By week 5 the focus is on the people-oriented SDGs (SDGs 1 to 5) along with an element of revision, where models introduced earlier in the module are revisited through the lens of human impacts. The readymade garment (RMG) sector in Bangladesh is used as a case study to look at people issues and from there Kate Raworth's ideas about Doughnut Economics (Raworth, 2017) are introduced. The tutorial explores how these ideas build on the idea of planetary boundaries (Rockström et al., 2009) and links to Maslow's hierarchy of needs which students are largely familiar with, and the Five Capitals model of Jonathan Porritt (2007) in order to understand the importance of all of the people-oriented SDGs and how they relate to each other, such that undermining people's ability to work undermines their ability to eat and to have shelter, and access to healthcare and education.

In the final week, there is a return to issues of governance with a focus on SDG 17 (Partnerships for the Goals). Week 6 emphasises leadership and partnership thereby topping and tailing the module with two cross-cutting themes that hold the rest of the module together and reflect the original emphasis on leadership and partnership in the on-campus residential. Week 6 takes a personal approach to partnerships for the SDGs by acknowledging that all partnerships and other collaborative arrangements begin as interpersonal relationships between individuals (Stott and Murphy, 2020; Murphy and Stott, 2021). All partnerships – from global multistakeholder partnerships to local community networks – are based on relationships that are forged and developed by people with their own values, worldviews, motivations, needs, attributes, and capabilities. One of the key messages of week 6 is that we bring ourselves to all our relationships, whether they are in the home, at work, in the community or indeed when we represent our organisations and the issues that we care about in cross-sector social interactions for sustainable development. At the end of week 6, we encourage our students to consider the power and potential of SDG 17 and invite them to reflect on this question: *How do we develop the partnerships that we need (or may not yet know we need) to help us to deliver our personal, organisational, and wider community commitments towards the SDGs?* Tutor interactions with business and other organisational leaders and managers throughout the module are aligned with PRME Principle 5 (Partnership) as it enable us to 'extend our knowledge of their challenges in meeting social and environmental responsibilities and to explore jointly effective approaches to meeting these challenges' (PRME, 2007).

Final reflections on the use of the SDGs in authentic assessment

The module captures the intensity of the original week-long, on-campus residential, and students find the course challenging but also relevant and rewarding. The teaching takes an empowering approach, acknowledging that students need to feel inspired to act. Otherwise, the enormity of the issues we face as a planet can become overwhelming and disempowering, and as students and management professionals, they risk becoming demotivated and disengaged from global challenges if they do not feel they can make a difference. In each week of their study, students are asked to identify three specific ideas from the learning (with each idea clearly presented, specific, and referenced) that they could carry forward into their organisation or community.

Once more several examples of student feedback:

> *Virtual communication was not just to network with other students, but academically valuable for clarifying some challenges while studying. Furthermore,*

group discussion was an excellent method to make the students feel like a student despite distant learning and time differences. The feeling of being in a group motivates everyone to network and be more aware of individualities. Our accountability towards our surroundings made us mindful that, as social beings, we need each other.

While there can be a tension between writing a business case for their organisation and writing a good assessment answer, students are asked to anchor the final report in their own organisation by using the introduction to identify their organisation, to lay out the scope of the report in relation to the organisation and to explain their individual role within it. After carrying out a 400-word critical analysis in answer to a specific question based on five or six readings from the weekly TRP, students then outline the current efforts of their organisation related to the issue. For example, if the organisation is not doing anything to address biodiversity, they are expected to say so, but they are still expected to outline the organisation's major impacts on biodiversity. Or if they do have policies in place to ensure good governance and clear leadership policies, the students are expected to outline what these are. Many students find the invitation to research how the SDGs are already applied within their organisations to be a rewarding part of the assignment.

The final part of their assessment each week is to identify three specific ideas from the linked TRP resources and to outline explicitly how they could carry that idea forward to improve practice. The inclusion of specific re-commendations helps students demonstrate their experiential learning as well as empower and enable them to make global issues local. Given the number of students engaged through the module, each cohort (up to 50 per class) and the high proportion of students being in leadership roles (or aspiring leaders) within international, national, business, NGO and governmental organisa-tions, is reminded of the significant potential and opportunity that they have to make a difference. We find that students even within relatively small or-ganisations often have positions within a community that allows them to make a difference and they may be explicitly using their MBA studies to help lift their communities out of poverty. Even if students only genuinely apply a handful of the recommendations put forward, and engage other people with that implementation, the sheer number and quality of leaders on this module means that, together, the alumni are making a difference – and students find that empowering. At the end of the module, students have produced an action plan in which they have selected the SDGs to implement within their own organisations or communities.

Conclusion

In summary, the RME example discussed in this chapter is using the SDGs as a framework for teaching international students from 180 different countries about ethics, responsibility, and sustainability. The teaching demands that senior (or aspiring) leaders think about their own ethical decision making, about responsibility in its broadest sense – from the individual to the supply chain, and the extent to which their personal and organisational actions are promoting sustainable development for people, planet, and prosperity. In doing so, the module has moved beyond replicating an authentic on-campus experience to developing a successful model of teaching that is using authentic assessment to engage business and other organisational leaders with real-word issues, delivered within the framework of the SDGs and consistent with the six PRME principles. This authenticity starts with students anchoring the assessment work in their role within their own organisation or community, and then very specifically engages them with teaching, which is up to date, relevant and inclusive, and with explicit and specific tasks that all link to real life. In addition, the exercise of writing a business report under time and work pressures and other constraints within a global pandemic is an authentic task within the business world. Student answers need to be specific and make use of module resources with a focus on depth of answer to demonstrate their understanding, along with appropriate academic skills such as critical analysis and application to their own context. This helps to keep the work authentic and to encourage students to engage with the SDGs as a framework for applying and implementing sustainability initiatives within their own organisations.

References

Ali, H.I.H. and Alhassan, A. (2021). 'Fighting contract cheating and ghostwriting in Higher Education: Moving towards a multidimensional approach,' *Cogent Education*, 8(1), 1–18.

Ali, S., Naseer, S. and Nadeem, A. (2021). 'Perceived teachers' support and academic achievement: Mediating role of students' satisfaction with online learning in medical and non-medical students during covid-19,' ASEAN Journal of Psychiatry, 22(9), 1–10.

Amigud, A. (2020). 'Cheaters on Twitter: An analysis of engagement approaches of contract cheating services,' *Studies in Higher Education*, 45(3), pp. 692–705

Bax, N., Novaglio, C., Maxwell, K.H. et al. (2021). 'Ocean resource use: Building the coastal blue economy,' *Reviews in Fish Biology and Fisheries*, 32, 189–207.

Custer, R.L. and Schell, J.W. (2000). Using authentic assessment in vocational education (No. 381). ERIC Clearinghouse on Adult, Career, and Vocational Education, Center on Education and Training for Employment, College of Education, the Ohio State University.

Esposito, M., Tse, T. and Soufani, K. (2018). 'Introducing a circular economy: New thinking with new managerial and policy implications,' *California Management Review*, 60 (3), pp. 5–19. 10.1177/0008125618764691

European Commission (2008). 'EU Waste Framework Directive, Waste Hierarchy,', *Directive 2008/98/EC of the European Parliament and of the Council of 19 November 2008 on waste and repealing certain Directives (Text with EEA relevance)* Brussels: EC DG

Environment, https://ec.europa.eu/environment/topics/waste-and-recycling/waste-framework-directive_en

Gulikers, J., Bastiaens, T.J. and Kirschner, P.A. (2004). 'A five-dimensional framework for authentic assessment,' *Educational Technology Research and Development*, 52(3), pp. 67–86. https://ec.europa.eu/environment/topics/waste-and-recycling/waste-framework-directive_en

Hurford, G. (2019). 'Promoting responsible leadership and sustainability: A case study in management education,' in Sharma, R.R. (ed.) *Human resource management for organizational sustainability*, New York: Business Expert Press, pp.177–184.

Hurford, G. and Chapman, P. (2018). 'Let's get sustainable: a five-day MBA residency adventure,' in Steffen, S.L., Rezmovits, J., Trevenna, S. and Rappaport, Shana (eds.) *Evolving leadership for collective wellbeing: Lessons for implementing the united nations sustainable development goals*. Bingley, UK: Emerald Publishing, pp. 313–329.

McCarthy, C. (2021). 'Address the rise in contract cheating amid the virtual learning environment,' *Student Affairs Today*, 24(1), pp. 1–5.

Murphy, D.F. and Stott, L., (eds.) (2021). *Partnerships for the sustainable development goals (SDGs)*. Basel: MDPI Books.

Newton, P.M. (2018). 'How common is commercial contract cheating in higher education and is it increasing? A systematic review,' In *Frontiers in Education*, 3(67), pp. 1–18, 10.3389/feduc.2018.00067

Parent, M.M. and Deephouse, D.L. (2007). 'A case study of stakeholder identification and prioritization by managers,' *Journal of Business Ethics*, 75(1), pp. 1–23.

Pauli, G.A. (2010). *The blue economy: 10 years, 100 innovations, 100 million jobs*. Taos, New Mexico: Paradigm Publications.

Porritt, J. (2007). *Capitalism as if the world matters*. London: Routledge.

PRME (2007). *Principles for responsible management education*. New York: UN Global Compact.

Raworth, K. (2017). *Doughnut economics: Seven ways to think like a 21st-Century economist*. London: Random House Business.

Rockström, J., Steffen, W., Noone, K., Persson, Å., Chapin, F.S., Lambin, E., Lenton, T.M., Scheffer, M., Folke, C., Schellnhuber, H.J., Nykvist, B., de Wit, C.A., Hughes, T., van der Leeuw, S., Rodhe, H., Sörlin, S., Snyder, P.K., Costanza, R., Svedin, U., … Foley, J. (2009). 'Planetary boundaries: Exploring the safe operating space for humanity,' *Ecology and Society*, 14(2), pp. 32. https://www.ecologyandsociety.org/vol14/iss2/art32/ http://www.jstor.org/stable/26268316

Rowland, S., Slade, C., Wong, K.S. and Whiting, B. (2018). '"Just turn to us': The persuasive features of contract cheating websites,' *Assessment & Evaluation in Higher Education*, 43(4), pp. 652–665.

Stott, L. and Murphy, D.F. (2020). 'An inclusive approach to partnerships for the SDGs: Using a relationship lens to explore the potential for transformational collaboration,' *Sustainability*, 12(19), pp. 7905, 10.3390/su12197905.

Sagiv, L., Roccas, S., Cieciuch, J. and Schwartz, S.H. (2017). 'Personal values in human life,' *Nature Human Behaviour*, 1(9), pp. 630–639.

Schaefer, A., Williams, S. and Blundel, R. (2020). 'Individual values and SME environmental engagement,' *Business & Society*, 59(4), pp. 642–675.

Scheyvens, R., Banks, G. and Hughes, E. (2016). 'The private sector and the SDGs: The need to move beyond 'business as usual',' *Sustainable Development*, 24(6), pp. 371–382.

Sokhanvar, Z., Salehi, K. and Sokhanvar, F. (2021). 'Advantages of authentic assessment for improving the learning experience and employability skills of higher education students: A systematic literature review,' *Studies in Educational Evaluation*, 70, p. 101030.

Villarroel, V., Boud, D., Bloxham, S., Bruna, D. and Bruna, C. (2020). 'Using principles of authentic assessment to redesign written examinations and tests,' *Innovations in Education and Teaching International*, 57(1), pp. 38–49.

Villarroel, V., Bloxham, S., Bruna, D., Bruna, C. and Herrera-Seda, C. (2018). 'Authentic assessment: creating a blueprint for course design,' *Assessment & Evaluation in Higher Education*, 43(5), pp. 840–854.

Walker, M. and Townley, C. (2012). 'Contract cheating: A new challenge for academic honesty?,' *Journal of Academic Ethics*, 10(1), pp. 27–44.

Weick, K.E. (1995). *Sensemaking in Organizations: 3.* (Foundations for Organizational Science). London: Sage.

Williams, S. (2021). 'The changing nature of CSR in practice – Learning from each other: How UK-based MNEs are engaging with the SDGs and what SMEs can learn,' *9th Annual Responsible Business Research seminar*, 17–18 March 2021 (online). Hosted by Tampere University, Finland.

Williams, S. and Preston, D. (2018). 'Working with values: An alternative approach to win-win,' *International Journal of Corporate Strategy and Social Responsibility*, 1(4), pp. 302–319.

Williams, S., Kofinas, A. and Minett-Smith, C. (2018). 'Developing live projects as part of an assessment regime within a dispersed campus model,' *Journal of Pedagogic Development*, 8(2), 3–7.

11 Matters of measuring: Student learning and success in sustainability education

Lauren Verheijen

Introduction

A conversation with nearly any business owner will sooner or later touch upon the issue of profit: what is the business case for sustainability? Aside from the issue of staying afloat within our current socio-economic system, an underlying theme is that profit is very easily measurable and that in this world 'what can be measured, matters.' Along this trend, implementing sustainability in business has taken the turn to assessment and accounting to show the magnitude of positive impacts or rather by how much negative impacts have decreased. While it is good to see the increased attention towards societal impact, these approaches to dealing with sustainability fail to acknowledge the quality of impact (e.g., what if 200 trees were planted for CO_2 compensation, but none survived due to the depleted ecosystem?) and incites a cycle of only accounting for impact on those components that are already measurable.

When turning to education – specifically management education – a similar issue arises. Higher (management) education institutions have embraced a similar mentality by assessing the institution's societal impact in terms of alignment with the Sustainable Development Goals (SDGs) by presenting elaborate overviews of initiatives that contribute positively to society. One example is Rotterdam School of Management's *Positive Change* initiative, complete with an SDG dashboard, contributions from students, alumni and employees, Massive Open Online Courses and publications on business sustainability (RSM, n.d.). While the increasing acknowledgment of educational institutions' societal impact is a good development in terms of broader societal awareness, it misses a pertinent opportunity for impact: student learning and development. As with the business case for sustainability, not addressing student learning and development directly as an opportunity for impact again highlights an ignorance for the quality of impact that is made as well as the danger of accounting only for already measurable components. Student learning and development is unique to the individual student and may not always be directly measurable. Even if attempts were made to capture learning and development in a measurement, it might not always be

DOI: 10.4324/9781003244905-15

possible to formulate a quality measurement for learning and development. When a student receives a grade for a project or exam, what does that really say about what the student learnt, how they learnt, or how they developed?

This chapter advocates for taking seriously how student learning and development is conceptualised and operationalised in the context of sustainable development. Currently, education is highly outcome-oriented, favouring measurable indicators of success so that there is comparability within education as well as certainty towards the industry regarding what quality of students they can expect while educational institutions function as 'the centrepiece on the "supply side" of business talent' (Morsing, 2021, p. 4). However, with the turn towards preparing students to tackle societal (sustainability) challenges, including the introduction of, for example, UNESCO's Education for Sustainable Development (ESD) and the United Nation's (UN) Principles for Responsible Management Education (PRME), education aims to drive the market by enabling student development and learning that cultivate citizens and professionals that dare to challenge the status quo, rather than education being market driven. This chapter moves forward to first understand the way that learning is conceptualised in two key streams within ESD and PRME: that of competency development and transformative learning. Secondly, the function of assessment as well as its (so far limited) operationalisation for sustainability education is explored. At the end of the chapter several suggestions for future research and action are presented.

Conceptions of learning

Transformation of management education is linked closely to the PRME movement, which emphasises the necessity of management education institutions to recognise and enact upon their societal responsibility through six key principles (Purpose, Values, Method, Research, Partnership, and Dialogue). The aim of this vision is to cultivate pioneers of responsible management and responsible management education (RME) and educate societally responsible leaders. Likewise, UNESCO aims to realise ESD as transformative, as well as learner-centred, action-oriented, and competency-based education (Leicht et al., 2018). In doing so, UNESCO advocates for 'holistic and transformational education that addresses learning content and outcomes, pedagogy and learning environment' (UNESCO, 2017, p. 7), taking into account the entire learning journey of the student. While PRME places more emphasis on these key values through identifying such pioneers as outcome, ESD highlights the processes of education more directly in its ambitions. Within both these proposals two vast traditions of educational research are built upon: competency development and transformative learning. Both streams are briefly explored to understand what learning means, both in terms of the process and outcomes, in the context of sustainability education, focusing specifically on PRME and ESD.

Competency development

The past decade has seen a growing emphasis on competencies for sustainable development that should be developed by students to become well-versed sustainability citizens and professionals. Competencies are generally understood as a desired educational outcome (Gardiner and Rieckmann, 2015; Jarchow et al., 2018; Lozano et al., 2017; Wiek et al., 2015). Within the ESD debate, competencies are understood as a trifecta of skills, knowledge and attitudes a professional should develop capacity in to tackle sustainable development issues. Leicht et al. further separate this into the division of 'knowledge and skills' as well as 'values and motivations' (2018, p. 46). While holding these capacities is one matter, enacting them is another and requires a context that enables the individual to respond to a situation or challenge (Glaesser, 2019).

Within the PRME discussion little reference is made to competencies explicitly. Given the similar aims of PRME and ESD, a few words are dedicated to contextualising PRME here in relation to competency development. The six key PRME principles relate to both the development of students, as well as the role of the educational institutions. Notably, principle 1 (Purpose) highlights the student: 'We will develop the capabilities of students to be future generators of sustainable value for business and society at large and to work for an inclusive and sustainable economy' (PRME, 2022). Here a reference is made to capability rather than competency, yet the definition of competency as outlined within the ESD debate remains applicable here. These six principles have furthermore been translated to the CAMB competency model of cognitive (C), affective (A), moral (M), and behavioural (B) competencies for students, educators, and professionals (Sharma, 2017). In relation to this model the nature of competencies is outlined as knowledge, skills, and behaviour as visible components, as well as values, motives, and traits as hidden components. As such, the understanding of competencies remains relatively consistent between PRME and ESD, although their application varies.

Two key frameworks of key sustainability competencies dominate the ESD discussion. The first is presented by Wiek et al. (2011), the most cited ESD competency framework to date, which demonstrates five key competencies in an integrated framework. The second is that presented by UNESCO (2017) and elaborated on by Leicht et al. (2018), which is an overview of eight key sustainability competences (KSC). The overlap and differences between the two sets of competencies are shown in Table 11.1. While UNESCO's list is slightly more elaborate, it may read as a checklist. Wiek et al., on the other hand, bring forward a framework that demonstrates integration between competencies, pointing more towards the holistic ambitions of ESD. In any case, both competency frameworks – as well as the many others that have been proposed over the last decade – indicate what the intended outcomes are of ESD.

Table 11.1 The overlap and differences between the key sustainability competencies (as presented by Wiek et al. (2011) and Leicht et al. (2018))

Key Sustainability Competencies	
Wiek et al. (2011)	*Leicht et al. (2018)*
Systems Thinking Competency	
Anticipatory Competency	
Strategic Competency	
Normative Competency	
Interpersonal Competency	Collaboration Competency
	Critical Thinking Competency
	Self-Awareness Competency
	Critical Thinking Competency

However, the problem of operationalisability arises once educators attempt to implement these competencies. As Wiek and Redman (2022) point out, the literature highlights elaborate negotiation on which list or competency framework is most suitable for ESD. Brundiers et al. (2021) attempted to close off this discussion with a Delphi study amongst sustainability education experts, yet still little work has been done on the further operationalisation of any competency list or framework. This includes UNESCO, who after pitching the KSC has done no further development on developing learning objectives and activities beyond education per SDG (UNESCO, 2017). Most other instances in literature where competences have been implemented in education refer to either course design (Hesselbarth and Schaltegger, 2014), retroactively assessing competencies as tool for ESD alignment (Remington-Doucette et al., 2013) or assessing the framework's application to specific student project types (e.g., reflective journaling for self-awareness) (Gardiner and Rieckmann, 2015). Wiek et al. (2015) go one step further to classify mastery levels (novice, intermediate, advanced) based on the extent to which students reflect on their competency development process. Yet, all these proposals remain separated from the educational practice and student learning journey itself. Furthermore, the translation from identified and possible connections between KSC and education to assessment in educational practise remains unaddressed (Cebrián et al., 2020; Redman et al., 2021; Wiek and Redman, 2022).

The assessment of competencies within educational practice is certainly no easy task. As introduced, competencies are complex, covering the three dimensions of skills, knowledge, and attitude. Additionally, it is difficult to pinpoint the development of a competency as this is asymmetric with enacting on that competency. When we then assess competencies, should we focus on the disposition to act? Must students demonstrate an act as outcome of a competency alone, or also be reflective towards that process? Or should we focus on a student's reflective capacities as precursors to developing competencies? Yet, even if we are able to answer these questions, while the ESD proposal emphasises a holistic approach, the focus on competencies reflects a hefty weight on the outcomes, the end-goals of the student's learning journey. Beckett (2004) outlines that assessing competency development requires being sensitive to both the process as much as the learning outcomes. To bring further to the foreground the process of learning, the transformative learning dimension of ESD is further explored, as well as how it has been applied within the PRME context.

Transformative learning

According to Mezirow, transformative learning 'is the process of effecting change in a frame of reference' (1997, p. 1), a process which is divided across 10 learning phases (Figure 11.1). While transformative learning is the commonly used term, it was originally referred to as 'perspective transformation' by Mezirow. In the context of sustainability challenges this approach to learning highlights the opportunities to challenge accepted norms and the status quo to explore new possibilities, trajectories, and societal innovation. Students undertake transformative learning as an active form of learning by working through critical reflection and freely exploring their best judgment. In doing so they develop an awareness of their own frames of reference, while also reframing and applying these in their own lives in relation to the dilemmas that the individual faces. In this way individual transformation goes hand-in-hand with societal transition.

The relevance of the abovementioned competencies as outcomes of ESD is clear when acknowledging the sensemaking process of transformative learning: 'To become meaningful, learning requires that new information be incorporated by the learner into an already well-developed symbolic frame of

---

10 Phases of Transformative Learning
1. A disorienting dilemma
2. Self-examination with feelings of fear, anger, guilt or shame
3. A critical assessment of assumptions
4. Recognition that one's discontent and the process of transformation are shared
5. Exploration of options for new roles, relationships and action
6. Planning a new course of action
7. Acquiring knowledge and skills for implementing one's plans
8. Provisional trying of new roles
9. Building competence and self-confidence in new roles and relationships
10. A reintegration into one's life on the basis of conditions dictated by one's new perspective

Figure 11.1 Ten phases of transformative learning (adapted from Mezirow (2005)).

reference, an active process involving thought, feelings, and disposition' (Mezirow, 1997, p. 10). The process of learning here involves three dimensions that can be linked to the three elements of key competencies: thought to knowledge, feelings to values and attitude, and disposition to skills and behaviour. Yet, when further evaluating the connection between transformative learning and ESD, there is no emphasis on outcomes other than the aim to 'empower learners to question and change the ways they see and think about the world in order to deepen their understanding of it' (UNESCO, 2017, p. 55). As was shown with the competencies, extensive work has been done on conceptualisation of transformative learning, ranging from the 10 phases of transformative learning as outlined by Mezirow (1997), to Hoggan's typology of transformative learning outcomes (2016) synthesised from literature on transformative learning, and the recent attempt by Savicki and Price (2021) to make transformative learning success measurable through analysis.

Here, again, a delicate dance is performed between retroactive analysis of student development and the comfortable attempt to classify learning outcomes. Although transformative learning has diluted over the years (Hoggan (2016) proposes that it now functions as metatheory), when looking at the original proposal by Mezirow, there is no reference to assessment through the 10 phases of transformative learning. Rather, evaluating the success of the process is related to the stability of the change in perspective through reflecting on one's sensemaking processes, and the agency to do so:

> The theory's focus is on how we learn to negotiate and act on our own purposes, values, feelings, and meanings rather than those we have uncritically assimilated from others – to gain greater control over our lives as socially responsible, clear-thinking decision makers.
>
> (Mezirow, 2000, pp. 7–8)

Undoubtedly, (critical) reflection is a core component of the transformative learning process. A proposal referred to in PRME literature that constructively takes into account the continuous reflective processes embedded in transformative learning is that of the sustainability mindset as:

> a way of thinking and being that results from a broad understanding of the ecosystem's manifestations as well as an introspective focus on one's personal values and higher self, and finds its expression in actions for the greater good of the whole.
>
> (Kassel et al., 2016, p. 8)

Alike competencies, this approach appreciates that learning for sustainability is more than knowledge, while also going beyond by embracing the process dimension of sustainability learning through the lens of a mindset. Hermes and Rimanoczy (2018) explored the translation of the sustainability mindset to course design by specifying three key themes (developing awareness, exploring paradigms and action) and connecting these with types of projects that might fit pedagogy for the sustainability mindset (as do Fairfield (2018) and Rimanoczy (2021)). However, as with the KSC, no assessment formats have been established as of yet that are suitable to these student projects and that simultaneously encapsulate the development of that which is coined the sustainability mindset. An assessment tool to measure the sustainability mindset in students has in fact been developed (Rimanonczy and Klingenberg, 2020), yet the question of integration into educational practice and constructive course alignment within management education still stands.

Bringing transformative learning further to the foreground in conceptions of ESD as a core descriptor of the learning process will help move ESD away from the outcome orientation within education. Doing so is no radical proposal, as transformative learning is already present in UNESCO's conceptions of ESD (Leicht et al., 2018). Likewise, in the case of RME specifically, PRME still provides a fertile ground to grow the emphasis on transformative learning through for example the principles of purpose and value. Shining a brighter light on student learning and development in sustainability education can be achieved by placing more weight on proposals such as the sustainability mindset or shifting the competency development indicators away from outcomes towards the process of learning. In both cases the reflectivity of the students and how they articulate any shifts in their perspectives decidedly play a key role with regards to classifying any transformative change in students. However, to avoid falling again in the same trap of measuring the ability to articulate reflection processes rather than measuring quality of actual development, it is pertinent to look beyond how students present their reflection process and instead move towards evaluating the developmental process itself – leaving aside for a moment the question of whether it is then still necessary to assess the student.

The function of assessment

The previous sections explored the current state of understanding regarding learning, as it is linked to outcomes, learning process, and assessment, within ESD and PRME. This chapter moves towards a research agenda and call to action within educational practise regarding the role of assessment within sustainability education. To do so it is crucial to first revisit the function that assessment currently plays within (higher) education to then identify potential conflicts with RME and ESD aims.

Assessment, when standardised, ensures comparability and predictability. Particularly in the European Union, the introduction of the Bologna Process sought coherence across higher educational institutions in the European Higher Education Area (EHEA) with the European Credit System (ECTs) (European Consortium for Accreditation, 2014). The benefit of this system is that it facilitates a consistent approach across institutions that enables comparability and supports predictability in education. This is useful for both prospective students looking to apply to university or switch courses within a university, and for the industry to recognise with what expertise and qualifications graduates apply to their job offerings. While the UK and USA hold different standardised credit systems, and other universities may apply a 'local credits' policy, the principle of standardised comparability remains the same. For an outcome-oriented education approach, this is a dream. However, for any education emphasising transformative learning and student development, this seems a nightmare.

For the credit system to work there must be measurable success markers as output for every course, whether that be learning objectives, competency profiles or otherwise. For example, in the management education context specifically, a student graduating from a Master's in Business Administration should hold all the qualities necessary to function as an adequate manager. In doing so, the diploma functions as a quality marker for the student as well as the industry. This may be likened with the economic model of education (Laurie et al., 2016), where education is a key factor in economic development as it serves the market. Quality in education is then intimately linked to quantitative indicators such as enrolment, drop-out numbers, investment in education, and measurable student achievement through standardised indicators (Kadji-Beltran and Zachariou, 2022). In contrast, the emphasis on process and holistic student development discussed in previous sections (learner-centred, participative, and democratic) that is so crucial to ESD reflects a humanist paradigm of education. UNESCO (2004) refers to this educational paradigm explicitly as leading prior to the conception of ESD. Quality markers in this case are for instance personal goals, development of personal talent and wider social/societal goals. So, the overarching question now becomes: what kind of quality markers are relevant for ESD? And by extension, how can we shift to meaningful assessment for learning and development in ESD?

Assessment in sustainability education: the missing link

The issues regarding assessment in ESD are several-fold. Firstly, the competency approach to ESD mentioned earlier lacks operationalisability regarding how to assess student development of competencies. Established indicators for student success are missing, also for other proposals such as the sustainability mindset. Where they are available, they are retroactively attributed to student performance in relation to the ESD aims as a means of assessing course alignment (e.g., evaluating whether students demonstrate 'success' in relation to the KSC after completion of the course or program). Research thus far has primarily rested upon two main questions: (1) how to conceptualise markers of success (mastery levels) for sustainability professionals? and (2) have existing courses been effective in cultivating student learning towards becoming successful sustainability professionals?

In the previous section assessment was outlined as a quality marker for stability, comparability, and predictability. Yet, sustainability challenges are anything but stable. Rather, they are the hallmark of uncertainty, unpredictability, and complexity. Additionally, sustainability is a moving target (Kemp and Martens, 2007), so engaging with it demands that learners be resilient in the face of uncertainty (Sterling, 2010). Any and every element of sustainability education, from course design to assessment, must take this into account, and adequately address how the learner relates to this. So long as the 'end' of the learning journey is marked by an assessment – ignoring for a moment the contradiction with ESD's position towards lifelong learning – that is oriented towards uniform and stagnant markers of success, it is impossible to account for the dynamism of sustainability issues as well as how individual students position themselves and their own role against societal challenges.

To elaborate on this position, the typology of learning outcomes for transformative learning as proposed by Hoggan (2016) is constructive. Hoggan stipulates six categories of learning outcomes: worldview, self, epistemology, ontology, behaviour, and capacity. For each of these, Hoggan outlines that we should be looking for not just whether an incident (or learning activity) is transformative, but rather to what extent it is. Criteria to classify this may be the depth (How deep is the impact?), breadth (Does the impact exist across multiple contexts?), and stability (Is there evidence that the change is not temporary?). This typology indicates again the need to turn our attention towards understanding the process of transformation as well as the outcomes. Furthermore, it also highlights the profound intimacy between the learning outcomes and the individual's experience. Should there ever be a standardised approach towards assessing this type of learning, it must at the very least provide space for the individual to define their own outcomes in relation to the transformations they have undergone/are undergoing (or have been/are resistant to) and how this relates to their own sensemaking processes and lived experiences.

Moreover, so far the assumption has been that we should keep a form of assessment within educational practice, but maybe we need to ask the question that makes some educators squirm: do we even *need* assessment? The relevance of this question can be illustrated by the fact that in Mezirow's conception of transformative learning not one of the 10 phases refers to assessment. Maybe the ultimate measure of success of sustainability education should be to see societal challenges being addressed by our students, that our students enact on their agency and societal role by creating tangible impact? Assessment has a role in safeguarding the quality of education if it is market-driven, but what role does assessment play within the development of sustainability professionals?

All this together points towards various calls for further research and a call to action for those involved with (setting the stage for) educational practice to explore whether assessment, and if so, in what format would be most fruitful for ESD, PRME and sustainability education more broadly. The operationalisation of frameworks for learning within the ESD and PRME context is missing on a broad scale, as well as how to address this. To repeat the call made by Wiek and Redman (2022): we do not need more frameworks to conceptualise learning, competency frameworks, or further discussion about what exactly it entails to be a sustainability professional. Work needs to be done on integrating these conceptualisations and frameworks into educational practice. This cannot be done without determining which quality and in which terms we assess within education (Kadji-Beltran and Zachariou, 2022).

Moving forward: focus on learning rather than metrics

This chapter opened by exploring the limitations of output-oriented education, arguing that education that strives to contribute to sustainable development, whether it be management education or otherwise, should be emphasising learning process as well as the actual and ongoing development of students. This conception is also implicit in both the ESD approach and PRME under the mantra of transformative learning. There is however a contradiction with the way that assessment has been used thus far as marker for stability and uniformity within education. To provoke further exploration within sustainability education, several open-ended questions are posed that demand an answer. Therefore, to close this chapter, the various themes discussed are brought together to stipulate a call to action to chart and sail the unknown waters of assessment for sustainability education.

To start, further work is necessary on conceptualising the process of learning within the ESD context generally. Any approach to sustainability education that emphasises holistic, transformative, and learner-centred education should be founded upon an elaborate understanding of what it means to learn for sustainable development. It should substantiate what we aim for students to get out of ESD, or instead what we would like to see students engage in as sustainability citizens. In this vein, questions such as the following are relevant:

- What kind of learning and development is expected from students?
- How do students communicate and present their own learning and development?
- How are students expected to contribute to sustainable development?
- What do students define as 'success' in their own learning and development journeys?

This contrasts with the current approach, where end markers – in the form of a mindset, set of competencies or otherwise – are defined without much sensitivity towards the learning process. Any studies done in this regard should advocate the student perspective. A starting point, for example, is using student reflective journals as data or conducting focus groups or interviews with students to reflect on their development in courses. To take it a step further, students should also be actively engaged in the design of educational programmes based on their expectations of learning, passions they wish to activate and ways in which they hope to engage in sustainable development. If the learning and development of students is to be highly valued, this should be reflected through the co-creation of learning spaces and instructional methods from start to finish. Even within the current method of course design where teachers set learning outcomes or course objectives there is an immense amount of room for experimentation regarding the format of classes and the type of projects which students engage in, even for assessment.

Building on this, the role of assessment (if there is one) within the context of transformative learning as central tenet to ESD deserves careful scrutiny. Again, this follows the notion that the process of learning should be prioritised over the output. As mentioned, it is crucial to also give a voice to the student perspective on their understanding and use of current education and assessment frameworks as well as to be open to listening to their critiques on their use and adjusting these frameworks accordingly. The final question of the series listed above is a particularly important one. How various students define success may in fact be very different from one another, and especially in the context of transformative learning it is essential to provide room for individualised learning and development trajectories. Engaging in these conversations, by allowing students to design their own learning goals and grading forms, is an important starting point for the alignment between student learning and development and the operationalisation of sustainability education. Given that the topics of flexibilisation and personalisation of education are already prominent with regards to the choice of content and courses, why not extend this liberty further to allow students to truly become the drivers of their learning and development journey?

Asking students to define their own learning paths, set learning goals, determine measures of success and outline grading sheets is a daunting task for individuals who have never been exposed to this kind of 'freedom' and personalisation within their education. Of course, educators should be careful not to throw students in the deep end without any structure or guidance. However, rather than holding back on innovating assessment practice and pedagogy more broadly by engaging students in co-creation, perhaps it is more suitable to hold a discussion how continuity can be created within higher education, and with primary and secondary education, in line with societal sustainability demands.

The avenues mentioned so far all are confined to the wiggle room within the current educational structures and systems. These are important first steps to take to explore what is already possible. However, when businesses propose an incremental change or innovation these are dismissed as 'not enough' to address societal sustainability issues. Should the same expectations not be held for education? Incremental changes within the current educational structures undermine what is truly necessary to support societal transformation. This chapter has shown that there is a fundamental asymmetry between the goals of ESD, PRME, and sustainability education at large and the assessment structures within education. It is therefore essential to raise the question: is assessment a necessary component of sustainability education?

To move forward in answering this question, the underlying assumption that first needs to be addressed is the question: if there is an 'end' marker for success in sustainability, what is it? Sustainability is often understood as a moving target, for which there is no 'finish line' (contrary to what sustainability agendas such as the SDGs might presuppose). If that logic also applies to sustainability education, markers of success in the way that they have been used in assessment, such as meeting a minimum passing requirement, are nonsensical. Likewise, the competency debate explored earlier highlights a necessity to focus on the enactment of behaviour, attitude, and skills, and not just their development. This would indicate a need to evaluate students based on real societal impact and contribution towards sustainable development. Such a form of assessment may be termed *Transformation Assessment*, where the emphasis lies on the way in which the student's personal background (including perspectives and values), learning and development (in relation to sustainability competencies), and context come together in how the student engages with societal challenges as a way of demonstrating the transformative learning process. Doing so would require evaluating for instance a student's passion for a certain societal theme, determination to create societal impact and ability (both in terms of individual, but also enabled by the context) to act, if not having acted already. These elements resist measurement, and even if attempts were made to measure these: what value would that add?

Assessment as it is known in higher education does not capture such elements, traditional assessment has focused on the cognitive domains of 'knowing' or 'knowing how to use.' Various researchers have made bold steps in exploring non-traditional forms of assessment that either move away from traditional success metrics such as grades in favour of feedback loops and other qualitative assessment forms or explore new trends such as authentic and compassionate assessment. Further experimentation in operationalising the current competency frameworks by building on these growing bodies of research presents a fruitful opportunity to allow new assessment formats to bloom in both conceptualisation and operationalisation. Within the context of sustainable development there is increasing evidence of the need for learning in non-cognitive domains, emphasising the importance of for example emotions and collaboration, as several other chapters in this book have argued. Holistic assessment for these non-cognitive dimensions of learning should also be further explored. Another route is one already mentioned, namely allowing students to define success and have them lead the way in articulating what they would like to achieve in their courses. A third route is to explore what might happen if formal assessment is entirely removed from educational programs. This is not to say that there should never be any feedback given to students, but that the format may dramatically change.

One of the key criticisms to the introduction of more qualitative assessment, as well as the focus on assessing learning processes rather than outcomes, is that it is seen as more subjective. This certainly should not be ignored, but it is often forgotten that open question papers and exams have long been assessed by individuals and even multiple-choice exams as the holy grail of objectivity in assessment are written by humans, so there will always be an element of subjectivity. Objectivity may be protected by for instance the use of multiple assessors (from both within education and the professional field), as well as implementing different moments and types of assessment in a course. However, the flip side of the coin might be to ask how objectivity is beneficial once learning and assessment are contextualised based on the individual's personal transformation and engagement with societal challenges. In the assessment formats proposed here, the comparison between students is much less of an indicator of learning and development; rather the focus lies on how the individual evolves in relation to where they stood before. A similar critique is that if students are provided with the option to grade themselves, they may abuse the opportunity and all score themselves with top grades. Anecdotal evidence from conversations with fellow educators suggests the opposite, that many students translate self-criticism into grades lower than the educator would have awarded them. Instead of abusing the system, they have become more aware of their development and where mistakes and room for improvement may lie.

The research and action called for here is certainly a daunting one. It requires educators, and students, to step far outside their comfort zones and the safe harbours of predictability. Current practice in arts education may prove a useful starting point in this regard. Education in the arts emphasises the development of the individual's artistic practice rather than comparing the student to established markers of knowing or doing. Particularly education that crosses disciplines, even providing inter- or transdisciplinary education, wrestles with the question of assessment in a way that adequately aligns with all disciplines and may again provide further inspiration for sustainability education. Non-formal education – separated from the credit systems that supposedly safeguard quality in education – additionally is an area to explore best practices regarding educational innovation and the boundaries of what we consider education, particularly as these programs rarely hold any form of assessment.

And still, many of these proposals assume that assessment still has a role to play within education. It somehow seems unthinkable to allow the student to leave our educational institutions without any sort of markers that clearly communicate 'this student is ready for the "real world".' Yet, sustainability education is all about impact in the 'real world,' where transforming the individual perspectives and ways of doing goes hand-in-hand with societal transformation. This chapter has paved the entrance to a path by which further alignment between the ways of doing education and sustainability can be bettered. In sum, three main streams of research and action are advocated for here. First, the conceptualisation of transformative learning within sustainability must be strengthened. An important element of this is bringing the student voice to the foreground by, for example, co-creation of educational programmes between students and educators. Questioning the role of assessment within transformative learning is a second stream. In relation to this, it must become more transparent what the markers of success are within sustainability education and, even more importantly, what the markers of success are for the students regarding their learning and development. Developing *Transformation Assessment* as a form of holistic assessment that focuses on the student's engagement with societal sustainability challenges in both research and practice is an important step in this regard. Thirdly, while the possibilities within the current educational structures and systems should be explored, incremental change is not enough for sustainability. To truly transform society and the role education plays within it, the role of assessment within sustainability education should be fundamentally questioned and reimagined.

Concluding remarks

The aim of this chapter was to present an overview of the state of sustainability education as it is being implemented in practice, particularly highlighting assessment as the missing link for operationalisation. ESD is a holistic, transformative, learner-centred approach to education. If we, educators, are to take this seriously, we must also address the implementation of ESD in a holistic way. Simply stated, the directions towards measuring student success within ESD currently do not align with ESD ambitions or key principles. We must be willing to explore what happens to students' motivation and engagement with their learning process if we adjust the forms of assessment and entertain the idea of throwing assessment in the current teacher-student dynamic out of the window in favour of regular reflection check-ins and revision loops on projects. If the aim of education is to aid students in developing as autonomous, independent professionals and citizens, we must equip students with the capability and confidence to determine at what point they regard themselves as 'successful.' If the aim of sustainability education is to prepare students to become professionals with the competencies or mindset to address wicked problems such as societal sustainability issues, what better way to lead them into the unknowns and uncertainties of sustainability problem solving than to let them lead the way in determining what it is that they need. Whereas our current model of assessment supports predictability, certainty, and comparability, assessment for sustainability education should help us find comfort in uncertainty, reflection and reflexivity, and adaptability to context.

References

Beckett, D. (2004). 'Embodied competence and generic skill: The emergence of inferential understanding,' *Educational Philosophy and Theory*, 36(5), 497–508. 10.1111/j.1469-5812.2004.086_1.x

Brundiers, K., Barth, M., Cebrián, G., Cohen, M., Diaz, L., Doucette-Remington, S., Dripps, W., Habron, G., Harré, N., Jarchow, M., Losch, K., Michel, J., Mochizuki, Y., Rieckmann, M., Parnell, R., Walker, P. and Zint, M. (2021). 'Key competencies in sustainability in higher education—Toward an agreed-upon reference framework,' *Sustainability Science*, 16(1), 13–29. 10.1007/s11625-020-00838-2

Cebrián, G., Junyent, M. and Mulà, I. (2020). 'Competencies in education for sustainable development: Emerging teaching and research developments,' *Sustainability*, 12(2), 579. 10.3390/su12020579

European Consortium for Accreditation. (2014, March 10). *Framework for Qualifications of the European Higher Education Area*. ECA. http://www.ecahe.eu/w/index.php?title=Framework_for_Qualifications_of_the_European_Higher_Education_Area#Source

Fairfield, K. (2018). 'Educating for a sustainability mindset,' *Journal of Management for Global Sustainability*, 6(1), 21–44. 10.13185/JM2018.06102

Gardiner, S. and Rieckmann, M. (2015). 'Pedagogies of preparedness: Use of reflective journals in the operationalisation and development of anticipatory competence,' *Sustainability*, 7(8), 10554–10575. 10.3390/su70810554

Glaesser, J. (2019). 'Competence in educational theory and practice: A critical discussion,' *Oxford Review of Education*, 45(1), 70–85. 10.1080/03054985.2018.1493987

Hermes, J. and Rimanoczy, I. (2018). 'Deep learning for a sustainability mindset,' *The International Journal of Management Education*, 16(3), 460–467. 10.1016/j.ijme.2018.08.001

Hesselbarth, C. and Schaltegger, S. (2014). 'Educating change agents for sustainability – learnings from the first sustainability management master of business administration,' *Journal of Cleaner Production*, 62, 24–36. 10.1016/j.jclepro.2013.03.042

Hoggan, C. (2016). 'A typology of transformation: Reviewing the transformative learning literature,' *Studies in the Education of Adults*, 48(1), 65–82. 10.1080/02660830.2016.1155849

Jarchow, M.E., Formisano, P., Nordyke, S. and Sayre, M. (2018). 'Measuring longitudinal student performance on student learning outcomes in sustainability education,' *International Journal of Sustainability in Higher Education*, 19(3), 547–565. 10.1108/IJSHE-11-2016-0200

Kadji-Beltran, C. and Zachariou, A. (2022). 'ESD competences for deep quality in education,' in Vare, P., Lausselet, N. and Rieckmann, M. (eds.) *Competences in education for sustainable development: Critical perspectives*. Springer International Publishing, pp. 69–75. 10.1007/978-3-030-91055-6_9

Kassel, K., Rimanoczy, I. and Mitchell, S.F. (2016). 'The sustainable mindset: Connecting being, thinking, and doing in management education,' *Academy of Management Proceedings*, 2016(1), 16659. 10.5465/ambpp.2016.16659abstract

Kemp, R. and Martens, P. (2007). 'Sustainable development: How to manage something that is subjective and never can be achieved?,' *Sustainability: Science, Practice and Policy*, 3(2), 5–14. 10.1080/15487733.2007.11907997

Laurie, R., Nonoyama-Tarumi, Y., Mckeown, R. and Hopkins, C. (2016). 'Contributions of education for sustainable development (ESD) to quality education: A synthesis of research,' *Journal of Education for Sustainable Development*, 10(2), 226–242. 10.1177/0973408216661442

Leicht, A., Heiss, J., Byun, W.J. and UNESCO. (2018). *Issues and trends in education for sustainable development*. https://unesdoc.unesco.org/ark:/48223/pf0000261445

Lozano, R., Merrill, M., Sammalisto, K., Ceulemans, K. and Lozano, F. (2017). 'Connecting competences and pedagogical approaches for sustainable development in higher education: A literature review and framework proposal,' *Sustainability*, 9(10), 1889. 10.3390/su9101889

Mezirow, J. (1997). 'Transformative learning: Theory to practice,' *New Directions for Adult and Continuing Education*, 1997(74), 5–12. 10.1002/ace.7401

Mezirow, J. (2000). 'Learning to think like an adult,' In Mezirow, J. et al. (eds.) *Learning as Transformation: Critical Perspectives on a Theory in Progress*, San Francisco: Jossey-Bass, pp. 3–33.

Mezirow, J. (2005). 'An overview on transformative learning,' In Sutherland, P. and Crowther, J. (eds.), *Lifelong Learning*. Routledge, 1st ed., pp. 90–105.

Morsing, M. (2021). 'PRME – principles for responsible management education,' in Morsing, M. (ed.) *Responsible Management Education*. Routledge. 1st ed., pp. 3–12. 10.4324/9781003186311-2

PRME. (2022). *What we do*. Principles of Responsible Management Education. https://www.unprme.org/what-we-do

Redman, A., Wiek, A. and Barth, M. (2021). 'Current practice of assessing students' sustainability competencies: A review of tools,' *Sustainability Science*, 16(1), 117–135. 10.1007/s11625-020-00855-1

Remington-Doucette, S.M., Hiller Connell, K.Y., Armstrong, C.M. and Musgrove, S.L. (2013). 'Assessing sustainability education in a transdisciplinary undergraduate course focused on real-world problem solving: A case for disciplinary grounding,' *International Journal of Sustainability in Higher Education*, 14(4), 404–433. 10.1108/IJSHE-01-2012-0001

Rimanoczy, I. (2021). *The sustainability mindset principles: A guide to develop a mindset for a better world* (1st ed.). Routledge. 10.4324/9781003095637

Rimanonczy, I. and Klingenberg, B. (2020). *SM Indicator*. https://smindicator.com/

RSM. (n.d.). *How we contribute to positive change*. Rotterdam School of Management (RSM). Retrieved May 6, 2021, from https://www.rsm.nl/positive-change/our-positive-changes/

Savicki, V. and Price, M.V. (2021). 'Reflection in transformative learning: The challenge of measurement,' *Journal of Transformative Education*, 19(4), 366–382. 10.1177/15413446211045161

Sharma, R.R. (2017). 'A competency model for management education for sustainability,' *Vision*, 21(2), x–xv. 10.1177/0972262917700970

Sterling, S. (2010). 'Learning for resilience, or the resilient learner? Towards a necessary reconciliation in a paradigm of sustainable education,' *Environmental Education Research*, 16(5–6), 511–528. 10.1080/13504622.2010.505427

UNESCO. (2004). *Education for all: The quality imperative* (EFA Global Monitoring Report). UNESCO.

UNESCO. (2017). *Education for sustainable development goals: Learning objectives.*Geneva: UNESCO.

Wiek, A., Bernstein, M.J., Foley, R.W., Cohen, M., Forrest, N., Kuzdas, C., Kay, B. and Keeler, L.W. (2015). 'Operationalising competencies in higher education for sustainable development,' in *Routledge handbook of higher education for sustainable development.* Routledge.

Wiek, A. and Redman, A. (2022). 'What do key competencies in sustainability offer and how to use them,' in Vare, P., Lausselet, N. and Rieckmann, M. (eds.) *Competences in education for sustainable development: Critical perspectives.* Springer International Publishing, pp. 27–34. 10.1007/978-3-030-91055-6_4

Wiek, A., Withycombe, L. and Redman, C.L. (2011). 'Key competencies in sustainability: A reference framework for academic program development,' *Sustainability Science*, 6(2), 203–218. 10.1007/s11625-011-0132-6

Index

Note: Page numbers in *italics* indicate a figure and page numbers in **bold** indicate a table on the corresponding page.

Printed in the United States
by Baker & Taylor Publisher Services